*Metaphysics
and its Task*

SUNY series in Philosophy
George R. Lucas, Jr., Editor

Metaphysics and its Task

The Search for the Categorial Foundation of Knowledge

JORGE J. E. GRACIA

STATE UNIVERSITY OF NEW YORK PRESS

Published by
State University of New York Press, Albany

For information, address State University of New York
Press, State University Plaza, Albany, N.Y., 12246

Production by Diane Ganeles
Marketing by Nancy Farrell

Library of Congress Cataloging-in-Publication Data

Gracia, Jorge J. E.
    Metaphysics and its task : the search for the categorial
foundation of knowledge / Jorge J.E. Gracia.
        p.   cm. — (SUNY series in philosophy)
    Includes bibliographical references and index.
    ISBN 0-7914-4213-6 (alk. paper). — ISBN 0-7914-4214-4 (pbk. :
alk. paper)
    1. Metaphysics. I. Title. II. Series.
BD111.G7   1999
110—dc21   98–48000
                                                                CIP

10 9 8 7 6 5 4 3 2 1

. . . scientia de aliquo et nihilo, ente et non ente, re et modo rei, substantia et accidente. . . .

—Leibniz

[A]s in this age to be practical is everything, I shall go back to Philosophy and study Metaphysics.

—Oscar Wilde

Contents

Preface

The continued resilience of metaphysics is perhaps one of the most obvious facts in the history of philosophy. From its very beginnings, metaphysics has been under attack; indeed, it has appeared at several times as if a coup de grace had been delivered to it. But the discipline has always managed to recover itself.

The attacks against metaphysics have had different motivations. Some have been inspired by a skeptical attitude against knowledge in general. This is the sort of assault which first surfaced in ancient Greece, when the Sophists rejected certainty in knowledge in favor of expediency. Their objections were not specifically aimed at metaphysics, for metaphysics had not at the time developed as a separate enterprise, rather they were directed toward the possibility of the acquisition of any knowledge with certainty. Skeptics such as Gorgias questioned the very basis of our understanding and sought, thereby, to undermine any attempt to develop what later came to be known as metaphysics.

The skeptical assault did not succeed, for Socrates arose out of the very midst of the Sophists. Explicitly acknowledging his ignorance, he set the foundations for Plato's theory of forms, one of the most influential metaphysical theories of all times. Indeed, it was Plato's student, Aristotle, who first explicitly tried to distinguish metaphysics from other disciplines of learning. And it was as a result of Aristotle's editor, Andronicus of Rhodes, that the very term 'metaphysics' came to be attached to the discipline.

During the Middle Ages, an altogether differently motivated attack was carried out against metaphysics. The primary concern of Latin medieval authors was the relation of human beings to God and the understanding of what the age considered to be God's revelation of His plans for humanity. In this context, it was to be expected that any enterprise based exclusively on human natural powers would be regarded as, at best, secondary to the fundamental aim of the age. In fact, all philosophical and nonreligious knowledge, including metaphysics, was considered suspect, for some of the views of those who practiced it seemed to conflict with views regarded as founded on God's revelation. The opposition to all worldly learning reached extremes at various periods of the age. Peter Damian, for example, accused the Devil of having invented grammar, for grammar made possible the declension of *deus* in the plural. Other attacks were less absurd than this, but, for that very reason, were more dangerous to the future of secular knowledge in general and of philosophy and metaphysics in particular. The carefully reasoned arguments of Bonaventure against all knowledge considered apart from revelation, and his attempt to reduce all disciplines of learning to theology, seriously threatened the independence of the metaphysical enterprise. And the same can be said about late medieval authors who emphasized the reliability of faith and unreliability of reason.

The religious offensive against metaphysics, however, did not succeed. Opposition arose from within the very ranks of deeply religious thinkers. Authors such as Thomas Aquinas and John Duns Scotus not only defended the metaphysical enterprise and wrote extensively on the nature of metaphysics and metaphysical topics, but also developed metaphysical views which influenced generations of future philosophers and produced, in the thirteenth and fourteenth centuries, what can only be considered a renaissance of the discipline.

The growth of empiricism in the early modern period constituted a different challenge to metaphysics. If all knowledge must be based on sense experience and if metaphysics, as many had claimed, both is concerned with nonphysical entities and proceeds a priori, then metaphysics cannot be regarded as a kind of knowledge. The program of Hume, for instance, entailed the destruction of the metaphysical enterprise and, if not that, at least its substantial modification.

But Hume gave way to Kant, who saw his task precisely as the establishment of metaphysics on a firmer ground. His response to the empiricist challenge was to find a place for metaphysics in the discovery of the conceptual structures which constitute the necessary conditions of our knowledge. Thus, metaphysics, considered dead by many at the time, rose again, like a phoenix from its ashes, although in a new form. Indeed, Kant's answer to Hume produced one of the richest periods of metaphysical investigation in the West.

The nineteenth century witnessed another challenge to metaphysics, this one inspired by the growth and success of the natural sciences. Nineteenth-century positivism held the experimental method of the natural sciences as exemplary and, therefore, dismissed any conclusions based on methods which did not resemble it. Because many post-Kantian metaphysicians engaged in speculation uncontrolled by observation, their views were bound to be dismissed by positivists as unscientific and, hence, not truly knowledge. Moreover, positivists had practical ends in mind; they saw their aim not only as theoretical, but also as the promotion of progress in society. They thought that metaphysics, with its purely theoretical goal and its speculative method, was an obstacle to progress. The challenge of the positivists was very strong, particularly because it appealed to practical needs and desires.

The revolt against this anti-metaphysical wave, however, was not long in coming. The demise of nineteenth-century positivists was prompted by their dismissal of ethical and aesthetic values. In their attempt to reduce all discourse to scientific discourse, they reduced ethics and aesthetics to empirical psychology, leaving no place in their scheme for human freedom and the self. Even some of those who had been trained in positivism found this approach inadequate and, therefore, turned against it. The result was a return to metaphysics, to a metaphysics of life, humanity, and values.

One of the most recent criticisms of metaphysics has been based on certain semantic theories. As a consequence of the important—some would say revolutionary—ideas of Frege and others, a strong connection was established in this century between meaning and truth conditions. This, coupled with a strong empiricist emphasis, set the stage for the verificationist theory of meaning. According to this theory, proposed and popularized by logical positivists, meaning is necessarily conditioned by empirical verification, so that, any sentence which is not empirically verifiable must be regarded as meaningless. Naturally, this view has devastating consequences for metaphysics, for most metaphysical sentences are unverifiable in empirical terms. Judged by this criterion, metaphysical sentences become nonsense and, therefore, metaphysics must be abandoned as a legitimate enterprise.

The attack of logical positivists on metaphysics has had a powerful influence on the Anglo-American philosophical tradition. Even though the view of meaning as verification was quickly challenged and eventually abandoned by most members of the Anglo-American philosophical mainstream, the semantic criticism of metaphysics as a spurious discipline proved highly effective.

The first important attempt to bring metaphysics back into the Anglo-American tradition was made by P. F. Strawson, among others, in the fifties. Strawson argued that there are two sorts of metaphysics, one legitimate and one illegitimate. The latter he called "revisionary," because it aims to change the way we think about the world; as he put it: "to produce a better structure [of our thought] about the world." "Descriptive metaphysics," in contrast, "is content to describe the actual structure of our thought about the world."[1] Examples of revisionary metaphysicians are Descartes, Leibniz, and Berkeley; examples of descriptive metaphysicians are Aristotle and Kant. Strawson's view of metaphysics is quite different from the view of his predecessors and, whether one agrees with it or not, it is one of the first significant steps toward the legitimation of the practice of metaphysics among members of the analytic philosophical tradition. Indeed, in recent years, metaphysics has become a regular pursuit of analytic philosophers, although they generally approach it from a linguistic and semantic perspective. Metaphysics has arisen from its ashes once again, albeit under a different form.

The other most important recent criticism of metaphysics has come from the camp of post-modernists. The roots of this criticism go all the way back to Kant and the historicism of the nineteenth century, but it is in Heidegger that one finds its immediate source. The hermeneutic circle, as formulated by Heidegger and others, is taken to imply that understanding is dependent on language and because language is culturally relative and contextual, understanding cannot transcend culture and language. Some, then, have gone further, claiming that all knowledge, including metaphysical knowledge, is ideological and reflects the attempt of some groups to dominate and repress others. Whence the accusations that metaphysics has been a Western creation, an imperialistic tool to exploit non-Western cultures, and reason, as understood in the West, an invention of white males to maintain their hegemony over females and nonwhite males. Metaphysics is regarded as one more instrument in the struggle among groups who seek power. This legitimizes the calls for the end to the discipline.

---

1. Strawson, *Individuals*, p. 9.

Still, even within the ranks of this radical opposition, we find attempts at a kind of rehabilitation of metaphysics, although under a different garb. And not only this, but we also find a continuous preoccupation with metaphysics and its possibility. The work of Habermas, for example, is testimony to this direction, and even the most radical post-modernists, like Derrida, occasionally grant the inevitability of the discipline.

Many of the attacks which have been made against metaphysics throughout the history of Western philosophy have not been merely a matter of argument. They have often been accompanied by actions aimed at suppressing the development of metaphysics or metaphysical views in social institutions. In the Middle Ages, for example, there were repeated condemnations of metaphysical views and books which were considered threatening to the accepted orthodoxy. These condemnations were not mere empty proclamations. Often they meant that the views in question could not be taught and the pertinent books could not be used. In not a few cases, teaching licenses were taken away and thus voices of dissent were silenced. Another, quite explicit example of repression is found in the attempts of nineteenth-century positivists to banish metaphysics and other "nonscientific" disciplines from the curriculum, particularly at the secondary school level. These attempts were not always successful in democratic societies, where pluralistic viewpoints were accepted, but in politically controlled societies the efforts of the positivists paid off handsomely. In countries like Mexico, for example, where a dictatorial regime was in charge at the end of the nineteenth century and the beginning of the twentieth, metaphysics became a thing of the past to be confined to "the dustbin of history."

Clearly, metaphysics always manages to reestablish itself in spite of all the obstacles put in its way. But why? Why is it that, in spite of the challenges it has encountered throughout its history, metaphysics not only survives but always returns with renewed vigor? One answer to this question is quite simple: Metaphysics seems to be a natural thing for human beings to do. As Kant put it: "That the human spirit will ever give up metaphysical speculations is as little to be expected as that we should prefer to give up breathing altogether, in order to avoid impure air."[2] Even if what we get in metaphysics is less than desirable, we just cannot give it up. And we cannot give it up precisely because the questions raised by

---

2. Kant, *Prolegomena* ("Solution"), p. 116, and also § 57, p. 102.

metaphysics are the most fundamental questions that can be asked; they have to do with what underlies everything else in our experience. To give them up is unthinkable, even if we never reach completely satisfactory answers.

Still, this answer itself is not satisfactory to the extent that it is unclear what metaphysics is, particularly because philosophers disagree concerning the nature of the discipline. If we are going to understand why philosophers always go back to metaphysics, we must begin by determining what, in fact, metaphysics is. To do so, however, is not easy not only because there is wide disagreement about how to answer this question, but also because there are various conceptual confusions which vitiate the question as raised by different authors. In this book, I give a direct answer to this question, while indirectly providing a rationale for the survival of the discipline.

I begin with some preliminary conceptual distinctions which should help to clarify the task ahead of us. To some, the task I undertake might appear useless or uninteresting. My first response to them is that it is a necessary step in the understanding of many other philosophical issues and that, as such, it should be of concern to anyone who has an interest in philosophy. Metaphysics is at the very core of philosophy and much that is called by other names today is in fact metaphysics. Large parts of the philosophy of language, the philosophy of science, the philosophy of mind, logic, ontology, semantics, and even hermeneutics are nothing but camouflaged metaphysics.

The definition of metaphysics will also help to answer one of the most often asked questions about its subject matter: Whether its object of study is words, concepts, or things. In this sense, I attempt to settle one aspect of the controversy concerning nominalism, conceptualism, and realism. The book does not discuss logical relations between metaphysical concepts or epistemological questions which deal with metaphysical knowledge or certainty; it does not explore semantic issues concerned with the meaning of metaphysical statements or terms; and it does not attempt to determine what value metaphysics may have. To this extent, the book differs from many other books devoted to metaphysics. Indeed, most contemporary discussions of metaphysics are concerned primarily with epistemological and semantic issues which are not discussed here. The contemporary interest in these issues is in part the result of the fact that, for the greatest part of the last two centuries, metaphysics has been under fire and those who openly write about it feel that its justification should be primary: one cannot, or at least should not, do metaphysics unless it is proven that metaphysics is possible.[3] The influence of Kant, British empiricism, and nineteenth- and twentieth-century positivism have played key roles in this connection.[4]

Most treatises on metaphysics that do not concern themselves with the epistemology of metaphysics or the semantics of metaphysical statements and terms, in general try to present more or less complete metaphysical systems or at least to discuss what their authors consider to be the most basic issues and concepts in metaphysics. An early, postclassical example of a treatise, which tries to consider the most basic issues and concepts in metaphysics, is Thomas Aquinas's *On Being and Essence*. The earliest example of an influential treatise, which presents a complete metaphysical system, is Francis Suárez's *Metaphysical Disputations*. The contemporary literature displays many examples of both approaches.[5] The present book, in contrast, has a much narrower focus; it aims to explore the nature of metaphysics; its purpose is neither to present a metaphysical system nor to investigate the most fundamental issues and concepts of metaphysics.[6] In carrying out its aim, however, it does discuss various metaphysical notions, but these discussions are only propaedeutic to the main objective of the book. Its task, then, is both ambitious and modest. It is ambitious because, in presuming to propose a satisfactory definition of metaphysics, it aims to achieve what twenty-five hundred years of Western philosophy have not succeeded in doing; it is modest because of its very narrow topic, and the tentative character of its theses. If nothing else, the history of philosophy has taught us that definitive philosophical answers to philosophical questions are difficult to obtain, if they can be obtained at all, and that often we must settle for only more or less accurate approximations.

This book is not intended as a chronological survey of the various views concerning metaphysics proposed throughout the history of Western philosophy. Its approach is systematic. The conceptual framework it presents, however, should help us understand and evaluate the history of the attempts to define metaphysics. For those

---

3. Ibid., § 5, p. 25.
4. See Carnap, "The Elimination of Metaphysics," and Ayer, *Language, Truth and Logic*, ch. 1.
5. More frequent are books of the first kind. See, for example, Taylor, *Metaphysics*, and Hamlyn, *Metaphysics*.
6. Two precedents are the collection edited by Pears, *The Nature of Metaphysics*, and Collingwood, *An Essay on Metaphysics*.

interested in the history of these attempts, I have provided historical references in the footnotes, although this is limited to the most
obvious signposts in the development of the discipline, and reveals
my partial knowledge and obvious preferences. Because of the non-
specialized character of the discussion, references have been made to
texts available in English whenever possible. Those readers who do
not have a historical inclination may ignore them and pay attention
only to the main text. The argument is intended to be self-sustaining
and independent of the historical apparatus included in the notes.

Nor is it my intention to introduce a drastic change in the way
metaphysics is practiced. The book aims to present a theory which
makes sense of the practice of metaphysics throughout its history. Its
goal is not to change practice but to understand it, that is, to fit it
within a conceptual framework which makes sense of our collective
experience. The theses I have defended are rooted in the practice of
the discipline, even if they contradict what many metaphysicians, in
fact, say about metaphysics. I will be content, then, if these theses are
regarded as sensible rather than revolutionary; I am not interested in
novelty, but in truth. Indeed, I believe I say nothing here that is not
already implicit in what other metaphysicians have said or done.

For these reasons, I have avoided the summary dismissal of
views which contradict mine simply because they do so. Indeed, I
have tried to look at what other metaphysicians have said and done
about metaphysics as data to be explained in the theory I propose.
The reader should be the final arbiter of my success in this regard.

Two further points about the book in general: One concerning
conventions, the other strategy. With respect to the first, apart from
standard uses, single and double quotes are both used to indicate
mention rather than use, but single quotes are used to indicate the
mention of linguistic entities such as words, terms, verbs, names, ar-
ticles, sentences, phrases, expressions, and the subjects and predicates of sentences.

With respect to the second, it should be clear that the comprehensive and satisfactory treatment of any of the many positions I
discuss would require much more space than I could give it in a book
of this size and character. Consider, for example, the view that metaphysics is the study of being *qua* being. Much space and effort have
been devoted to this position in the history of philosophy, so to do justice both to its history and to its complexity would require at least a
substantial book. Rather than attempting comprehensive discussions of this and the other views I consider, then, my strategy has
been to present basic formulations of these views not tied to partic-

ular historical figures and to present, as briefly as possible, what appear to me to be the main advantages and disadvantages of the views in question. In short, I have tried to capture the elements of each view that are pertinent for the general argument of this book without engaging in a protracted analysis of it. Those who wish to delve more deeply into the history and context of these views will find some guidance in the footnotes.

The discussion is divided into ten chapters. The first is introductory. Chapters 2–6 present a systematic analysis and criticism of the main positions concerning the nature of metaphysics in terms of the object it studies, the method it uses, the general aim it pursues, and the character of the propositions in which it is expressed. Chapters 7–9 develop my own position with respect to the nature of metaphysics, the role reduction plays in discussions of the nature of the discipline, and the consequences of my view for the controversy concerning one brand of realism, conceptualism, and nominalism. The study closes with a brief concluding statement, a bibliography, and indexes.

This book may be read in various ways. One may begin at the beginning and end at the end. Or one may pick a chapter here and there, for most chapters stand on their own, even if they are part of a larger argument and rely on support from other parts of the book. But perhaps the best way to approach the book is to read chapters 1 and 2 and then go to 7 through 10. After this, the reader can go back and consult other chapters, depending on interest and inclination. Indeed, in many ways, chapters 3 to 6 are meant to be consulted here and there, as one does with a work of reference, rather than read through, for they contain short capsules on various positions I find inadequate.

Three main theses are defended. The first is that metaphysics is the part of philosophy that studies categories, but that it studies different categories in different ways because it seeks to establish different things about them. Concerning the most general categories, metaphysics seeks to identify them, to define them whenever possible, and to determine the relations among them. Concerning less general categories, metaphysics seeks to establish their relations to the most general categories. The second thesis is that categories are neutral with respect to the question of whether they are linguistic, conceptual, or real in the sense that there are categories of each sort but not all categories are of one sort. Now, since metaphysics studies categories and categories are neutral in the explained sense, it is a mistake to think of metaphysics in exclusively nominalistic, conceptualistic, or realistic terms. Metaphysics does not study only one kind of category, but rather all kinds. Finally, I argue that it is an attempt at reduction that is responsible for the mistaken understanding of metaphysics exclusively in one of the ways mentioned.

The most fundamental of these theses is the first. Generally, philosophers have distinguished metaphysics from other disciplines in terms of the object it studies (being *qua* being, first principles, God, etc.), the method it uses (a priori, a posteriori, deductive, etc.), the aim it pursues (theoretical, practical, aesthetic, etc.), or the propositions of which it is composed or to which it arrives as conclusions (analytic, synthetic, synthetic a priori, etc.). According to the view I defend, metaphysics is distinguished from other disciplines both because of the object it studies and the specific aim it pursues. Moreover, that metaphysics tries to identify and relate the most general categories and to establish the relations of less general categories to the most general ones explains both why metaphysics is fundamental—it is logically prior to every other discipline—and inescapable—metaphysical views are presupposed by every other view. It is for this reason that one can regard metaphysics as the categorial foundation of all knowledge.

There are, moreover, three further corollaries of this position. First, the conception of metaphysics I present makes it possible to think of widely different philosophers—Aristotle and Kant, Aquinas and Ricoeur, Quine and Habermas—as engaged in one enterprise. The history of metaphysics, and to a certain extent the history of philosophy as a whole, can be seen as a single endeavor in which many different approaches and viewpoints are present. This conception gives the discipline intelligibility, promotes dialogue between different schools, makes easier the study and comparison of radically different positions, and contributes to the elimination of artificial divisions and boundaries among philosophical traditions. Anyone who is familiar with the recent history of the discipline and its almost schizophrenic manifestations will, I believe, agree that this is much needed.

Second, the conception of metaphysics I present explains the unity of metaphysics, a topic which has worried philosophers from the beginning of the discipline. There is, indeed, a discipline we can call "metaphysics" and that discipline derives its unity from the object it studies and what it aims to establish about it.

Finally, if I am right and metaphysics is both fundamental and inescapable, then any satisfactory understanding of philosophers, whether past or present, must take into account their metaphysical views regardless of whether they explicitly stated them or left them implicit in their work. Until that is done, no philosopher can be properly understood. For this reason, the task of this book becomes essential to any serious attempt at understanding the thought of any philosopher. But this is not all, for the fundamental character of metaphysics makes the practice of this discipline and the understanding of its nature necessary steps in the development of a comprehensive view of the world or any of its parts. In this sense, the issue discussed here is at the basis of all human understanding.

In the preparation of this book, I have used some materials which have appeared elsewhere. The discussion of categories in chapter 9 relies on the discussion of universals presented in chapter 2 of *Individuality: An Essay on the Foundations of Metaphysics* (1988) and of categories in "The Ontological Status of Categories," *International Philosophical Quarterly* 45 (1998); and the discussion of transcendentality in chapter 2 relies on "The Transcendentals in the Middle Ages," *Topoi* 11, No. 2 (1992).

Let me finish by thanking those who have read parts of this book in draft form and have made suggestions for its improvement. I am particularly indebted to John Kearns and Michael Gorman. They read parts of the book and raised fundamental questions which forced me to rethink and revise aspects of my view. Peter Hare and John Kronen read an early draft of the manuscript and made useful suggestions about its scope and topic. Barry Smith read a later draft of chapters 7–9, and Mariam Thalos of chapter 8, and posed specific questions which proved useful. I am also grateful to the faculty and students of the department of Philosophy at Fordham University for the issues they raised during the Suárez Lecture, where I presented parts of chapter 7, and to Joseph Seifert, who raised some objections in a conversation we had concerning my conception of metaphysics. Kenneth Shockley, Yishaiya Abosch, and William Irwin also made valuable comments. Robert Delfino helped with the footnotes and bibliography, and made many perceptive observations about content. I profited also from class discussions carried on in three graduate seminars in which I used parts of the manuscript in the spring semesters of 1994, 1995, and 1996. The students who most actively participated in discussion and, thus, contributed to my thinking were Richard Main, Kenneth Shockley, Robert Delfino, and Elizabeth Millán. Thanks also to William Fedirko who checked the proofs and compiled the Author Index.

Jorge J. E. Gracia

CHAPTER ONE

Introduction

A book of this size cannot be expected to explore all the issues which can be raised concerning metaphysics. There are, indeed, many issues which could claim the attention of the philosopher. Epistemically, for example, one may raise questions concerning criteria for the certainty with which we hold metaphysical views. How do I know with certainty that sentences such as, 'The universe is finite' or 'Minds are immaterial,' are true or false? With respect to semantics also, one may raise questions such as: Do sentences which express metaphysical views have meaning? Do terms used by metaphysicians to refer to so-called metaphysical entities have reference? For instance, is the sentence, 'The soul is a substance,' meaningful? And does the term 'God' have any reference? There are logical issues which arise and have to do with the relations among concepts used by metaphysicians. For example, one may ask whether the concept of person is equivalent to the concept of mind or rather to the concept of mind and the concept of body taken together. And there are also many axiological issues that could be explored. What value does metaphysics have? Does metaphysics have a practical application? And so on.

One issue of particular importance concerns what has been called the "ontological status of metaphysics." This issue should not be confused with that involved in the definition of metaphysics, insofar as the former involves what is often referred to as its "ontological characterization." By this is meant the identification of the broadest categories within which metaphysics fits. An example

should help us see the difference between these two issues. Consider
the case of bachelor. A bachelor is defined as an unmarried man. But
this definition does not tell us the most general categories to which a
bachelor belongs. Within an Aristotelian metaphysical framework, a
bachelor turns out to be a substance, because that is the one general
category, of those Aristotle adopts, into which bachelors fit. Moreover, Aristotle would conceive that substance to be composed of two
principles, matter and form. Other philosophers, however, might
think otherwise. For example, Descartes would think of a bachelor
as a thinking substance of a certain sort and for Leibniz, it would be
a monad. Indeed, some philosophers reject the notion of substance
altogether and thus maintain that a bachelor is something other
than a substance. Hume, for example, would classify a bachelor as a
bundle of perceptions.

The categorization of metaphysics too has been of concern to
philosophers and they have frequently differed as to what that categorization is. For example, some have held that metaphysics, like
any other kind of scientific knowledge, is a feature (often referred to
as a quality) of the mind.[1] Others have held that metaphysics is a set
of propositions.[2] Others still have spoken of a set of sentences or
texts,[3] and so on. But settling this matter is not the concern of this
book, although some of the things I say in chapter 2 have implications for it. Rather than attempting to discuss the ontological status
of metaphysics or to deal with all the logical, metaphysical, epistemological, semantic, and axiological issues that can be raised about
it, I concentrate my efforts on one issue, the definition of metaphysics, although by finding a solution to it I also provide an answer
to the question of whether metaphysics should be understood nominalistically, conceptualistically, or realistically.

Definitions come in a wide variety, but these can be divided into
two broad groups: nominal and real.[4] A nominal definition consists of
a sentence whose predicate specifies the necessary and sufficient conditions of the correct use of the subject of the sentence. Nominal defi-

---

1. Aristotle, *Categories*, 8b26, p. 23.
2. Ockham, "On the Notion of Knowledge or Science" (*Expositio super viii
   libros Physicorum*, Prologus), p. 11.
3. If propositions turn out to be sentences, and metaphysics is no more
   than a set of propositions, then metaphysics is a set of sentences. Quine
   holds the view that propositions are nothing but sentences in *The Roots
   of Reference*, p. 35.
4. See Robinson, *Definition*, p. 16; Suppes, *Introduction to Logic*, p. 152.

nitions are the province of semantics, for they concern the meaning of terms. A real definition also consists of a sentence, but the conditions its predicate specifies have to do with the kind of thing to which the subject of the sentence refers. Both, nominal and real definitions, are supposed to express essence.[5] In the first case, it is what some philosophers call "nominal essence," that is, the necessary and sufficient conditions of the correct use of terms; in the second case, it is what some philosophers call "real essence," that is, the necessary and sufficient conditions that make a thing the kind of thing it is.[6]

In ordinary language, nominal and real definitions are frequently expressed by the same sentence, which is nonetheless understood differently, depending on whether one understands it in nominal or real terms. Consider the sentence, 'A bachelor is an unmarried man.' On one hand, when this sentence is understood to express a nominal definition, it is taken to mean something like: The term 'bachelor' means unmarried man. In this case, the predicate of the sentence is understood to specify the conditions of the proper use of the term 'bachelor.' On the other hand, the sentence, 'A bachelor is an unmarried man,' can also be understood to express a real definition, that is, something like: To be a bachelor is to be an unmarried man. In this case, the predicate of the sentence is understood to specify the conditions that must be satisfied for something to be a bachelor. Nominal definitions have to do with conditions of language use; real definitions have to do with conditions of being.

Note that I take predicates to specify certain conditions which are claimed to be satisfied by the entities to which the subjects of the sentences of which they are predicates refer. Moreover, I regard subjects and predicates as linguistic entities. In the sentence, 'Ebony is black,' both the subject 'ebony' and the predicate 'black' are linguistic entities. Occasionally, however, for the sake of brevity, I adopt the widespread custom of speaking about predicates as if they were not linguistic entities and of saying that predicates are predicated of the entities to which the subjects of the sentences refer rather than of the terms that are used to refer to those entities. I particularly adopt this way of speaking when I discuss the views of authors who speak this way.

---

5. Aristotle, *Topics*, 102a1, p. 191.
6. Locke, *An Essay Concerning Human Understanding*, vol. IV, ch. 6, 4; vol. 2, p. 253. The term 'real definition,' however, is also used to refer to all sorts of other things. For a list of these, see Robinson, *Definition*, pp. 189–90.

Traditionally, metaphysics has been taken to deal with real rather than nominal definitions. Whether it does or not, of course, depends among other things on the nature of its object, that is, on whether metaphysics studies linguistic or nonlinguistic entities. This means that the issue cannot be determined until we have established the object of metaphysics. But this is not what is at stake here. My concern at this point is with the kind of definition metaphysics itself can have: Is it real or nominal?

Some might argue that it must be nominal, for real definitions apply only to natural kinds, such as human being and tree, and metaphysics is not a natural kind, but the product of human intention and design. It is possible to respond to this argument that metaphysics is indeed a natural kind. Although metaphysics originates as a result of human intentional activity, it is not the result of human design. In this sense, it is very much like running, for example, which is a human activity originating from a decision to run, but it is not the result of human design.

This response relies on a distinction between natural and artifactual in which something artifactual is conceived as having been produced by human beings. But this conception of artifactual is too narrow. In a broader, more effective conception of artifactual, an artifact would be either (1) something which is the product of intentional activity and design, or (2) something which is not the product of intentional activity and design but has undergone some change or its context has undergone some change, and the change in either case is the product of intentional activity and design.[7] If we accept this view, then running is artifactual, for the way one runs is always the product of a process of learning, imitation, and thus of design. And the same applies to metaphysics, for even if there were some natural core to what we call "metaphysics," it is surely modified in many ways as a result of intentional activity and design.

In short, metaphysics is artifactual rather than natural. But can it, in this case, have a real definition? This brings me to an alternative answer to the argument that the definition of metaphysics must be nominal: That metaphysics is not a natural kind does not preclude it from having a real definition, for the distinction between real and nominal definitions is not based on the fact that the first applies only

---

7. Gracia, *A Theory of Textuality*, ch. 2, p. 48. For this understanding of artifact to be effective, the notion of design must be, of course, understood to refer to the fact that humans have determined the necessary and sufficient conditions of the kind to which the artifact belongs.

to natural kinds and the second only to artifactual ones. The distinction is based on whether the necessary and sufficient conditions specified in the definition are conditions that apply to a kind or are conditions that apply merely to the correct use of a linguistic term. Hence, there can be real definitions of artifactual kinds as well as of natural kinds as long as the conditions apply to the kind and not to the effective use of a linguistic term. It is irrelevant whether or not the kind is the result, at least in part, of human intention and design, as long as the conditions apply to the kind. Chair can have a real definition even though it is an artifactual kind, as long as the conditions specified in its definition refer to the kind and not to the proper or effective use of the term 'chair.' And the same applies to metaphysics.

One may want to argue, indeed, that the real definition of artifactual kinds is in fact easier than the definition of natural kinds, for the conditions of a kind of artifact are established by those who design it. In this sense, the definition of a coat hanger is rather easy to determine, insofar as it was a human being who first thought and designed a coat hanger. In contrast, the definition of a tiger is difficult, for tigers are not the products of human design.

Obviously, if as some philosophers hold, it is impossible to reach definitions of any sort, whether real or nominal, then it would seem that we have no business trying to do so. But this is a position which is not to be accepted uncritically by any means. The position is the result to a great extent of a recent philosophical tradition which goes back to Wittgenstein. The objections raised against definitions run along two lines. One goes back to Wittgenstein himself and his view that it is not possible to identify common features to the things which are designated by common terms such as 'cat' and 'white.'[8] Wittgenstein illustrated his point with reference to the term 'game.' 'Game' is used to refer to all sorts of things, such as basketball, canasta, chess, and so on, but if one tries to identify some common feature to the things we call "games," we will find none. Games share no more than a family resemblance. Now, if this is so, then it is clear that a definition intended to establish necessary and sufficient conditions, whether of the use of a term or of the sort of thing to which the term refers, is fruitless.

I have discussed possible answers to this objection elsewhere, so I will not repeat them here.[9] For our present purposes, it should

---

8. Bambrough, "Universals and Family Resemblances," pp. 207–22.
9. Gracia, *Individuality*, pp. 10–12.

suffice to say two things. First, if I can come up with an acceptable definition of metaphysics, that should be enough to answer this objection. But, even if I am not able to come up with a definition that is acceptable to everyone, still the effort to develop a definition should have proven useful in many ways, increasing our knowledge of the difficulties faced by the task of defining and of the reasons why certain definitions are unacceptable and why others appear more promising.

The second objection is based on the theories concerning the meaning and reference of common terms that Kripke and others have developed. According to this view, common names are very much like proper names, but proper names do not have a meaning which may be expressed through a description. We use proper names effectively because there is a causal chain which ties us to a moment when a baptism occurred. At that moment, the name was imposed on something, but the name still refers to that thing in spite of the fact that the thing in question may not be at all as it was when the name was imposed. In short, proper names are not descriptive in any sense. Now, so the argument goes, common names are also like that. That is why tigers do not need to have any common set of characteristics, just as games do not.[10] A tiger may turn out not to have stripes, for example.

The detailed answer to this objection, which I have also discussed elsewhere, need not detain us.[11] For our present purposes, we can use the same answer we gave to the first objection. If our enterprise is successful, it will show that this objection is ineffective. But, even if our enterprise is not completely successful, it would have helped us to understand in greater detail the problems involved in coming up with a definition of metaphysics and, presumably, will have deepened, even if only negatively, our understanding of the nature of the discipline or of our use of the term 'metaphysics.'

One thing must be added to this discussion of definition. The necessary and sufficient conditions specified in a definition, whether nominal or real, are usually specified in terms of genus and specific difference (*differentia*). The genus is the class to which the kind of thing which is to be defined immediately belongs. Thus, the genus of human being is often taken to be animal, and so is the genus of cat. The identification of a genus reveals a set of necessary conditions,

---

10. Kripke, *Naming and Necessity*, p. 121.
11. Gracia, *Individuality*, pp. 12–13.

but to make the conditions sufficient, the specific difference must be added. This is the condition or set of conditions which distinguish the kind of thing being defined from other things which satisfy the generic conditions. In the case of human beings, the capacity to reason has been traditionally identified as the specific difference. Of course, the kind of condition that will function as a specific difference will vary depending on the kind of thing in question.

Neither generic nor specific conditions are sufficient conditions, considered separately and by themselves, for the determination of the *definiendum*. Considered by themselves, they are merely necessary conditions. Generic conditions are distinguished from specific ones in that the first are necessary for the second. In the example cited earlier, the conditions specified by animal are supposed to be necessary for rational. To be rational requires to be animal, but to be animal does not require to be rational.

The example I have provided to illustrate what is involved in a definition is not uncontroversial. Indeed, as explained, it turns out that all rational beings must be animals, and this is a view that some may not wish to accept. The reason: There does not seem to be any contradiction in the notion of a rational being which is not an animal. This difficulty, however, should not obscure the point about the relation between specific and generic conditions. For the difficulty in question concerns only the proper *differentia* of human beings, not the distinction between generic and specific conditions. Yet, even if that distinction itself is found to be wanting, this does not undermine what will be said in this book about the definition of metaphysics, for what will be said does not depend on the viability of the distinction. The use of genus and difference is convenient, however, not only as a device to understand the substantive position that will be developed in the rest of the book, but also as a way to tie that position to traditional discussions of the nature of metaphysics.

The definition of metaphysics, then, requires the determination of the genus to which metaphysics belongs and of the specific difference that sets it apart within the genus. Considering the long history of metaphysics, one would expect the task of defining metaphysics to be rather simple. In fact, however, this task encounters many difficulties.

CHAPTER TWO

Generic and Specific Conditions

It might appear that the determination of the genus of metaphysics is fairly uncontroversial. After all, everyone agrees that metaphysics is a branch of philosophy, so such determination might just require to make this explicit. This is not sufficient, however, for at least two reasons. First, because the term 'philosophy' itself is too vague to be sufficiently informative; second, because such a description does not make clear how and in what order metaphysics is related to other branches of philosophy. The identification of the genus of metaphysics must involve a more determinate understanding of philosophy and a specification of the relation of metaphysics to other branches of philosophy. Reflection reveals, however, that it is not possible to provide a credible specification of the relation of metaphysics to other branches of philosophy without having first determined what metaphysics is. So we must postpone an attempt to do the former until we have arrived at a definition of metaphysics we consider acceptable. A more determinate understanding of philosophy, however, need not delay our progress. Although philosophers have debated the nature of philosophy from time immemorial, and, to this day, they regard the topic as unsettled, we can make some headway by staying away from radical and extreme conceptions and adopting one which is largely in agreement with our ordinary use of the term both in the classroom and outside of it. Later, I return to this issue and the implications it has for metaphysics.

We speak of philosophy in various ways, but these tend to fall into two kinds. In the first, we speak of philosophy as something we have, hold, study, develop, adopt, commit ourselves to, discover, admire, believe, formulate, state, and so on. In the second, we speak of philosophy as something we do, practice, engage in, carry out, and so on. When we speak of it in the first sense, generally we are thinking of it as a view, that is, a set of beliefs concerning anything, although there are differences with respect to the beliefs in question. Sometimes these beliefs are simply those regarding anything which an ordinary person may have. Thus, we speak of the philosophy my car mechanic has with respect to fixing cars: She believes in not taking on jobs she is not sure she can finish. Or we speak of the philosophy someone may have about feeding cats: never feed them scraps from the table. The examples I have given are rather pedestrian, but we also speak about more lofty cases of having a philosophy in this sense. The quality of the particular examples is not important for the understanding of this use of the term 'philosophy'; the important point is that the only condition necessary for a philosophy in this sense is that of being a belief someone holds or may hold. I say "may hold" because there are beliefs probably no one would hold, or could consistently hold, and yet these would nonetheless qualify as philosophy in this sense. There is no reason why we cannot think of a view that not only has never been held but will never be held by anyone. We might examine such a view, consider why it is untenable, and argue against it, even though it will always remain a straw figure.

Apart from the conception of philosophy as any view an ordinary person may hold about anything, philosophy may be conceived as a view of the world, or any of its parts, that seeks to be accurate, consistent, and comprehensive, and for which evidence is given as support. It is a view of the world or any of its parts because the object which philosophy studies does not seem to be restricted to any individual thing or any particular kind of thing. Philosophy seems to concern itself with everything which is subject to human experience. In this sense, there is no difference between this conception of philosophy and the previous one examined. The differences arise only because philosophy, in the latter sense, seeks to be accurate, consistent, comprehensive, and supported by sound evidence. Note I do not say that it is or must be so. Indeed, I do not yet know of any philosophy which is generally regarded as having fulfilled these conditions. If these conditions were to be applied as criteria of what constitutes a philosophy, then, based on what we know, we could not call philosophy any of the things which are generally called philosophy. And this makes no sense.

In order to qualify as philosophy, then, a view need not be accurate, consistent, comprehensive, and supported by sound evidence, but it does need to seek to be so. It must seek to be accurate in the sense that it must aim to be faithful to experience understood broadly to include both empirical experience and nonempirical intuitions. It must seek to be consistent because it must attempt to avoid contradiction. It must seek to be comprehensive in that it must try to present as complete a picture of the object it describes as possible. And it must seek support in evidence which is thought to be sound because philosophy wishes to achieve the status of knowledge, and views without sound support are matters of opinion, not knowledge.

In the first two and the last specified conditions, philosophy is not very different from science, for science also aims at accuracy, consistency, and sound support. The difference between science and philosophy rests on the third condition. Particular sciences do not aim at comprehensiveness; they restrict themselves to certain aspects, areas, and modes of investigation. Indeed, even if all sciences were pooled together into one super science, the picture given by this superscience would not be comprehensive insofar as there would be epistemic, ethical, and metaphysical dimensions which would be missing from it and which this super scientific view would not cover or aim to complete. Only philosophy aims to be fully comprehensive. Philosophy aims to produce a big picture even of partial aspects of the world; it is not content with partial pictures of the world or any of its parts.

One might object that I have not been faithful to my original intention of adopting a conception of philosophy generally in accordance with the use of the term both within and without the classroom. The reason is that the view of philosophy I have presented conflicts with at least one widely accepted conception of philosophy as the attempt to do away with views of the world or any of its parts which seek to be accurate, consistent, comprehensive, and supported by sound evidence.[1] What do we make of philosophers like Gorgias, Nietzsche, Derrida, and others, who have considered themselves, *qua* philosophers, as fulfilling a primarily critical function?

Two ways out of this difficulty suggest themselves. The first is to reject the credentials of these philosophers and say that what they

---

1. For other objections, see Grice, Pears, and Strawson, "Metaphysics," pp. 4–7.

do is not philosophy because their aim is not the aim I have identified as appropriate for philosophers. But this way out only confirms
the charge that I am not trying to be inclusive in the conception of
philosophy I have given. For what these critics do has been traditionally called philosophy even though there have been repeated
attempts at disenfranchising them. I cannot adopt this answer without having also to abandon the pretense of doing at least some justice to the way the term 'philosophy' is used in the classroom, and
that I do not wish to do.

A second way out is to argue that, in spite of initial appearances,
critics in fact fit the mold of philosophers. But, we may ask, how can
this be when they explicitly aim not only to undermine views of the
sort I have described, but more significantly, to undermine the whole
process of production of such views by questioning the possibility of
the enterprise? The way to include critics in the conception of philosophy I have proposed is to point out that those who aim to undermine noncritical philosophers do, in fact, have a view of a part of the
world, namely, of philosophy, which they believe to be accurate, consistent, comprehensive, and supported by sound evidence. Their
view must be regarded as seeking to be accurate because they believe, indeed, that philosophy is the way they believe it is. It must be
regarded as seeking to be consistent because they believe it applies
to all philosophies, including their own. It must be regarded as comprehensive because it seeks to apply to the whole of philosophy, not
just to some of its branches. And it must be regarded as seeking support in sound evidence, because it is thought to be effective in reaching its conclusions. In short, even the position which holds that one
cannot have a view is a view. Moreover, it is a view which concerns
one part of the world, for philosophy, whatever it is, is part of the
world when one conceives the world as including everything.

So much, then, for the understanding of philosophy as a view.
Now we must turn to the second, although related, understanding of
philosophy. This is the understanding of philosophy as something one
does, practices, or engages in, rather than something one has, holds,
or believes. In this sense philosophy is an activity rather than a view.
But the activity in question is not just any kind of activity. Running is
not doing philosophy, although one may do philosophy while one runs.

It appears at first that the activity in question may be of two
sorts. One is the activity whereby a view of the world, or any of its
parts, that seeks to be accurate, consistent, comprehensive, and
supported by sound evidence is produced. Another is the activity
whereby one seeks to develop the formulation, explanation, and jus-

tification of rules according to which the production of such a view of the world or any of its parts must proceed. But clearly the latter activity also involves the production of a view which itself seeks to be accurate and so on. This sort of activity concerns the production of a view of proper philosophical method and, therefore, strictly speaking, should be subsumed under the general heading of philosophy. In essence, there is no fundamental distinction between these two sorts of activities.

This discussion, however, has brought to the fore another conception of philosophy, namely, philosophy as a view concerning philosophical method. In this sense, philosophy consists of the set of rules that must be used to guide the activity that yields other philosophical views. In this sense, philosophy is often called a "discipline," for it consists in a set procedure that must be followed to achieve philosophical knowledge, although its disciplinary character is also associated with the activity involved in the implementation of the rules. Obviously, philosophy, understood as a set of rules, can be subsumed under the notion of philosophy as a view. Still, it may be convenient to keep it separate because of its peculiarity and in order to prevent confusion.

There is, moreover, another sense of philosophy that must be added to the three mentioned. It refers to the sort of ability a philosopher has to do philosophy. We often speak of someone as a philosopher or as having become a real philosopher even when the person is not at the time engaged in any kind of philosophical activity or does not hold any kind of philosophical view. Under these conditions, it cannot be said that the person is a philosopher because of a certain activity in which the person is engaged or because of a certain view the person holds. What is it that makes the person a philosopher, then? It is the ability to engage in philosophical activity or to develop philosophical views that makes us speak of the person in question as a philosopher.

We have, then, four different genera of metaphysics, that is to say, we have four different sets of generic conditions for metaphysics, although none of these four sets taken by itself is sufficient to distinguish metaphysics from other disciplines within and without philosophy:

1. A view of the world, or any of its parts, which seeks to be accurate, consistent, comprehensive, and supported by sound evidence;

2. The activity whereby 1 is developed;

3. The rules which are to be followed in the formulation of 1;

4. An ability to produce 1, to engage in 2, or to develop 3.

Obviously, 1 takes precedence over the others and must be considered the appropriate genus of metaphysics. It is the aim of all the others and presupposed by them. None of the others makes sense apart from it, even if 1 cannot be developed without the others.

Next we must inquire as to what gives metaphysics its distinctive character within philosophy, that is, we must determine the specific conditions which will complete, with the mentioned generic conditions, the set of necessary and sufficient conditions of metaphysics. It will take the greater part of this book to answer this question, but I begin by discussing various strategies which have been used to answer it.

Although philosophers have often differed as to what is peculiar or distinctive about metaphysics, one can easily discern four different traditions as well as various ways of integrating them.[2] One tradition distinguishes metaphysics on the basis of the object with which metaphysics is concerned. This is well exemplified in various other fields of learning. For example, astronomy is concerned with celestial bodies, theology is concerned with God, and human anatomy is concerned with the human body. If we adopt this approach, then we should be able to point to an object, group of objects, or kind of object, studied by metaphysics and only by metaphysics. Note that by object here I do not necessarily mean anything like an individual thing. I mean by object whatever it is that metaphysics studies.

A second tradition finds the distinguishing characteristic of metaphysics in its method. Again, other fields of inquiry serve as support and illustration of this approach. For example, it is customary to distinguish so-called revealed theology, that is, theology based on revelation, from other fields of inquiry by noting that it proceeds on the basis of authority, whereas in other fields of learning authority does not count or does not count as much. Likewise, one may argue that it is the method of investigation used by chemistry which distinguishes it from physics, for example, and not the object of each science for that can be, and often is, the same.

A third tradition finds the distinguishing difference of metaphysics in its aim. As in the previous cases, there are similarities

---

2. Kant points to three of these in *Prolegomena*, § 1, p. 13. For some others, see Grice, Pears, and Strawson, "Metaphysics."

with the way other disciplines are distinguished which support this claim. For example, one may point to the fact that the difference between ethics and politics concerns their aims: in ethics it is the good of the individual; in politics it is the good of the state. Or one may cite the cases of medicine and veterinary science, whose aims are the health of human and nonhuman animals respectively.

Finally, a fourth tradition identifies the difference that sets metaphysics apart from other disciplines with the kind of knowledge it yields. Often, this is understood in terms of propositions (or statements, sentences, or judgments, depending on the philosopher). Philosophers who distinguish metaphysics in these terms point out that metaphysical propositions are different from the propositions of other disciplines of learning. And, indeed, even a simple inspection of metaphysical propositions indicates they are quite different from the propositions of other disciplines. A proposition such as, "Being *qua* being is indefinable," seems to be quite different from the propositions physicists and psychologists entertain when they are practicing their disciplines.

It is difficult to find philosophers who exclusively argue in favor of one of these approaches and against the others. Most often we find that philosophers argue for one of them and either neglect the others or subordinate them to the one they favor.[3] Moreover, there are many attempts to integrate two or more into one.[4]

We need not go very far into the history of philosophy before we find these various approaches at work. One of the earliest examples of the attempt to make distinctions among our beliefs based on their objects is illustrated by Plato's divided line in the *Republic*.[5] The purpose of this line appears to be to distinguish among various kinds of knowledge on the basis of their objects. Knowledge properly speaking is only of intelligible entities whereas opinion concerns only sensible objects. It is the kind of object, then, that determines how we can know it and what we can know about it.[6] Naturally, because this view can be used to distinguish among various disciplines of learning, it gives rise to the view that it is the object that determines the disci-

---

3. Kant, *Prolegomena*, § 1, p. 13.
4. Boethius, *On the Trinity*, vol. II:8.
5. Plato, *Republic* 510, p. 745.
6. In *Ion*, Plato is quite explicit about this point; see 537d, p. 769. But compare this text with *Republic* 346, p. 595, where arts seem to differ by function or aim rather than object, and also with *Theaetetus* 146e, p. 851, where Socrates chides Theaetetus for confusing the question concerning the objects of knowledge with the question of what knowledge is.

pline whether considered as a view, as an activity, as a set of rules, or as an ability. Often, those who adopt this position speak of the subject or subject matter of the discipline, rather than its object.[7] There are several reasons for this terminology: Some think in terms of a subject in which features or characteristics inhere; others think of subjects of sentences of which predicates are predicated; and still others conceive the subject as the object considered in relation to a knower or under a certain perspective, whence the use of the term 'formal object' as well. Moreover, they contrast these with the objects toward which mental or perceptual faculties are directed.[8]

Aristotle's attempt to develop criteria of scientific knowledge in *Posterior Analytics*, on the other hand, may be taken to illustrate a different approach, which holds that method distinguishes among disciplines.[9] For Aristotle, scientific knowledge is characterized by the use of demonstrative reasoning. Demonstrative reasoning is deductive reasoning known to be valid and based on true premises which are known to be true because they are immediate. If Aristotle had ended with this, one could say that, contrary to Plato, he distinguished scientific knowledge exclusively on the basis of the method by which it is attained.[10] But Aristotle went further and added that scientific knowledge must be knowledge of the universal and of what is real, and that the premises of the reasoning which yields scientific knowledge must be related to the conclusions as causes are to effects.[11] Obviously, these conditions go beyond method and concern the object of knowledge itself.

The aim has also been used to distinguish among different disciplines. Aristotle's own distinction between theoretical and practical sciences illustrates the point.[12] What distinguishes these sciences is

---

7. Avicenna, *Metaphysica* I, p. 11; Aquinas, *Commentary on "On the Trinity" of Boethius*, q. 5, 4, p. 42.
8. Ockham, "On the Notion of Knowledge and Science" (*Expositio super viii libros Physicorum*, Prologus), pp. 8–9; Aquinas, *Summa theologiae* I, 1, 7, p. 12, and *Commentary on "On the Trinity" of Boethius*, q. 5, a. 4, pp. 44–45. There is plenty of disagreement about these notions in the history of philosophy.
9. Aristotle, *Posterior Analytics* 71b20, p. 112.
10. Indeed, Averroes did just that in *On the Harmony of Religion and Philosophy*, pp. 49, 59, 68.
11. Aristotle, *Posterior Analytics* 71b20, p. 112. See also *Metaphysics* 1064a1–3, p. 860.
12. Aristotle, *Metaphysics* 981b, 1026a17, pp, 690–1, 779, and *Nicomachean Ethics* 1141a20–1141b10, p. 1028.

that the former have knowledge as their aim, whereas the latter are intended to guide action.

Finally, the kind of knowledge or the kind of proposition has also been used to distinguish metaphysics from other disciplines. There are antecedents of this attempt in the Middle Ages. Ockham's view that sciences are distinguished by the subjects and predicates of the propositions of which they are composed sets an important precedent for this position.[13] But it is with Kant's characterization of metaphysical judgments as synthetic a priori that this position enters the mainstream.[14]

Naturally, there have been intermediary positions or positions that combine two or three of the mentioned ways of distinguishing the disciplines. For example, Aquinas, although emphasizing the object, finds that it is that object considered under the formal aspect under which it is studied that yields disciplinary differences and, in that way, recognizes the importance of method as well among the distinguishing factors of the disciplines.[15]

Let me begin, then, by considering some views which distinguish metaphysics in terms of the object it studies. Following these, I shall turn to those which establish its distinction from other disciplines of learning on the basis of the method and the aim. Finally, I shall briefly discuss those which see the character of the propositions it contains as determining its distinctive character. These four lines of inquiry will take up in the next four chapters.

---

13. Ockham, "On the Notion of Knowledge and Science" (*Expositio super viii libros Physicorum*, Prologus), p. 15.
14. Kant, *Prolegomena*, §§ 1 and 2, pp. 13–19.
15. Aquinas, *Commentary on the "De Trinitate" of Boethius* 5, 1, resp. And ad 1, pp. 7, 10, 16, ad 6; 5, 4, ad 7, p. 38; 6, 1, ad 4, p. 62. Also Boethius, *On the Trinity*, vol. II:8.

CHAPTER THREE

Object

Views which distinguish metaphysics by its object fall into two broad groups. In one of these, metaphysics is conceived as being concerned, in some sense, with everything. In the other, metaphysics is conceived as being concerned only with some things. There are four main views of the first sort; they identify the object of metaphysics as one of the following: being(s) and nonbeing(s), being(s), being *qua* being, and transcendental being(s). There are many views of the second sort, but they can be gathered into two main classes, depending on whether they identify some things in general or some things in particular as objects of metaphysics. Those which constitute the first of these two classes list as objects the following: transcendentals/being *qua* being and its properties, transcendental properties of being *qua* being, categorial being(s), real being(s)/reality, existential being(s)/existence, essential being(s)/essence(s), formal being(s)/form(s), natural being(s)/nature(s), substantial being(s)/substance(s), causal being(s)/cause(s), and intelligibles/knowables. Those which constitute the second of the two classes list as objects the following: God, necessary being(s), immaterial being(s), person(s), ultimate cause(s), relations, abstract entities, concepts, consciousness/lived-world/phenomena, noumena, language(s), texts, meaning(s), propositions, presuppositions/first principle(s), the most general predicates, end(s), and combinations of some of these.

A. Everything

In this group, the common view is that, in some sense, metaphysics studies everything and that is the distinguishing mark of the discipline.[1] Whereas this or that discipline studies an individual being, say God, or a particular kind of being, say the human body, metaphysics studies every individual being and particular kind of being. But 'everything' can be understood in at least two ways. In one way, distributively. To say that metaphysics studies everything in this sense is to say that it studies the members of a set or collection.[2] Consider a universe composed only of three things—a, b, and c—and their relations—aRb, aRc, bRa, bRc, cRa, and cRb. If metaphysics studies everything in this universe and this is understood distributively, this gives us two possibilities:

1. Metaphysics studies a, b, and c.

2. Metaphysics studies a, b, c, aRb, aRc, bRa, bRc, cRa, and cRb.

However, we can also understand 'everything' nondistributively, as a whole. In this sense, metaphysics studies the set or collection considered as a group.[3] This seems to yield the following possibilities:

3. Metaphysics studies the set composed of a, b, c, aRb, aRc, bRa, bRc, cRa, and cRb.

This means that metaphysics studies the set or collection of members and the interrelations among the members taken together, as forming a whole. But there is also another possibility:

4. Metaphysics studies the set of aRb, aRc, bRa, bRc, cRa, and cRb.

In this understanding, metaphysics does not study the members of the set or collection considered independently of their relations among themselves, but rather the set of relations among the mem-

---

1. Aristotle, *Metaphysics* 982a10–20 and 1004a15, pp. 691, and 733.
2. Grossmann, *The Categorial Structure of the World*, p. 4; Hampshire, "Metaphysical Systems," p. 33.
3. Bradley, *Appearance and Reality*, p. 1; see also Quinton, in "Final Discussion," p. 142.

bers. But if metaphysics studies only relations, then it does not, in fact, study everything, unless the study of relations is considered to include the study of relata or one holds that there are only relations. That the study of relations includes the study of relata does not seem to be necessarily the case. I can study the relation of sisterhood holding between Jane and June and yet not study either Jane or June. Indeed, Jane and June may be considered only insofar as the relation of sisterhood holding between them requires two relata. If this is so, then 4 cannot be considered a legitimate understanding of the view that metaphysics studies everything, but rather a view which conceives the object of metaphysics to be a certain kind of thing, that is, relations. The view that metaphysics studies only relations because, in fact, there are only relations, relies on a very peculiar view which requires considerable support. I shall leave the discussion of this view for later.

A similar point can be made about 1, for this understanding of metaphysics excludes relations. 'Everything' must be taken in the most inclusive way possible if the view that metaphysics studies everything is to be taken as distinctive. Indeed, if metaphysics is understood in this way, it does appear that metaphysics is different from other disciplines, for no discipline studies everything in this broad sense. But, under these conditions, can metaphysics be conceived as anything more than the collection of all other disciplines, that is, as the encyclopedia of all knowledge?[4] Is metaphysics anything more than physics, chemistry, literary criticism, sociology, ethics, and so on taken together? This is one of the three fundamental difficulties we shall see apply to all views of metaphysics that conceive it as studying everything.

A second difficulty concerns its distinction from philosophy. If metaphysics is taken to be the discipline that studies everything, then, can it be distinguished from philosophy? The object of philosophy was identified as the world or any of its parts. If the world were composed of only two things and a single relation between them—say a, b, and aRb—the object of philosophy would be a, b, and aRb or a, or b, or aRb, where the 'or' is not understood exclusively. But how would this be different from the object of metaphysics, which in such

---

4. Warnock, in "Final Discussion," p. 143. This is a concern of all those who try to define the limits of a most general discipline. See Meinong, "The Theory of Objects," p. 78, and Aquinas, *Commentary on "On the Trinity" of Boethius*, q. 5, a. 1. *ad* 6, p. 16.

a world would also be a, b, and aRb? For $(a.b.aRb) \rightarrow a$, and $(a.b.aRb)$
$\rightarrow b$, and $(a.b.aRb) \rightarrow aRb$. The only possibility would be to emphasize that philosophy can be content with the study of any part of the
world, whereas metaphysics cannot. But this does not appear to be a
very significant difference, for the ideal of a philosophy would surely
be to cover the full extension of the world.

If metaphysics is understood as studying everything, it does not
appear possible to maintain a distinction between it and philosophy.
Indeed, some philosophers have identified philosophy and metaphysics, possibly for this very reason.[5] This view, however, is contrary to a long tradition which considers them to be distinct and it
should be adopted only as a last resort; as we shall see, there are
other ways of conceiving metaphysics which do not require its identification with philosophy.

Finally, there is a third recurring difficulty that affects views of
metaphysics which conceive it as studying everything. In order to
avoid the two difficulties mentioned, supporters of these views distinguish the object of metaphysics by noting that, although it is extensionally the same object of other disciplines, it is that object
considered differently. That is to say, metaphysics studies the same
object as other disciplines, but it studies aspects of it which are not
the same as those studied by other disciplines.

Unfortunately, this way out is not successful to the extent that
it is not clear what about the object metaphysics can study that is
not studied by other disciplines. This solution leaves us with an
empty discipline, for it appears that anything that could be said
about the object of metaphysics is part of one discipline or another.

Let us turn now to some particular ways of understanding the
object of metaphysics conceived as everything.

1. *Being(s) and Nonbeing(s)*

One way to understand that metaphysics is concerned with
everything is to hold that the object of metaphysics includes both being and nonbeing.[6] The full development of this position is a rather

---

5. See, for example, Popper, "Metaphysics and Criticizability"; Broad, "Critical and Speculative Philosophy"; and Moore, "What Is Philosophy?"
6. Aristotle, *Metaphysics* 1004a10, p. 733; Heidegger, *An Introduction to
Metaphysics*, pp. 2, 20. For Meinong, the "science of objects" studies both
being and nonbeing, but he distinguishes this science from metaphysics
proper. "The Theory of Objects," pp. 79, 82.

recent event in the history of philosophy. Traditionally, nonbeing has generally been spoken of only as the opposite of being and as incapable of investigation in its own right. Indeed, when investigations of it were made, they were presented as investigations into being, namely, being considered as imperfect or as lacking something.[7] Many systematic treatises on metaphysics which followed the model established by Suárez's *Disputationes metaphysicae* (1596) relegated the discussion of nothing, mental entities, apparent being, and similar things to an appendix to the discussion of being.[8] Only a few included them within the object of metaphysics.[9] In recent times, however, authors like Heidegger, put nonbeing at the very center of metaphysics.[10]

The advantages of a position which incorporates both being and nonbeing into the object of metaphysics should be obvious. It is able to distinguish metaphysics from any other discipline by giving it an object so general that no other discipline is concerned with it. Even within philosophy, no other branch of the discipline appears to be concerned with both being and nonbeing.

Yet, does it make any sense to say that metaphysics is concerned with nonbeing? The fact is that this view appears to be reducible to another view, the view which holds that metaphysics is concerned with being.[11] This can be shown by asking about the meaning of 'nonbeing.' 'Nonbeing' can be understood in two ways: either as nothing, that is, as nonbeing taken strictly; or as something, that is, as some individual being or some kind of being. If nonbeing is understood as nothing, then the view reduces to the view that metaphysics is concerned with being, for being and nothing amount to being, just as one plus zero amount to one. But if nonbeing is understood as something, that is, as some being or some kind of being, again, the view reduces to the view that metaphysics is concerned with being.

---

7. Scot, *Periphyseon*, vol. I:3 ff.; Fredugis, "Letter on Nothing and Darkness," pp. 104–8.
8. Suárez, *Disputationes metaphysicae* 54, vol. 26.
9. Timpler argued that the object of metaphysics is comprised of intelligibles and that "nothing" is intelligible and, therefore, must be included in it. *Metaphysicae systema methodicum*, Bk. I, ch. 1, probl. 5, p. 6, and ch. 2, probl. 1, p. 21.
10. Heidegger, *An Introduction to Metaphysics*, p. 23.
11. This objection does not impress Heidegger, although he does not consider as clear a formulation of it as I have presented here. Ibid., p. 33. I shall return to this objection in chapter 7.

Because being comprises all individual beings and all kinds of being, to be concerned with being and some individual being or some kind of being is nothing other than to be concerned with being. In short, the view that the object of metaphysics includes being and nonbeing seems to be reducible to the view that the object of metaphysics is being. So we must next turn to the view which argues that metaphysics studies being.

2. Being(s)

At first, the view that metaphysics in concerned with being and only with being may, indeed, appear to make sense insofar as it can serve to distinguish metaphysics from other branches of philosophy as well as from other sciences and arts, for none of them has this scope.[12] Every discipline appears to be concerned only with some individual beings or some kinds of beings rather than with all being(s). Upon reflection, however, this position seems untenable. One difficulty with it is that metaphysics amounts to nothing but a conglomerate of other disciplines. If metaphysics studies being, that is, everything (whether distributively or not), and various disciplines study different individual beings and kinds of being, that is, different portions of being, then metaphysics would appear to be nothing over and above those disciplines. Of course, one could argue that the disciplinary conglomerate which metaphysics would turn out to be, according to this view, would have characteristics which the various disciplines that constitute the whole would not have. But, in order to argue this, one would have to find the origin of those distinguishing characteristics in something other than the fact that metaphysics studies being. Let me illustrate this point with reference to history.

Some philosophers argue that a general history is not equivalent to the sum total of special histories.[13] They do so not on the basis of their objects, because the object of a general history is nothing but the sum total of the objects of special histories. Rather, they base this claim by arguing that the method of a general history differs from the method of special histories. The problem for philosophers who might wish to argue for the distinction between metaphysics

---

12. Leibniz, *Philosophical Papers and Letters*, p. 76; Randall, *Nature and Historical Experience*, p. 125; and Pols, *Radical Realism*, pp. 178–9.
13. Mandelbaum, "The History of Ideas, Intellectual History, and the History of Philosophy," pp. 44–45.

and a merely cumulative discipline in a similar way is that they cannot refer to differences of method, for they are committed to the establishment of differences only in terms of object.

A second but no less serious objection against this position is that, if this view were correct, then the conclusions reached in metaphysics could not be different from the conclusions reached in other disciplines. Suppose that we considered metaphysics to be composed of certain understandings we have about the world. According to this view, those understandings would have to be indistinguishable from the understandings reached in other disciplines. Now it appears to be true that metaphysicians concern themselves with the same objects which concern physicists, chemists, and so on. They are concerned with colors, electrons, elements, and so on. But what they say about these objects is quite different from what physicists, chemists, and other practitioners of particular disciplines say. They say, for example, that colors are immaterial and elements are substances, which are not statements found in other disciplines. Therefore, the distinguishing feature of metaphysics cannot be found in the fact that metaphysics studies these objects, as this view proposes, for then its conclusions would have to be similar to those of the specialized disciplines which study only those objects and they, in fact, are not.

3. Being qua Being

A way out from these and other difficulties for those who wish to maintain that metaphysics is concerned with everything is to modify the formula so as to include everything, but everything taken in a certain way. Perhaps the most widespread view of this sort is the one which holds that the object of metaphysics is being *qua* being.[14] Although there are different understandings of what this formula means, most of those who use it have in mind that the object of metaphysics is not the same as being considered as the collection of

---

14. Aristotle, *Metaphysics* 1003a24 and 1005a2, pp. 731 and 735; Avicenna, *Metaphysica*, p. 14; Scheibler, *Opus metaphysicum*, p. 3; Maritain, *A Preface to Metaphysics*, p. 26. Another expression used in place of 'being *qua* being' is 'common being' (*ens commune*). See Aquinas, *Commentary on the "De Trinitate" of Boethius* 5, 1, ad 7, p. 16. See also Heidegger's idiosyncratic rendition of this position in *An Introduction to Metaphysics*, pp. 3, 15–16.

all the different individual things or kinds of thing there are. Being *qua* being is not the same as the sum total of all individual beings such as this table, this man, this pen, and so on; nor is it the sum total of all kinds of being such as table, man, pen, and so on; nor even of the sum total of all individual beings and kinds of being. Being *qua* being is not the same as the things or kinds of thing of which 'being' may be predicated or which can be said to be in some way or another. Being considered *qua* being is supposed to be these things not considered as the individual things or kinds of things they are, but only insofar as they are beings. Thus, a table is not studied by metaphysics insofar as it is an individual thing or insofar as it is a table, but only insofar as it is a being.

The advantages of this view are quite evident. If metaphysics is concerned with being *qua* being, and all other disciplines are concerned with individual beings or with particular kinds of being, then we should have no difficulty in distinguishing metaphysics from them, at least in principle. Whereas human anatomy is concerned with the human body *qua* human body, metaphysics is concerned with the human body *qua* being. Moreover, even though metaphysics is concerned with the collection of all kinds of being studied by the remaining disciplines, metaphysics could still be distinguished from these disciplines because it would study everything but only insofar as these things are beings and not the individual things or the particular kinds of thing they are.

There are difficulties with this position, however, at least three of which must be mentioned. The first difficulty is that, if the object of metaphysics is being *qua* being, then one would be hard pressed to argue that metaphysics studies everything, for being *qua* being excludes both individual beings and kinds of being. This, however, could not be considered a serious difficulty unless one were to insist both that metaphysics must study everything and that the study of individuals and kinds *qua* beings means that individuals and kinds are not studied.

The second difficulty is more serious. It makes no sense to say metaphysics studies being *qua* being, because being *qua* being is nothing other than the various individual beings and particular kinds of being which compose the universe. Being is nothing but being this or that, such as this cat, this chair, or that color, or being a kind of thing, such as a cat, a chair, or a color. To ask about being *qua* being is to ask about an abstraction. There is nothing over and above individual beings or particular kinds of being, and so the discipline concerned with being *qua* being amounts, after all, to the collection of disciplines concerned with the various individual beings or particular kinds of being which compose the total collection of what there is. Metaphysics is the encyclopedia of all knowledge.

Then, too, if being is taken as the most general category, there is nothing that can be said about it considered under any other category. To be the most general category implies that there is none above it and thus that being admits of no classification or analysis. This is what philosophers express by saying that being cannot be defined.[15] That is to say, being becomes a primitive notion. To say that a notion is primitive is to claim that the notion is such that it cannot be further divided and analyzed into simpler notions.[16] A notion such as bachelor is not primitive because it can be analyzed into the notions of unmarried and man. But not all notions are like bachelor. Some are such that they cannot be further broken down into other, more simple components. Indeed, some philosophers have argued that even some composite notions, such as person and characterized particular, are, or should be considered, unanalyzable and, therefore, must be regarded as primitive.[17] Most frequently, philosophers regard as primitive the most fundamental notions in their metaphysics, analyzing all the rest in terms of these basic building blocks.[18] Hence, if the object of metaphysics were being *qua* being, metaphysics would turn out to be an empty discipline, for nothing significant could be said about its object.[19] Only when being is considered as it appears in various garbs can one say anything about it. Granting this argument, however, leads to the position that metaphysics is rather about all individual and kinds of beings, and this

---

15. Aristotle, *Metaphysics* 998b22, p. 723; Suárez, *Disputationes metaphysicae* 2, 4, 1, vol. 25, pp. 87–88; Collingwood, *An Essay on Metaphysics*, p. 14. Aristotle is not the only philosopher who is not bothered by the notion of a study whose central notion is indefinable. Another is Moore, *Principia ethica*, p. 7.

16. Strawson, *Individuals*, pp. 98–9.

17. For the primitive character of persons, see ibid., p. 98; for the primitiveness of characterized particulars, see Long, "Particulars and Their Qualities."

18. For the reasons metaphysicians have for adopting primitive notions, see Gracia, *Individuality*, pp. 51–2.

19. For every science requires a genus and, as Aubenque points out, metaphysics has none. *Le problème de l'être chez Aristote*, pp. 222 and 229 ff.

would be to reduce metaphysics to the collection of all other disciplines, or to this or that being or particular kind of being, and this would be to reduce the discipline to a subdiscipline. Both moves we found to be unacceptable.

4. *Transcendental Being(s)*

A different way to argue that the object of metaphysics is everything is to say that metaphysics is concerned with transcendental being.[20] The notion of transcendentality depends on the notion of transcendence, and transcendence may be understood in at least four ways.[21] In one way we might say that,

> 1. *X* transcends *Y*, if and only if the extension of the term that names *X* is other than the extension of the term that names *Y*.

According to this conception of transcendence, cat transcends human being for the extension of 'cat' is other than the extension of 'human being.' The point is that the class cat transcends the class human being because the extension of the name for the class cat, namely, 'cat,' is other than the extension of the name for the class human being, namely, 'human being.' Note that for the purposes of this analysis and the others that will follow, I am assuming that the name of the class of things that are cats is 'cat,' the name of the class of things which are Plato is 'Plato,' and the name of the class of things which are Plato's teacher is 'Plato's teacher' (not 'Socrates').

In another way, we might say that,

> 2. *X* transcends *Y* and *Z*, if and only if the extension of the term that names *X* coincides with the extensions of the terms that name *Y* and *Z* taken together.

According to this understanding of transcendence, sibling transcends brother and sister, for the extension of 'sibling' coincides with the extensions of 'brother' and 'sister' taken together.

---

20. Scharf, *Theoria transcendentalis primae philosophiae* (1624).
21. For the sake of brevity, I am giving only an extensional analysis of transcendence, but intensional analyses are also possible. See my "Suárez and the Doctrine of the Transcendentals," p. 122.

In a third sense,

3. *X* transcends *Y*, if and only if the extension of the term that names *X* is greater than and includes the extension of the term that names *Y*.

In this sense, animal transcends human being because the extension of 'animal' includes that of 'human being' but is greater than it. The extension of 'animal' also includes, for example, the extension of 'cat.'

Finally, we might say that,

4. *X* transcends *Y*, if and only if the extension of the term that names *X* is at least partly other than, and does not completely include, the extension of the term that names *Y*.

According to this conception, just transcends human being because the extension of 'just' partly overlaps with the extension of 'human being' but there are some just things which are not human beings.

The notion of transcendence is fundamental to the doctrine that metaphysics is concerned with transcendental being, but it is not sufficient to make sense of this doctrine. To do so one must keep in mind that this view arises in the context of a broader attempt at a fundamental categorization of being such as the one undertaken by Aristotle. Aristotle's attempt, and what his followers did with it, can serve as an illustration.

According to Aristotle, there are some and only some basic categories into which being can be fitted, giving rise to what is called "categorial being," that is, being considered as divided into the basic categories.[22] These categories are substance, quantity, quality, relation, time, place, and so on. Within the Aristotelian framework, there are three ways in which being fits into these categories: (*A*) beings which fit into one and only one category such as a horse, which fits in the category of substance; (*B*) beings which fit into more than one but less than all the categories, such as three, which fits into the categories of quantity and time but not into all categories; and (*C*) beings which fit into all the categories, such as good. Because all

---

22. Aristotle, *Categories* 1b25, p. 3.

being for Aristotle is categorial being, C is to be understood as referring to beings which fit into all the categories but do not extend beyond them. However, Christian Aristoteleans see Aristotle's scheme as confining, for they believe that reality is greater than categorial being. This opens up three further possibilities: (D) beings which fit into all the categories but which also extend outside of them such as good; (E) beings which fit into some, but not all, categories, and which also extend outside the categories such as wisdom; and (F) beings which fall outside the categories altogether, such as God. Now, the term 'transcendental' as traditionally used applies only to C, D, F, and E, giving us four different understandings of transcendentality as follows:

a. X is transcendental, if and only if the extension of the term that names X coincides with the combined extensions of the terms that name each and every one of the basic categories into which categorial being may be divided.

b. X is transcendental, if and only if the extension of the term that names X is greater than and includes the extension of the terms that name each and every one of the basic categories into which categorial being may be divided.

c. X is transcendental, if and only if the extension of the term that names X does not coincide with the combined or separate extensions of the terms that name each and every one of the basic categories into which categorial being may be divided.

d. X is transcendental, if and only if the extension of the term that names X does not coincide with the combined or separate extensions of the terms that name each and every one of the basic categories into which categorial being may be divided, but the extension of the term that names X includes some but not all of the extensions of the terms that name each and every one of the basic categories into which being may be divided.

These understandings of transcendentality correspond to the four understandings of transcendence given earlier: a corresponds to 2; b corresponds to 3; c corresponds to 1; and d corresponds to 4.

If the transcendentality of being is understood in the first sense (a), and all being is considered to be categorial, then this view amounts to the one which holds that metaphysics studies categorial being, for transcendental being in this sense amounts to all categorial being. Metaphysics studies beings which fall under A, B, and C. The merits of the position which identifies categorial being as the object of metaphysics will be discussed later, under views which identify some things in general as the object of metaphysics.

If the transcendentality of being is understood in the second sense (*b*), then the view reduces to the already discussed position that metaphysics studies everything. Metaphysics studies beings included in *A–F*. Transcendental being in this sense includes both categorial and non-categorial being, and this appears to be as broad a class as possible.

If the transcendentality of being is understood in the third sense (*c*), then metaphysics will seem to study only non-categorial being, for transcendental being in this sense amounts to non-categorial being (beings falling under *F*). Non-categorial being has frequently been reduced to God. Apart from whether or not this is so, this position limits the object of metaphysics to an individual being or a particular kind of being and, therefore, its discussion must wait until we turn to views which do not include all beings in the object of metaphysics.

Finally, if the transcendentality of being is understood in the fourth sense (*d*), then metaphysics studies only some categorial and some non-categorial beings.[23] Metaphysics studies beings classified under *E*. Because these would have to be gathered under some common notion, which would identify the particular kind of being in question, the object of metaphysics would include only a particular kind of being. So, as in the previous case, we must wait until we get to views of this sort.

In conclusion, the identification of the object of metaphysics as transcendental being does not help us find the specific difference which characterizes metaphysics. Partly for this reason and partly for others, some philosophers have turned away from attempts at finding the object of metaphysics in everything and have sought to identify it with some things in general or some things in particular. There have been many attempts in this direction, and I shall refer only to those which have been more influential or which I have found useful. I should point out at the outset that none of them appears effective for reasons which will become evident as we go along.

---

23. Scotus, "Concerning Metaphysics" (*Opus oxoniense* 1, 8, 3), pp. 2–3.

B. Some Things in General

1. *Transcendentals / Being* qua *Being and Its Properties*

One of these views holds that the object of metaphysics is the so-called transcendentals.[24] The transcendentals are usually identified as being *qua* being and its properties.[25] Most of those who favor this view adopt a notion of transcendentality according to which the extension of a transcendental term coincides with the conjoined extensions of the terms which name all the basic categories of reality.[26] In terms of extension, this is explained by saying that a term is transcendental if and only if it can be truly predicated of every categorial term. 'One,' for example, is predicable of 'cat,' 'white,' 'fatherhood,' and so on. In terms of intension, it can be put by saying that the notion expressed by every categorial term includes the notion expressed by the transcendental term.[27]

This position holds not only that being is transcendental, but also that the properties of being are transcendental. By property is meant a feature that always and only accompanies that of which it is a property but which is not part of its definition.[28] Thus, for example, the capacity to laugh is a property of human beings because

---

24. Scotus, "Concerning Metaphysics" (*Quaestiones subtilissimae super libros Metaphysicorum Aristotelis*, Prologus 5), p. 5a; Albert the Great, *Metaphysica* 1, 1, 2, p. 5a; and Fabro, "The Transcendentality of *Ens-Esse* and the Ground of Metaphysics," p. 426. Jan A. Aertsen has recently claimed that this applies even, or perhaps particularly, to Aquinas, in *Medieval Philosophy and the Transcendentals*, p. 157.

25. Often the formula reads: Being and the properties of being. But the properties of being are also referred to as attributes (*passiones*). Aristotle, *Metaphysics* 1003a1, p. 731; Aquinas, *Commentary on the "De Trinitate" of Boethius* 6, 1, p. 64.

26. This is not so with everyone, however. See Scotus, for example, in "Concerning Metaphysics" (*Opus oxoniense* 1, 8, 3), p. 3. I have discussed Scotus's view in "Scotus's Conception of Metaphysics: The Study of the Transcendentals."

27. Many have a stronger reading of this formula. They conceive the transcendentals not just as coextensional but as identical in reality, although not in concept. The sources of this view are found in Islamic authors. See, for example, Averroes, *In Metaphysicam*, fols. 66va and 65ra.

28. Porphyry, *Isagoge*, p. 48.

there can be no human being without it, and everything which has it is a human being. This holds even if it is never exercised or its exercise is impeded, and even though the capacity to laugh is not part of the definition of human being. This example assumes the traditional definition of human being as rational animal, but the point being made does not depend on that definition. In a different example, it is a property of an Euclidean triangle that the sum of its angles measure 180 degrees. If properties are understood thus, then the properties of being are those which always accompany being, that is, they can be truly predicated of all beings. Obviously, as being has no definition, these features are not part of the definition of being.

According to this view, then, being has properties and these properties are transcendental. That they are transcendental means that, as with being itself, the extensions of the terms which name them coincide with the conjoined extensions of the terms that name all basic categories of reality, or, to put the matter in terms of intension, that the notion expressed by every term that names a basic category of reality includes the notions expressed by the terms that name the properties of being.

The identity of these properties has been a matter of debate among those who adhere to this doctrine. In the Middle Ages, it was common to list unity, truth, and goodness among them. But others were added as time went on, such as thing, beauty, disjunctive features, and so on.[29] For my purposes, the identity and number of these properties is not important.

There are several difficulties with the doctrine of the transcendentals. Because my concern is not with this doctrine, but with the view that being *qua* being and its transcendental properties constitute the object of metaphysics, I do not need to examine them here. However, I will discuss one to illustrate the seriousness of the difficulties.

It is not clear, for example, that it is possible to maintain coherently that being *qua* being can have any properties in the sense mentioned, when being is conceived as not having a definition. Those who hold the aforementioned conception of property maintain that

---

29. Cf. *Topoi* 11, 2 (1992), devoted to the transcendentals in the Middle Ages. Some authors included such things among them as cause and effect and substance and accident. See Albert, *Metaphysica* 1, 1, 2, vol. 16, p. 4.

predicates are of two classes: essential (part of the definition) and nonessential (not part of the definition). Animal and rational are essential predicates of human being because they are part of the definition of human being. Nonessential predicates are subdivided further into two classes. One class of nonessential predicates consists of predicates which refer to properties. These, although not part of the definition, are nevertheless truly predicated of every thing to which the definition applies. The capacity to laugh is a property of human beings and having angles which measure 180 degrees is a property of Euclidean triangles.

Another class of nonessential predicates consists of predicates which refer to accidents. These are not truly predicated of every being to which the definition applies. An act of laughter in which an individual human being engages is an accident of the human being and the color of the lines of an individual Euclidean triangle is an accident of the triangle. The distinction between property and accident makes sense only if there are nonessential features which are entailed by essential features, for then one can distinguish these (properties), which are entailed, from those (accidents), which are not entailed by the essential features of the entity to which the definition applies. In this way, properties necessarily apply, whereas accidents do not. De facto, there may not be any difference between these, for a particular accident may apply to every member of a kind of being. But, in principle, there is a difference, because the accident is not entailed by the essential features identified in the definition.

The problem, however, is that if being is not definable, then it can have no essential features. And if being has no essential features, then it can be argued that either everything predicated of it is an accident or everything predicated of it is a property. For the second position, one must accept that having no essential predicates implies that all predicates are necessary; for the first position, one must accept that having no essential predicates implies that no predicate is necessary. For our purposes, we need not choose between these two alternatives, as both are equally undesirable to the position we are discussing, although for different reasons: The second is undesirable because it would make all features of being transcendental properties of it; the first is undesirable because it would make no feature of being a transcendental property of it.

We might, at this point, ask whether the doctrine of the transcendentals is imperiled by this problem, or whether it is just the understanding of transcendental attributes of being as properties that is imperiled? The view that predicates such as 'being' and 'unity,' for example, refer to the same thing is not imperiled by the objection I have discussed. But the talk about transcendental attributes as properties is. So much, then, for the difficulties involved in the doctrine of the transcendentals. Now let us return to the object of metaphysics.

The strength of the view that metaphysics studies the transcendentals is that, according to it, metaphysics is concerned with both a very general object, namely, being, and with some, but not all, of the features that being may have. Thus, one can preserve the sense that metaphysics is not reducible to other disciplines and yet has something particular to say. By identifying some properties of being which are common to all beings, but not particular to any, this position extends the work of metaphysics beyond that of dealing with being *qua* being. This allows the metaphysician to speak of the relation of being to its properties, of the number and nature of those properties, and of other issues that arise from their consideration. Moreover, by excluding from metaphysics features of being which are not properties of being, the view makes room for other disciplines whose purpose is precisely to study such features. Thus, physics will study materiality, biology will study life, and so on.

The weaknesses of the position stem, first, from the controversial notion of properties of being. Second, they stem from the fact that, as with the other views which posit only part of everything as the object of metaphysics, this conception of metaphysics turns out to be too narrow, failing to do justice to metaphysical practice. Indeed, metaphysics as practiced by most metaphysicians extends well beyond the consideration of the transcendentals. The transcendentals have generally been considered part of the object of metaphysics, but metaphysics studies all sorts of other things in addition, as the very large variety of objects identified as the object of metaphysics by different philosophers illustrates. The presentation of these, then, will constitute an indirect argument against the view that metaphysics studies the transcendentals and only the transcendentals, even though we will find each of these views, considered by itself, to be inadequate to account for the distinctive character of the discipline.

2. *Transcendental Properties of Being* Qua *Being*

There is a variation on the position just mentioned, according to which it is not being *qua* being and its properties that is the object of metaphysics, but only the properties of being *qua* being.[30] The reason for this position is clear. Being *qua* being seems to be nothing other than the things that are and the properties of being *qua* being would seem nothing other than the properties which are common to all beings. Moreover, even if one were to hold that being *qua* being is something other than its properties, one would be hard pressed to say what that would be. A way out, then, is to make the properties of being *qua* being the object of metaphysics. These properties, unity, goodness, and so on, are called "transcendental."

Unfortunately, this view does not answer most of the objections raised against the view we just discussed. The doctrine that being *qua* being has properties is highly controversial and even if it were easily acceptable, a view of metaphysics that makes those properties the sole object of metaphysics would narrow that object in ways which do not do justice to what metaphysicians have done in the past and continue to do today.

3. *Categorial Being(s)*

We saw earlier that transcendental being can be contrasted to categorial being. This allows for the possibility that categorial being be considered the object of metaphysics. The advantage of this view is that categorial being presumably includes all there is, except for any being which falls outside categorial being. This limitation, of course, is unacceptable to those metaphysicians for whom non-categorial being is precisely the most important kind of being, thus constituting an essential part at least of the object of metaphysics. But, even if this were not a serious difficulty for all metaphysicians, there is another which would be hard to overcome: Categorial being is what all the other disciplines study and, therefore, if metaphysics were to have it as its object, metaphysics would amount to nothing more than the collection of those disciplines, the encyclopedia of all knowledge. And we have already seen that this would not be accept-

---

30. Aristotle, *Metaphysics* 1004b15, p. 734.

able. It is perhaps for these reasons that we do not find clear supporters of this view in the history of philosophy.[31]

4. Real Being(s) / Reality

Another possibility for the object of metaphysics is real being or, as some philosophers put it, reality.[32] The notion of real has been related to all sorts of other notions such as mental, possible, nonactual, potential, imaginary, and apparent. Different philosophers understand and relate these notions in different ways, so to say that metaphysics studies real being, or reality, is not helpful. Instead of arguing for particular understandings of these notions—a task that would take far too long—I shall adopt certain understandings of them for the purpose of the present discussion and hope that this will be sufficient to carry us through.

I shall consider mental to be the opposite of non-mental, so that such things as thoughts, anger, and remembrances are mental, and rocks, the color of this paper, and ghosts are non-mental. Mental is anything which exists, or can exist, in a mind and only in a mind. Non-mental is anything which exists or can exist outside a mind. And I will assume that the categories are mutually exclusive, so that what is mental cannot be non-mental, and vice versa. There is another sense of mental that is frequent in the literature.[33] According to it, the mental is always the product of a mind.[34] Thus, such things as chimeras and goat-stags are mental, because they are creations of the mind, but Socrates is not. Moreover, many who adopt this view

31. Leibniz, however, uses a formula which may imply this view. See *Philosophical Papers and Letters,* p. 76. And Suárez attributes this position to Flandria in *Disputationes metaphysicae* 1, 1, 18, vol. 25, p. 8.

32. Suárez, *Disputationes metaphysicae* 11, 26, vol. 25, p. 11; Broad, "Critical and Speculative Philosophy," p. 96; Bradley, *Appearance and Reality,* pp. 1, 3, 433; and Meinong, "The Theory of Objects," pp. 79, 106. Cf. Also Brentano, "Genuine and Fictitious Objects," p. 74. Not everyone conceives reality as real being. For example, Zubiri holds that reality antecedes being and it is the former that constitutes the point of departure of metaphysics. *Sobre la esencia,* pp. 400–401. Ryle, among others, rejects the notion of reality. "Systematic Misleading Expressions," p. 18.

33. For another sense less frequently found in the literature, see Suárez, *Disputationes metaphysicae,* 54, 1, 5, vol. 26, p. 1016.

34. Pols, *Radical Realism,* p. 177.

regard the mental as nonphysical and the non-mental as physical. But this is not the sense I wish to capture here. According to the sense I adopt, some non-mental entities are physical, such as a table or a cat, but some non-mental entities are nonphysical, such as minds and ghosts. Note that I am not making any commitments as to the existence of minds and ghosts here. I cite these merely as examples of entities which, if they exist or were to exist, would have to be considered neither mental nor physical. The distinction I adopt does not identify the mental with the nonphysical and the non-mental with the physical, nor does it identify the mental with the product of the mind and the non-mental with the product of causes other than minds.

By possible, I mean what is not contradictory and, by impossible, what is contradictory. Circles and squares are possible but square circles are not. But I distinguish between the merely possible, such as the son I had when I was twenty two (I did not have one), and the actualized possible, which includes my maternal great-grandfather. The difference between the merely possible and the actualized possible is that the merely possible is never actual, whereas the actualized possible is actual at some time or at all times.

One may speak of actual with respect to temporal and non-temporal entities. With respect to non-temporal entities, I shall take actual in the sense of existing at all times or, to put it differently, that there is no time at which the entity or entities in question do not exist. Thus, such entities as God, for example, if actual and non-temporal, cannot be said not to exist at any time, even if such entities are not supposed to exist in time.

With respect to temporal entities, one may speak of actual in two senses: (1) to be actual in the sense of existing at a particular time and at no other time, and (2) to be actual in the sense of existing at some time, whether in the past, the present, or the future. In the first sense, Napoleon was actual between 1769 and 1821, but was not actual before 1769 or after 1821. In the second sense, Napoleon is actual because he did exist between 1769 and 1821, even if he does not exist at other times. Likewise, if it turns out that I will have a grandchild named Ignatius, Ignatius is actual. What has been said about actual helps explain the distinction between the actualized possible and the merely possible. The actualized possible is actual at some time or at all times, whereas the merely possible is never actual, whether in the past, the present, or the future.

The notion of potential lies somewhere between the notions of actual and possible. It shares with the notion of possible the fact that it is not contradictory. But the potential is not merely noncontradictory, it is that which has some probability of becoming actual. My nonexisting uncle, Alexander, is possible in the sense of not being contradictory, but he is not potential, because under current circumstances he could never become actual. One might explain this by saying that there are at least five conditions for X to be potentially Y at t_1:

1. X is not Y at t_1

2. X is actual at t_1

3. Y is not actual at t_1

4. Under certain circumstances, X becomes Y at t_2.

Consider an example. Baby X is potentially adult Y at t_1, if and only if: Baby X is not adult Y at t_1; baby X is actual at t_1, that is, baby X exists at t_1; adult Y is not actual at t_1, that is, adult Y does not exist at t_1; and under certain circumstances, baby X becomes adult Y at t_2.

By imaginary, I mean what is exclusively the product of the imagination. A goat-stag, for example, is imaginary, and so is the $10 million I will make in royalties when this book is published. Note that the notion of imaginary has to do with a particular kind of cause. Something is imaginary because it is the product of imagination. In this, the notion is different from the others we have examined. Note also that what is imaginary cannot be actual in the second sense of actual examined earlier, but can be actual in the first sense. An artist may imagine a work and then produce it. Before the artist produces it, the work is imaginary, but after production, the work is no longer imaginary.

Finally, we come to the notion of apparent. For something to be apparent or, as philosophers are fond of saying, to be appearance, is for it to look as if it were what it is not. There are two requirements of the apparent: First, the apparent must look as if it were a certain individual or of a certain sort—X may look to be the individual Y (say, Peter) or to be of the sort Z (say, honest); second, the apparent must not be the individual Y or of the sort Z.

The various notions we have been discussing can be combined with the notion of being in the following ways: mental being, nonmental being, possible being, merely possible being, actualized possible being, impossible being, actual being, nonactual being, potential being, non-potential being, imaginary being, non-imaginary being, apparent being, and non-apparent being. Of these combinations, only four are generally used to understand real being. Real being has been taken as: (1) possible being, (2) actual being, (3) non-imaginary being, and (4) non-apparent being. The last two can be easily dismissed because they attempt to express what real being is in terms of a relation rather than in terms of what real being is in itself. In the case of 3, the relation is to the causes of being: non-imaginary being cannot be the result exclusively of some mind or minds. In the case of 4, the relation is to a knower who is not deceived by the way being may seem.

The first two, by contrast, try to identify what real being is in itself, apart from the relations it has or may have to causes or knowers. According to 1, real being is the same as possible being, that is, it includes every individual being and kinds of being whose notions do not involve contradictions. As such, real being includes actual and merely possible being, but it excludes impossible being. According to 2, real being is more restricted; it includes only actual being, leaving out merely possible being and impossible being. For some, real being also excludes potential being, but for others it does not—whether it does or not depends on the degree of actuality accorded to potential being.

Having provided two different understandings of real being, we are now in a position to judge whether real being is the object metaphysics studies when real being is understood in either of these two ways, as possible being or as actual being. The advantage of the first position is its comprehensiveness.[35] If the object of metaphysics is possible being, then metaphysics studies everything except contradictory entities, such as square circles, or negations, such as nothing. In this sense, this view would have to be reclassified as one which takes everything, and not just certain things, to be the object of metaphysics, for contradictory entities and negations are no entities at all.

Precisely because the position is so general, however, it runs into the standard objection against this sort of view: Metaphysics becomes no more than a composite of other disciplines. In addition, many philosophers have complained that to understand metaphysics in this way is to distance the discipline from what exists and, therefore, to make it a speculative enterprise of little value.[36] I

---

35. The position is advocated by Wolff. See *Preliminary Discourse*, § 29, and *Prima philosophia*, §§ 1, 70.
36. This is the basis of Gilson's attack on Wolff and his defense of Aquinas in *Being and Some Philosophers*.

should point out that I am not impressed by either of these objections, but I will leave them for the moment, as I shall have occasion to return to this matter at a later stage of my argument.

A third objection, however, is more convincing. It argues that this view excludes impossibilities, privations, and the like, from metaphysical consideration, even though these have been traditionally discussed by metaphysicians.[37] Indeed, metaphysicians discuss the impossible, the contradictory, and nothing. So it makes no sense to say that metaphysics studies only the possible.

The second alternative, that in dealing with real being metaphysics deals with actual and only actual being (whether actual at some time or always), has the advantage that it appears to avoid two objections raised against the previous view.[38] Metaphysics is not about everything, but only about everything that is actual. Moreover, metaphysics does not include the study of abstract possibilities, but is rather concerned with concrete actualities.

Apart from certain advantages, this position does encounter difficulties. One is that what is actual in our world is always presented to us as contingent. Existence, as we know it, is a contingent affair. And yet metaphysicians have frequently claimed that their interests lie in what is necessary.[39] Some philosophers have argued that the very notion of a necessary being implies the existence of the being in question and thus that actual being includes necessary being.[40] But such arguments are not by any means generally accepted as sound and it would be, therefore, difficult to rest the case against this position on them.

Another difficulty is that the consideration of logical possibility is perhaps one of the most important tools metaphysicians have at their disposal. Indeed, much argumentation aimed to show contradiction uses logical possibility. Therefore, it would not make much sense to eliminate a long-established practice merely in order to preserve the

---

37. Ockham, "On the Notion of Knowledge or Science" (*Expositio super viii libros Physicorum*, Prologus), p. 13.
38. Avicenna, *Metaphysica* 1–3, pp. 11–16, and P. Morewedge's commentary, p. 153. Georges C. Anawati's translation of the more extensive *Shifâ* (*Sufficientia*) is more explicit. See Avicenna, *La métaphysique du Shifâ'* 1, 2, pp. 93–94. If 'actual' means existing, then this is Grossmann's position in *The Categorial Structure of the World*, p. 9. See also Barnes, "Metaphysics," p. 70, and Taylor, *Aristotle*, p. 42.
39. Hamlyn, *Metaphysics*, p. 4.
40. Cf. Anselm, *Proslogium*, ch. 3, pp. 8–9.

view that metaphysics studies only actual being, that is, at least while there may be better alternatives. Some philosophers, impressed by these and other objections against this view, have turned to existence or existential being, as a proper object for metaphysics.

5. Existential Being(s)/Existence

There are at least two important ways in which existential being or existence may be understood. In one way, it is understood as nothing but actual being. If existential being is taken as actual being, then the view which holds that metaphysics studies existential being amounts to the view that metaphysics studies actual being. Because I already discussed that view (see section 4. Real), we may dispense with it and turn instead to the second alternative.

In another way, existential being or existence may be taken to be something other than actual being. There is a long philosophical tradition which holds that, in addition to what we ordinarily call a being, such as a cat or a feature of the cat, there is an act whereby the cat and its features exist.[41] This act is called existence or the act of existence and is distinguishable from essence, that is, from the kind of thing a cat or its features are. This distinction is established by noting that one can distinguish between what something is, the essence, and whether or not the thing in question exists, the existence. Moreover, this principle is not to be identified with the causes that bring something about, such as the parents of the cat we are considering, for causes are kinds of thing which cause precisely in virtue of their kind. Existence is not a cause at all.

Some of the philosophers who adhere to the view that existence is distinct from essence go on to argue that the proper object of metaphysics is precisely existence. Metaphysics, according to them, is not concerned with essences, namely, what things are, but with existence, namely, what ultimately makes them exist.[42]

If this view were correct, then without a doubt metaphysics would be a unique discipline distinct from all others, for no other discipline has existence as its object. All other disciplines are concerned with what things are and their relations; they deal with essences. The problem is that, under such circumstances, metaphysics would

---

41. Aquinas, *On Being and Essence*, ch. 4, § 6; p. 55.
42. Gilson, *Being and Some Philosophers*, p. 215; Sweeney, *A Metaphysics of Authentic Existentialism*, pp. 13–14, 317, 329; Fabro, "The Transcendentality of *Ens-Esse* and the Ground of Metaphysics," pp. 415–416.

end up having no content at all or, if it had some content, it would be very limited indeed. The reasons should be obvious. If metaphysics does not study what things are, but the principle through which or by which they exist, and such a principle is not reducible to what we generally call "causes" or "essences," then there is very little that can possibly be said about it. For the principle would have no definition, or properties, or relations of any kind; it would have to be considered primitive and, hence, subject to no analysis. Metaphysics would, therefore, turn out to be empty, and this does not appear at all appropriate or concordant with past practice.

6. *Essential Being(s) / Essence(s)*

Essential being/essence may be understood in at least two ways. It may be taken as the beings which have essences or it may be taken as simply essences.[43] In either case, in order to make sense of the claim that metaphysics studies essential being(s)/essence(s), we need to begin by establishing what an essence is.

I take an essence to be the set of necessary and sufficient conditions for a thing to be the kind of thing that it is and without which, therefore, the thing could not exist. Thus, for example, the essence of human beings is rational animality. Note that I do not say that the conditions are necessary and sufficient for the thing to exist. To say that would imply that to be a kind of thing is sufficient for existence and also to confuse the notions of essence and cause. To be something or other, to be a kind of thing (such as rational animal), is a requirement of existence, but it is not a sufficient condition of it, as there are kinds of things which do not exist (such as unicorns or Martians). Nor is an essence the same as a cause. To be an essence is to be a kind of thing, but to be a cause is to be related to something else in a certain way. This point can be illustrated by the fact that an essence is expressed by a definition, but a cause is not. The essence of human being is expressed by the definition: 'A human being is a rational animal.' The causes that give rise to human beings, say other human beings, are not expressed by the definition of human being.

This understanding of essence makes clear that it is not only actual beings which have essences. Essences extend to merely possible

---

43. For Plato, the highest science studies the essences of things, that is, what each thing is. He called this science "dialectic." *Republic* 532a, 533b, 534b, pp. 764, 765, 766.

beings, although they do not extend to impossible beings. The unicorn has an essence and so does the goat-stag, but the square circle does not. A merely possible being has an essence because, although it never, in fact, exists, it could exist. Therefore, there are necessary conditions of its existence. But impossible beings could not have essences because they can never exist and, therefore, there cannot be necessary conditions of their existence.

If essential being is understood as beings which have essences, then essential being is the same as possible being. Therefore, the view which holds that metaphysics studies essential being(s)/essence(s) reduces to the view that metaphysics studies possible being(s). But that view has already been discussed, so we need not take it up again.

If essential being/essence is understood to refer to essences, rather than to beings with essences, then the advantages and disadvantage of the view are different.[44] As an advantage, the extension of the term may be cited, for all beings except those that are impossible have essences. So metaphysics would have considerable breadth. Moreover, some might want to argue that many disciplines are not concerned with essences. For example, many natural sciences are concerned with external relations among various beings and these external relations among beings are not generally taken to be part of their essences. In this way, then, one could easily distinguish metaphysics from other disciplines.

But there are difficulties with this position as well. In first place, if metaphysics studies essence only, then existence is left out of its province; and existence, whether we can find much to say about it or not, is one of the topics which has been of constant interest to metaphysicians. Moreover, if metaphysics is not concerned with it, which discipline is?

In second place, much metaphysics is concerned with nonessentials as well as essentials.[45] A metaphysical analysis of something, say color, involves not only a discussion of its essence and what is implied by it, but of nonessential features and the relations that color may have to other entities, such as dimensions. Therefore, to restrict metaphysics to the study of essence would be to narrow it be-

---

44. Gilson has written a history of this sort of essentialism in *Being and Some Philosophers*. For Aristotle, see *Metaphysics* 1004b7, p. 734.
45. This even though many metaphysicians have explicitly rejected this view. Cf. Suárez, *Disputationes metaphysicae* 1, 1, 2–3, vol. 25, p. 2, and 1, 1, 18–20, vol. 25, p. 8.

low the scope it has. Moreover, in many ways it would preclude a satisfactory metaphysical analysis of any entity, for such analysis should include references to what is not essential to it, including its relations to other entities.

7. Formal Being(s) / Form(s)

Formal being, or form as I shall refer to it here, can be taken in at least two ways. In the first, a form is a transcendental entity in the sense of being something outside the world of experience. And here there are at least two positions that we may consider. One identifies forms with transcendental, non-abstract beings, such as celestial intelligences and angels.[46] The other identifies forms with abstract entities, such as justice and catness.[47] Because I have discussed transcendental beings already and I shall discuss abstract entities later, I dispense with these views at this point.

In another sense, however, form is taken to be an immanent principle in things, what organizes a thing's various parts, components, and features, making the thing what it is. In this sense, the form of X is the same thing as the essence or nature of X; for the form amounts to a set of necessary and sufficient conditions expressed in a definition. The form of a human being, then, consists of those internal conditions that make the human being what he or she is *qua* human. Philosophers who make a distinction between form and essence generally point out the distinction between the two is intensional (or conceptual), but extensionally 'form' and 'essence' are the same.[48] Now, for this reason and because we have already discussed essence in the previous section, we need not discuss further the position which identifies form as the object of metaphysics.

8. Natural Being(s) / Nature(s)

Metaphysics has also been conceived as the study of natural being(s) or nature(s). By natural beings sometimes is meant beings which are not supernatural and sometimes beings which have natures. If understood in the first sense, metaphysics could be quite restricted because it would exclude the study of what many have regarded as its object. Indeed, in one common interpretation of its

---

46. Averroes, *In Aristotelis libros Physicorum* 1, text 83, vol. 4, fol. 22vb.
47. Plato, *Parmenides* 134, p. 928; *Republic* 509 ff., pp. 744 ff.
48. Aquinas, *On Being and Essence*, ch. 1, § 4, p. 31.

name, metaphysics is conceived precisely as the study of what is beyond nature (*physis*). Moreover, if understood in the second sense, metaphysics would not study the single being which is regarded by some as not having a nature, namely, God. In either case the position is unacceptably narrow and goes contrary to important traditions in the history of the discipline.

On the other hand, nature, like form, can be understood in two main ways. In one way, a nature is the same as a transcendental being or an abstract entity. In another way, it is an immanent principle of things responsible for their change. We need not discuss the first sense because I have already discussed transcendental beings earlier and I shall discuss abstract entities later. In the second sense, nature is supposed to be extensionally the same as form and essence. The difference is only that a form is a nature considered as a structural principle and an essence is a nature considered as a principle of being, whereas a nature is the same as these but considered as a principle of change.[49] Hence, a nature is, like an essence, a set of necessary and sufficient conditions of a thing which explains why the thing in question changes in the way it does. As with form, what was said about essence also applies to nature and so we may dispense with further discussion of this view.

9. *Substantial Being(s)/Substance(s)*

The expression 'substantial being' is intended to mean substance, and substance has been one of the objects which, from the very beginning, has been identified as the object of metaphysics.[50] 'Substance,' however, has been used to designate many and different things. Hence, in order to understand the claim that metaphysics studies substance we must look at the most important meanings of the term.

One of the earliest senses of 'substance,' which goes back to the very origins of metaphysics, is that of being.[51] Because we have already discussed the view of being as the object of metaphysics, there is no need to say anything further about it.

---

49. Ibid., p. 32.
50. Aristotle, *Metaphysics* 1003b17, 1005b8, pp. 732, 737. Suárez attributes this position to Buridan. (*Disputationes metaphysicae* 1, 1, 21, vol. 29, p. 9) For a more contemporary adherent, see Mercier, *A Manual of Modern Scholastic Philosophy*, pp. 413–14.
51. Aristotle, *Metaphysics* 1028b4, p. 784.

Another view of substance is that it is what is neither predicable of nor present in something else.[52] In this sense a horse and a cat are substances, but the weight of the horse or the color of the cat's coat are not.

Substance is also identified with form by some of those who work within the Aristotelian tradition.[53] For them, form is the structural principle of beings. It is extensionally the same as essence and nature, but intensionally the terms 'form,' 'essence,' and 'nature' are not equivalent.[54] Nature is form considered as principle of change, whereas essence is form considered as principle of being (a necessary but not a sufficient condition of existence, as we saw earlier). In this sense, the substance of a human being, for example, is her humanity: the arrangement, as it were, of the various things a human being is into what makes a being human.

Substance is also understood as material or stuff;[55] the material or stuff out of which something is made is frequently called its "substance." The substance of a marble statue of Apollo is the marble out of which it has been carved. This sense of 'substance' is closely related to the notion of matter. But, whereas stuff is always understood as something physical, matter has not always been understood strictly in this way. It is common to understand matter as potentiality.[56] Here one must distinguish between pure potentiality and relative potentiality. Pure potentiality is nothing, for it is potentiality to anything and any determination of it would preclude its complete openness. Relative potentiality is restricted, depending on the conditions on which the potentiality is based. A boy is potentially a man in this relative sense, but a boy is not potentially a dog, which precludes the boy from being an example of pure potentiality.

Substance is also frequently understood as substratum.[57] Although it is the function of substratum to be the supporter of features, substratum itself does not have any features other than the

52. Aristotle, *Categories* 2a11, p. 11.
53. Aristotle, *Metaphysics* 1041a–b, pp. 810–11, and *On the Soul* 412a8, p. 554; Avicenna, *Metaphysica* 3, p. 16.
54. Aquinas, *On Being and Essence* 1, 4, p. 31.
55. Aristotle, *Metaphysics* 1017b10, 1029a18, pp. 761, 785, and *On the Soul* 412a8, p. 554; Avicenna, *Metaphysica* 3, p. 16.
56. Aristotle, *On the Soul* 412a10, p. 555.
57. Aristotle, *Metaphysics* 1028b35, pp. 784–5; Locke, *An Essay Concerning Human Understanding*, vol. I, 23:392. Compare this view with the contemporary notion of bare particular. See Allaire, "Bare Particulars."

ones it supports. Substratum is characterless in itself; it merely stands under features, supporting them. A cat is not a substratum; the substratum of a cat is that which takes on the features of cat- ness, blackness, and whatever else might characterize the cat.

Apart from these views of substance, there are two others which have been popular in the history of philosophy and which are closely related.[58] Both are related to formulas developed in the Mid- dle Ages. According to one, a substance is what needs nothing else in order to exist.[59] In one way, as later understood by Spinoza, for example, this view implies that there is only one substance.[60] The medievals understood the formula differently, however. For them, the formula referred to the fact that in the definition of a substance, unlike that of a feature of a substance, there is no reference made to something on which the substance depends for its existence. The definition of a substance such as a human being is, say, that a hu- man being is a rational animal; there is no reference in it to any other thing on whose existence a human being depends. By con- trast, in the definition of rationality there is a reference to the fact that it is a feature of something else on which it depends for its ex- istence, namely, a human being.

According to the second formula, substance is that which exists by itself.[61] Obviously, this understanding of substance is closely re- lated to the first, although it does not make any reference to depen- dence or independence for its existence from something else. What exists by itself is a horse or a cat.

For our purposes, it makes very little difference which of these different understandings of substance is adopted. Apart from partic- ular advantages, they all share one important advantage, namely, that metaphysics would have a definite object of study not shared by any other discipline.[62]

---

58. This is not by any means an exhaustive list of the different views of sub- stance that have been presented in the history of philosophy. For exam- ple, substance has also been understood as a composite, a fiery body, an immaterial entity independent of the body, an intelligence, and so on. See, Avicenna, *Metaphysica*, vol. 3:16.
59. Descartes, Reply to Obj. IV, in *Philosophical Works*, vol. II:103, and *Principles of Philosophy*, pt. I, 52, p. 156.
60. Spinoza, *Ethics*, vol. III:1.
61. Suárez, *Disputationes metaphysicae* 33, 1, 1, vol. 26:330; Aquinas, *Summa theologiae* I, 3, 5, ad 1, p. 32.
62. Aristotle, *Metaphysics* 1003b18, 1005b7, 1069a18, pp. 732, 736, 872.

Unfortunately, in addition to particular disadvantages, they also share one serious difficulty. If substance in any of the specified senses is taken as the object of metaphysics, then metaphysics excludes the study of many things with which it has concerned itself in the past. For example, metaphysics would not study qualities or relations. Of course, one could argue that, indeed, metaphysics would study them insofar as they are related to and affect substance. But does this make sense, when it is substance itself which is the object of metaphysics? It is one thing to say that metaphysics studies substance and another to say that it studies substance and features of substance which are not properties of it. Moreover, if it were the case that metaphysics studied only substance, which discipline or disciplines would be in charge of studying the things metaphysics has traditionally studied that are not the province of other particular disciplines?

But there are other difficulties as well. To say that metaphysics studies substance can be understood in two ways, regardless of what one understands substance to be. In one way, it would mean that metaphysics studies what substance is, that is, the nature of substance; in another way it would mean that metaphysics studies different kinds of substance and different individual substances. But neither of these alternatives is acceptable. The first one is unacceptable because there would be relatively little that could be said about substance itself apart from what could be said about various kinds of substance or individual substances and, moreover, this inquiry would leave out much that has traditionally been included within the purview of the metaphysician. The second alternative is also unacceptable because metaphysics would turn out, after all, to be a composite discipline, made up of the various disciplines which investigate particular kinds of substance and individual substances.

10. *Causal Being(s) / Cause(s)*

I understand a causal being simply as a cause. Thus, that the object of metaphysics is causal being means simply that metaphysics studies causes.[63] Causes, as already noted, should not be confused with essences. An essence is the set of necessary and sufficient conditions for something being the kind of thing it is and without which the thing could not exist. Causes, by contrast, are the necessary and sufficient conditions for something to exist. All essences are causes,

---

63. Ibid., 981b28, 982a28, 982b10, pp. 691, 692.

insofar as to be a kind of thing is necessary for the thing to exist, but not all causes are essences because there are causes which have nothing to do with making a thing the kind of thing it is. In this sense, the capacity to reason is part of the essence of a human being and thus a cause, in the stated sense of cause, of the human being, whereas the human being's parents are causes of the human being, but not part of her essence.

The conception of cause I have presented is more inclusive than the conceptions used in the sciences. Whether or not one accepts it is significant for our topic. If a narrower conception is used, then the scope of metaphysics would be narrower and, therefore, less adequate. I am proposing a broader notion of cause in order to make possible a broader and more adequate scope for metaphysics. I argue now on the basis of this broader notion, although conceived even in this charitable way, we shall see this understanding of metaphysics is inadequate.

To say that metaphysics studies causes may mean that metaphysics is concerned with the nature of causality, that is, with the necessary and sufficient conditions of something being a cause. Or it may mean that metaphysics is concerned with the things that function or can function as causes. Taken in the latter way, this view makes some headway toward avoiding the objection of being too narrow. Every possible thing in the universe seems to be related to something else either as an actual or possible cause of it. So, if metaphysics studies the things which are or can be causes, one could claim that metaphysics studies everything. Still, there are problems. One is that metaphysics would turn out to be no more than the composite of all other disciplines. The other is that metaphysics would still leave out much that metaphysicians have dealt with in the past, such as possibility, necessity, and the like. Indeed, it would also leave out of consideration impossibilities and the like, which are not beings properly speaking.

One way to avoid this difficulty is to argue that the object of metaphysics is causality, not the beings that are or can be causes, in accordance with the first understanding of the formula given. Still another way of avoiding the objection would be to combine both formulas and argue that metaphysics studies all beings, but only insofar as they are causes. But these alternatives lead back to the original obstacle, for metaphysics traditionally has studied beings not only in their causal connections but in all sorts of dimensions. Of course, one may still argue that all those dimensions must be studied in order to understand the causality of beings. And this may be true, but if so, would we not be going back to the study of everything and thus to the reduction of metaphysics to other disciplines? More-over, there is the obstacle that metaphysics is not concerned with many of the causal explanations found in other disciplines. I know of no book of metaphysics which discusses the causes of rain, for exam-ple. In short, the view that the object of metaphysics is causal being does not appear convincing.

Finally, one could argue that metaphysics studies a particular kind of cause, such as ultimate causes. But this implies that the ob-ject of metaphysics is something particular, so I leave the discussion of this view for the next section.

11. Intelligibles/Knowables

The seventeenth century saw the rise of a view which held in-telligibles or knowables to be the object of metaphysics.[64] The devel-opment of this view answered the felt need to include under the purview of metaphysics such things as nothing, contradictions, chimeras, and impossibilities.[65] Because these are discussed, and presumably understood, by metaphysicians, they must be incorpo-rated into the object of the discipline. Naturally, this position rejects the common view that only what exists or has being is intelligible or knowable and that it is so to the degree it exists or has being.

There are at least two ways of understanding this position. In one way, intelligible/knowable is understood relatively as intelligible/knowable to humans; in another it is understood absolutely as intelli-gible/knowable to anyone. Obviously, the second yields a stronger for-mulation than the first. Yet, it is not without difficulty. One is that it makes intelligibility/knowability both the necessary and sufficient con-dition of the object of metaphysics, and this is not accepted by many metaphysicians who argue that the supreme object of metaphysics is ultimately ineffable. Another is that it considers intelligible/knowable such things as nothing and contradictions, but many philosophers con-sider these to be unintelligible/unknowable in themselves even though they can be described and analyzed in terms of other notions.

---

64. Timpler, *Metaphysicae systema methodicum*, Bk. 1, ch. 1, probl. 5, p. 6; Clauberg, *Metaphysica de ente* 1, nn. 4–5, vol. 1:283; Ulloa, *Logica ma-jor*, d. 3, ch. 1, n. 3, p. 242. But there are antecedents; see Aquinas, *Com-mentary on the "Metaphysics" of Aristotle*, Prologue, pp. 1–2.

65. Timpler, *Metaphysicae systema methodicum*, Bk. 2, ch. 2, probl. 1, p. 21; Izquierdo, *Pharus scientiarum*, Bk. 1, Prefatio.

Apart from the merits of these two difficulties, there is a recurring objection we have seen which is also applicable here. The intelligible/knowable seems to include the objects of every discipline and, therefore, would convert metaphysics into the encyclopedia of all knowledge.

C. Some Things in Particular

In the previous section, we looked at various conceptions of the object of metaphysics which restrict that object to some things in general, although it often turned out that these views implied that metaphysics studies everything. None of these conceptions, however, aimed at narrowing the object of metaphysics to individual objects or particular kinds of objects, even if in some cases they turned out to do just that. Yet, there have been many attempts precisely in this direction in the history of philosophy. Indeed, the very term 'metaphysics' has suggested to some that the object of metaphysics is to be found outside the physical realm and, therefore, that it studies a being or kind of being distinct from physical being. Here are some examples of these objects.

1. God

God is frequently identified by many philosophers as the object of metaphysics.[66] One of the advantages of this view is that it can be taken to include a number of other views we have discussed. For example, if God transcends the fundamental categories of reality, and is the only being to do so, then metaphysics turns out to study non-categorial being. If God is paradigmatic of substance, then metaphysics might be taken to study substance *per excellence*. If God is the ultimate, as well as the paradigmatic, cause of everything, then metaphysics can be taken as the study of causal being. There are other possibilities also. Moreover, by making God the single object of metaphysics, the discipline becomes unique and different from all others, for no other discipline is exclusively devoted to the study of God.

---

66. Aristotle, *Metaphysics* 1069b1, 1026a10, pp. 872, 779; Boethius, *On the Trinity*, vol. II:9; Avicenna, *Metaphysica*, vol. 2:14; Aquinas, *Commentary on "De Trinitate" of Boethius* 5, 1, p. 8; Averroes, *In Aristotelis libros Metaphysicorum* 6, text 2, fol. 69rb.

There are, however, disadvantages to this view. Perhaps most important, like the other views which identify particular objects for metaphysics, this view appears to reduce metaphysics to a particular discipline; in this case, to theology. Not, of course, to theology conceived as the understanding of divine revelation, for that discipline falls outside philosophy. Theology, in this context, must be understood naturally, as the study of what can be known concerning God based on evidence independent of God's revelation. Indeed, some argue that this study includes the study of the world insofar as God is the cause of the world and the world reflects such causality. So that, in order to find out something about God, we need to begin with the world. But this means, of course, that metaphysics does not study the world as such, but only the world as related to God, and that does not seem to correspond to much that metaphysics has been doing throughout history.

Moreover, if this is as the supporters of the view claim, then why not use revelation in metaphysics? If metaphysics deals with God and revelation purports to tell us something about him, there is no good reason, based only on the consideration of the object, to rule out the study of God *via* revelation. Indeed, it makes no sense to reject what might be the best source of information on the matter. But this conclusion, I believe, does not concur with what most metaphysicians have done or with what they have conceived themselves to be doing. Indeed, even most of those who have subscribed to religious views have also kept revelation separate from metaphysics.[67]

Finally, there is the difficulty involved in the knowledge of God, for there seems to be very little we can say about God if we do not use the information religions presume he has made available through revelation. Indeed, the very possibility of meaningful speech about God is a matter of acrimonious disagreement among theologians, and this extends even to God's existence. Therefore, if God is the object of metaphysics, it looks as if there is very little, if anything at all, that metaphysics can establish.[68]

2. Necessary Being(s)

A view which was considered seriously during some periods of the history of philosophy, although there is very little support for it

---

67. Aquinas, *Summa theologiae* I, 1, 8, pp. 13–14.
68. For other objections against this position, see Avicenna, *Liber de philosphia prima* 1, 1, 1, p. 5, and Scotus, "Concerning Metaphysics," (*Reportata parisiensia*, Prologus, q. 3, a. 1), pp. 10–12.

today, maintains that metaphysics studies necessary being(s).[69] By a necessary being is understood a being whose nonexistence is impossible, although some philosophers interpret this formula epistemically to mean a being whose nonexistence is inconceivable. I will consider only the first, which is, of course, the strongest formula. Note also that this view should not be confused with the position which holds that metaphysical propositions are necessary, for according to this view, metaphysics studies more than propositions.

There are two important advantages to this view. First, by identifying necessary being(s) as the object of metaphysics, it becomes easy to distinguish metaphysics from other disciplines. Moreover, in this case, the advantage is greater insofar as no other discipline claims to study this object. Indeed, the notion of a necessary being is peculiarly metaphysical insofar as it is only metaphysicians who use it. The second important advantage is that many metaphysicians claim that metaphysical propositions are necessary and it would appear reasonable to expect that the study of a necessary being will yield necessary propositions.

Apart from the well-known difficulties posed by the notion of a necessary being, one of the problems with this position is that it excludes from metaphysics all the beings to which we have access through experience. None of the beings we experience is necessary, so these beings must be excluded from metaphysical consideration. But does this make sense? Judging from what most metaphysicians have studied in the past, it does not. Of course, one could argue that the study of necessary being(s) requires the study of non-necessary being(s) and, therefore, that it includes the study of all being(s), as the categories necessary/non-necessary are complementary. But understood thus, this position becomes indistinguishable from the position which argues that metaphysics studies all being(s) and is, therefore, subject to the objections discussed earlier concerning that position.

Then, too, there are epistemic questions concerning how we can have access to necessary being and the kind of knowledge we can have of it: Is that knowledge itself necessary or contingent? And finally, if necessary being is the same as God, then this position turns metaphysics into theology, opening the doors to the objections raised earlier.

---

69. Aquinas, *Commentary on the "De Trinitate" of Boethius* 5, 2, ad 4, p. 24.

3. Immaterial Being(s)

A more popular view in the history of philosophy has argued that metaphysics studies immaterial being(s). Indeed, this line of thought was suggested from the very beginning of the discipline and was inspired by its name. 'Metaphysics' means beyond physics and thus metaphysics was identified with the discipline that studies nonphysical objects. This conception of metaphysics is much broader than the ones which identify the object of metaphysics with God and necessary being(s). Other beings such as minds, spirits, souls, angels, and so on would also be studied by it; indeed, one might want to argue that even logical principles, concepts, and abstract entities could be included, but most authors who adopt this view identify metaphysics with theology.[70]

Even understanding the category generously, however, there are still many objects metaphysics has traditionally investigated which would be excluded from its purview if this view were adopted. Indeed, from the very beginning metaphysicians have been interested in the nature of the physical universe, the nature of matter, volume, dimensions, colors, figures, physical motion, and so on. But all these would have to be banished from metaphysics, if the discipline were to be restricted to the study of immaterial beings, unless, of course, what we call the "physical universe" were to be regarded as immaterial, as some early modern philosophers did.[71] To do so in a credible way, however, would require considerable courage today, and would hardly contribute to an easy resolution of the issue concerning the object of metaphysics.

A variation on this view, quite popular in the medieval world, held that metaphysics studies beings which are immaterial and not subject to change (or motion, as they put it).[72] But this modification does not strengthen the position against the objection raised.

4. Person(s)

The interest in the notion of person that developed in the late nineteenth century and the early twentieth century, has led some philosophers to hold that the proper object of metaphysics is the

---

70. Boethius, *On the Trinity*, vol. II:9; Averroes, *In Aristotelis libros Physicorum* 1, text 83, vol. 4, fol. 22vb.

71. Berkeley, *Three Dialogues Between Hylas and Philonous*, p. 58.

72. Avicenna, *Metaphysica*, vol. 1:12–13.

person.[73] The person is conceived as the highest ontological reality, as integrating lower levels of reality such as the individual and the organism, and as the foundation of the community. The person, moreover, is the source of value and finds its loftiest expression in the supreme being, namely, God.[74] The person represents autonomy and transcendence, exemplifying the very essence of being. For this reason, some supporters of this position present it as a correct interpretation of the classical view in which metaphysics studies being.[75]

The main problem with this position is its narrow focus. Persons have never been the only object of metaphysics. Nor is it easy to argue that everything one studies in the discipline, even if not persons, is somehow related to persons. This position tries to avoid the charge of being too narrow with two doctrines: First, it identifies the Supreme Being, regarded as the ontological ground of everything there is, with a person; second, it makes the person a kind of microcosm, that is, a reality which includes in it every other kind of reality. But these doctrines have problems themselves, and even if accepted without question, would not completely answer the charge of being too narrow. The problems have to do with the very controversial nature of the claims. Claims about God are extremely difficult to establish on firm philosophical ground and, therefore, it makes no sense to use them to support some other views unless it is absolutely necessary because there are no other ways of supporting such views. Moreover, even if one were to disregard this problem, there is a further difficulty: If metaphysics is the study of persons, and ultimately and primarily of the supreme person who is the model for all others, then metaphysics properly speaking is the study of God. But we have already seen the problems that result from the identification of metaphysics with theology.

The view that the person is a kind of microcosm is also very controversial, for what exactly could this mean? Does it mean, for example, that the person is somehow like the universe, except on a smaller scale? This does not seem promising, for a person does not

---

73. The personalist movement in the United States goes back to Borden Parker Bowne and Edgar Sheffield Brightman; in France, to neo-Scholastics like E. Gilson and Jacques Maritain; and in Germany to phenomenologists like Max Scheler. Seifert has recently rearticulated the view of metaphysics as the study of the person in *Essere e persona*, pp. 384, 408.
74. Seifert, ibid.
75. Ibid., pp. 406–8.

prima facie appear to be in any way, considered as a whole, like the universe. Alternatively, could it mean that the parts of the person resemble the parts of the universe? Again, this sounds strange, for where are the planets and stars in persons? Again, does it mean that the intension of 'person' somehow implies the intensions of all other terms in our language? This is clearly wrong, for to be a person does not imply the notion of uranium, for example.

All these are serious problems, but there are also other problems, even if one does not regard the ones mentioned as insurmountable. For the escape from the charge of being too narrow opens the possibility to the charge of being too broad. If a person is a microcosm, then in a sense, to study the person involves the study of everything and metaphysics, as the study of the person, turns out to be the study of everything. Metaphysics becomes the conglomerate of all sciences, the encyclopedia of all knowledge and this is a view we have already rejected.

5. Ultimate Cause(s)

A more frequently found view in the history of philosophy conceives metaphysics as the study of ultimate causes.[76] Ultimate causes are frequently understood to be the most fundamental causes. It is generally agreed that ultimate in this context does not refer to time, but rather to those causes which completely explain the universe in the sense that they explain the existence of everything else without needing explanation themselves. For this reason, they are sometimes called "first causes." Of course, if metaphysics is conceived thus, then it is easy to distinguish it from other disciplines within and without philosophy. It is distinguishable from disciplines outside philosophy, because sciences, one might wish to argue for example, are concerned with the study of immediate, not ultimate causes. The astronomer wants to know the relation of some observable phenomena to other observable phenomena, and not the ultimate, non-observable reasons which make possible the relation of causality among the phenomena she observes. On the other hand, metaphysics would be easily distinguishable from disciplines within philosophy, because various branches of philosophy deal with specific areas which are not related to ultimate causality. For example, the epistemologist is concerned with the justification of knowledge

---

76. Aristotle, *Metaphysics* 981b27, 982b10, 1003a27, pp. 691, 692, 731; Avicenna, *Metaphysica* 2, p. 14.

and the ethicist with the justification of action, and neither of them deals with the ultimate causes of the universe.

But this advantage is not sufficient to overcome the disadvantages of the position which conceives metaphysics as the study of ultimate causes. Among these, perhaps the most serious is the unclarity as to the nature of the ultimate causes the metaphysician is supposed to study. If these causes do not refer to God, then what are they? If causes are understood as sets of conditions which are necessary and sufficient to bring about an effect, then either ultimate causes are simply the causes which in our experience bring about effects, or they are causes other than those. If they are the first, then they are no different from the causes studied in science, and metaphysics would not be distinguished from science. If they are the second, then they can be nothing other than what philosophers over time have referred to as God, and then metaphysics would turn out to be theology. But this, also, is unacceptable.

6. Relations

Relations are very peculiar entities; indeed, most philosophers have been puzzled by the status of relations, and many have thought that relations are nothing other than the relata and their features[77] or that they are merely appearances.[78] But others have conceived relations as the very stuff out of which the world is ultimately constituted.[79]

Earlier I pointed out that most science is interested in relations. Indeed, science is interested in causes and to be a cause is to be related to something else in a certain way. So we must begin by asking whether the relations metaphysics is supposed to study are the same as or different from the relations studied in the sciences. If they are the same, then metaphysics cannot be distinguished from the sciences. So the relations metaphysics studies must be different from the relations the sciences study. But this poses two problems: First, it is not clear which relations metaphysics studies and, second,

---

77. Weinberg, "The Concept of Relation," p. 63; and Suárez, *Disputationes metaphysicae* 47, 2, 22, vol. 26, 792b.
78. Bradley, *Appearance and Reality*, p. 28.
79. Those who conceive the world in terms of facts must hold this view, for a fact is a kind of relation. Wittgenstein, *Tractatus*, vol. I:31. This view seems to be implied as well by Jonathan Edwards' position. In Howard, *"The Mind" of Jonathan Edwards*, p. 42.

whatever relations these are, they seem to exclude much that metaphysics has traditionally studied. Indeed, the idea that metaphysics
studies only relations is highly exclusionary unless one accepts the
controversial view that the world is composed of nothing but relations. This view is controversial on various counts, two of which are
quite evident: First, our experience seems to vouch for the existence
of things other than relations, and second, the very notion of relation
seems to presuppose the notions of non-relational entities, the relata
which are tied by the relation. In short, this line of thought does not
seem promising.

7. Abstract Entities

By abstract entities, I mean the referents of abstract nouns, such
as justice, beauty, catness, tableness, goodness, unity, redness, and the
like.[80] These were the sorts of things Plato thought philosophy in general should study, but there have been other philosophers who have
made them the object of metaphysics alone.[81] Sometimes they have
done so in their desire to find a place for them in our disciplinary studies when the sciences or the arts seemed to offer none. At other times,
philosophers have placed abstract entities within the realm of metaphysics because they thought these entities reflect the character of scientific propositions: universality, necessity, immutability.

Even those metaphysicians who have not found in them the exclusive object of metaphysics, however, have been concerned and are
concerned with them. Moreover, by making abstract entities the object of metaphysics, the discipline could be easily distinguished from
other disciplines, whose objects are part of the concrete world of experience. From the view that metaphysics studies abstract entities,
it does not follow, however, that metaphysicians are concerned only
with abstract entities. But this corollary is irrelevant, for the view
we are discussing holds precisely that the object of metaphysics is
abstract entities and only abstract entities.

At least three objections may be brought up against this view.
One argues that there is really no difference between this view and

---

80. Some philosophers have identified abstract entities with immaterial
    substances (in the Aristotelian sense) such as God and celestial intelli-
    gences. Boethius, *On the Trinity*, vol. II:9. This position was discussed in
    § 3 above.
81. Plato himself seems to speak in this way in places, where he calls the sci-
    ence in question "dialectic." *Republic* 532a, 533b, 534b, pp. 764, 765, 766.

the view which identifies essence as the object of metaphysics. After all, to study justice is to study the essence of justice and similarly with any other of these abstract entities. Of course, if abstract entities are the same as essences, then the objections raised against the view that metaphysics studies essences apply here as well.

The second objection argues that a metaphysics concerned only with abstract entities must necessarily be an abstract discipline with little relation to the concrete world of our experience. What exists cannot enter into this study, for what exists is concrete. Then there is the further consequence that this discipline, contrary to the belief of many metaphysicians, has little to do with the actual, that is, with what exists. Moreover, as Plato found out, it is not easy to explain how the study of the abstract is related or relevant to the study of the concrete.[82]

The third objection points out that this view could not easily distinguish between metaphysics and other disciplines which also deal with abstract entities, such as geometry and mathematics. Of course, proponents of this view could argue that metaphysics is broader, extending to abstract entities not studied by any other discipline. But that does not do away with the fact that mathematics, geometry, and other disciplines concerned with abstract entities would have to be considered parts of metaphysics. And this goes contrary to what most metaphysicians and scientists have thought.

8. Concepts

A concept may be taken in at least three ways. It may be taken, first, as an event which takes place in a mind, when 'event' is used broadly to include anything that is present or goes on in a mind.[83] In this sense, the concept cat, for example, is whatever is present or goes on in my mind when I think of cat. Concepts, understood thus, have been characterized by philosophers in different ways as forms, qualities, acts, events, and so on. Often they have been called "ideas."

Obviously, if what metaphysics studies are concepts understood in the stated sense, its scope is very narrow; metaphysics turns out to be a branch of the philosophy of mind. This would distinguish

---

82. Plato, *Parmenides* 133b, p. 927.

83. Dummett, *The Logical Basis of Metaphysics*, pp. 1, 15; Strawson, *Analysis and Metaphysics*, pp. 7, 18, 22, 34. Many philosophers reject concepts (or ideas), for example: Ryle, "Systematically Misleading Expressions," pp. 11–12, 29; Quine, "On What There Is," p. 2.

metaphysics from other disciplines, but it certainly goes contrary to what many metaphysicians have held. For, according to this view, metaphysics would not study God, say, but the mental event which goes on in a mind when it thinks about God, and the same applies to other sorts of things metaphysics has traditionally studied.

Concepts may also be understood as the intensions of the terms we understand when we have concepts understood in the sense just explained.[84] In this sense, the concept of human being is the intension of 'human being' about which I think when I think about human being. But if this is so, then one might argue that there is little difference between essences and concepts and, thus, metaphysics amounts to the study of essences. Because we have already discussed the advantages and disadvantages of the view which identifies the object of metaphysics with essences, I need not dwell further on this version of the view we are considering.

A proviso should be added here, however. For I have been assuming that concepts are universal. I have been speaking of concepts such as cat or table. If one accepts the view that concepts can be individual, so that there can be a concept of Socrates, for example, then essences and concepts are not the same, unless of course one also adopts the view that essences can also be individual. Moreover, if one's view is that essences are principles which are in some sense responsible for the existence of the things of which they are essences, as some Aristoteleans have thought,[85] then essences are not the same as concepts when the latter are understood as intensions. For essences, in this sense, are more than intensions. The essence of Socrates, for example, is his humanity, a non-mental principle which, as a form, has a causal influence on Socrates.

Finally, concepts may be understood in a third way as (1) the views we hold, reject, or merely consider, or as (2) the views someone may hold, reject, or merely consider.[86] There is considerable support for 1 in certain quarters of the philosophical world. After all, even Plato seems to have been concerned with what people held. And G. E. Moore never tired of saying that what prompted him to philosophize

---

84. Perhaps this is the way to understand Ockham's view. "On the Notion of Knowledge and Science," (*Expositio super viii libros Physicorum*, Prologus), p. 11, and "The Possibility of Natural Theology" (*Reportatio* 3, 8), pp. 113–114. See also previous note.

85. Aquinas, *On Being and Essence*, ch. 1, § 4, p. 31.

86. Strawson, *Individuals*, p. 9.

were precisely the things philosophers said.[87] Moreover, this position would make it easy to distinguish metaphysics from other disciplines which clearly deal with the world rather than with what human beings hold about the world.

But there are difficulties, for if metaphysics studies only views we hold, reject, or merely consider, then the scope of metaphysics is quite narrow. It is true that it extends to all our views, but it excludes views which we do not hold, reject, or consider. Of course, the 'we' here can be understood to include all human beings, and the time frame could be extended to cover the past, present, and future. But even then, there may be some views which no one ever, de facto, has held, rejected, or considered, does hold, reject, or consider, or will hold, reject, or consider, and according to this position, metaphysics could not concern itself with these.

Alternatively, if concepts are understood as 2, namely, the views someone may hold, reject, or merely consider, then the scope of metaphysics is broader, for it includes not just past, present, and future views, but any view regardless of the time in which it is held, rejected, or considered. So the main disadvantages against 1 are overcome.

Yet, other disadvantages surface which are no less threatening. One is precisely that, according to this position, metaphysics cannot deal with the world; metaphysics is only about our views about the world. As such, much of the traditional talk of metaphysics as dealing with reality, dealing with what is, and the rest turns out to be misguided and must be translated as meaning "reality as we believe it to be," "what is as we think it is," and so on.

From this objection follows another. If the object of metaphysics reduces to the views anyone does or could hold, rejects or could reject, and considers or could consider, then it becomes impossible to arbitrate among those views. No judgment of truth can be made.[88] Metaphysics can only be a descriptive and comparative enterprise,[89] and the metaphysician's task amounts to the presentation of the views someone holds, rejects, or considers, and the comparison of those views with those other persons hold, reject, or consider. No adjudication among them is possible.

---

87. Moore, "A Reply to My Critics," p. 14.
88. Or, as Plato put it, in his discussion of Protagoras, everything that seems is true. *Theaetetus* 170, p. 875.
89. Indeed, that is precisely how some philosophers characterize it. Strawson, *Individuals*, p. 9.

Finally, it is not clear how this position can distinguish between metaphysics and other branches of philosophy, unless other branches of philosophy are taken not to deal with views. But on what basis could it be argued that branches of philosophy other than metaphysics do not deal with views, when metaphysics does?

9. Consciousness / Lived-World / Phenomena

Consciousness is one of the most disputed notions in philosophy, particularly since the nineteenth century. This has not deterred philosophers from identifying it as the primary or the single object of philosophical or metaphysical reflection. Among the many views of consciousness which have been proposed, two in particular stand out, although it is not always easy to distinguish them, and different authors have offered idiosyncratic understandings of them. One conceives consciousness as phenomena. Now, phenomena, ever since Kant, have been conceived as the things presented to us in experience considered as they are presented to us. Phenomena are what we perceive and, in a broader sense, what we experience and are aware of. By contrast, noumena are the things which lie beyond experience; things as they are in themselves.[90] This should suffice to understand the view which makes phenomena the objects of metaphysics.

The advantage of this position is that it provides empirical grounds for metaphysics; it moves the discipline away from abstraction and speculation into the realm of experience, particularly if one adopts a strictly phenomenological method of inquiry. But there are several difficulties with this position. First, it moves metaphysics to the level of the empirical sciences and, because of that, it is not clear that it can preserve a distinction between it and them. Empirical sciences study phenomena and, if metaphysics also studies phenomena, then how can the latter be differentiated from the former?

Second, it has been a standard view of metaphysicians that metaphysics goes beyond phenomena in order to study reality, when reality is understood to be other than phenomena. Indeed, even those who maintain that metaphysics is nonsense, or yields no knowledge, hold that to be the case precisely because metaphysics aims to go beyond what is given in experience, which is quite impossible.[91]

---

90. Kant, *Prolegomena*, §§ 13, 22, 32, pp. 34–5, 52, 61.
91. Ayer, *Language, Truth and Logic*, p. 36.

The second way of conceiving phenomena is as the lived-world, as the awareness the self has in life, although how this is further analyzed differs again from author to author. Some think of it in terms of common, experienced linguistic structures in a practical, action-oriented context.[92] Others conceive it as human life, and particularly "my life," for it is my life, my living, concrete, and individual self and its circumstances, that is the source of all I know and can know.[93] My life is a radical reality in the sense that it is the root of everything else. Metaphysics, then, must not only begin with the study of my life, but cannot go beyond it, because everything that it can study is in some sense part of my life, for an awareness of an object is nothing but a means to living.[94] This entails that metaphysics becomes a kind of personalized philosophical anthropology in which the central and only topic of investigation is my life in its full particularity and concreteness.

There are many problems with this position, regardless of the way in which it is interpreted. For example, there is the question of what exactly this life is and how it is different from what we normally call life. But none of these difficulties especially concern the object of metaphysics. A more pertinent difficulty has to do with the narrow scope of that object the position entails. For life in general and my life in particular are objects which exclude much that metaphysicians in the past have claimed metaphysics studies.

If, in answer to this objection, the supporter of this view were to say that my life includes everything I can know because in some sense it includes everything of which I can have an experience, then one may respond as follows: First, to frame the whole universe in terms of *my* experience appears to undermine the objectivity and independence of the objects of experience; second, this position becomes indistinguishable from several of the positions we have discussed, depending on how exactly the formula is unpacked. For example, one could argue it amounts to the view that metaphysics studies phenomena, that is, the world as presented to, or as it appears in, my experience. Or, giving the position a more realistic turn, one could argue it amounts to the view that metaphysics studies being. And so on. None of these avenues, however, are satisfactory, as we have seen.

---

92. Habermas, *Postmetaphysical Thinking*, pp. 16, 43–4, 50.
93. Ortega, *Obras*, vol. XII:33, 99, 103, 127.
94. Ibid. VI, p. 13, and Zubiri, *Teoría fenomenológica del juicio*, p. 92.

10. Noumena

Noumena are the things which are beyond experience. There are at least two ways this may be understood. In one way, noumena are beyond experience because they have not yet been experienced. In this sense, traveling to Pluto is part of noumena because no one has yet done so. This is in fact what some philosophers have said metaphysics studies.[95] For them, metaphysics is an ever-shrinking field, for its object is constantly being reduced by the increasing number and kinds of experiences of human beings as a result of technological development, increases in the number of human beings, and anything else which might cause the expansion of the horizon of human experience.

Taken in this way, metaphysics is only a provisional field which produces conjectures as to that about which we do not have sufficient information. It might be called a hypothetical, conjectural, or speculative science; it is the first step on our way to knowledge which, with time, yields to science properly speaking. Only particular metaphysical views are abandoned for the sake of science. Metaphysics as such does not cease to exist, for the field of human experience is unlimited; there will always be something we have not yet experienced in spite of how much we may have in fact experienced. In this way, metaphysics is always ensured to have an object. At the same time, this view subordinates metaphysics to science, relegating it to a prescientific level of conjecture.

Although many positivists would agree with this characterization, few metaphysicians would. They would argue that, regardless of the discoveries of science and technology, and the corresponding expansion of human experience, metaphysics has an object whose breadth and depth increases rather than decreases with these discoveries. And, indeed, there is sense in this response, for the areas of metaphysical speculation have expanded rather than shrunk with the development of science. Consider how recent discoveries about computers, neuroscience, and physics have opened, rather than closed, areas of metaphysical inquiry.

Moreover, many metaphysicians would argue that metaphysics is not exclusively, or even primarily, about what we have not yet experienced but, to a great extent, about what we have experienced or

---

95. Ingenieros, *Principios de psicología*, p. 79.

do experience. Metaphysics is concerned, so the argument goes, with tables, colors, properties, and relations, among other things, and these are given in experience. So to conceive the object of metaphysics as that which has yet to be experienced is inadequate.

A second understanding of noumena is to take them, as Kant did, as what cannot ever be experienced.[95] It is not that we have not yet experienced them, but that it is impossible to do so. The advantage of this view is that it draws a sharp distinction between metaphysics and the empirical sciences, even sharper than the one drawn between the two when 'noumena' is interpreted to refer to what has yet to be experienced. But this is not sufficient to make this view acceptable. For, like the previous view, this one makes metaphysics a purely speculative enterprise, divorced from our experience, and subject to no checks from experience. Moreover, what could its value be if it has to do with what we cannot possibly experience? And how can we discourse about objects and understand them if they are in principle not subject to experience? Perhaps it is possible to mention what is beyond experience, but how could we do any more than merely mention it?

Philosophers who have opposed this view have frequently pointed out, moreover, that there is a contradiction in holding that metaphysics is about noumena when all we can know is phenomena. Indeed, they argue there is a contradiction even in mentioning noumena when we know and can know nothing about it. For, how can we know that what we experience is phenomena and, therefore, that there is noumena when all we know is phenomena?[96] This kind of argument led post-Kantian idealists to conclude that all there is, indeed, is phenomena and thus that reality is ideal. But this seems rather an unsatisfactory conclusion. Also unsatisfactory to those who wish to preserve the legitimacy of the discipline is the positivist inference that metaphysics is a pseudoscience and must be done away with.

11. Language(s)

A position that tries to keep the advantages of the view which holds the object of metaphysics to be phenomena and yet preserves its distinction from empirical disciplines argues that the object of

---

95. Kant, *Prolegomena*, § 32, p. 62.
96. Moore, "What Is Philosophy?", p. 18.

metaphysics is language.[97] Language is very much part of what we experience but at the same time it is not what the empirical sciences study, except for linguistics. One could avoid the identification of metaphysics with linguistics by noting that language may be understood in two senses. In one sense, it may be understood as the natural languages which have developed or may develop, such as English, Latin, and Spanish. In another sense, language may be understood to refer to the common structures which are fundamental to all languages. Language understood in the first sense, one might argue, is the object of linguistics, and language understood in the second sense is the object of metaphysics.

Few linguists, however, will agree that language, understood in the second sense, is not studied by linguists, even if they count themselves as descriptive linguists, whose primary task is to describe natural languages. Most linguists will argue that there are parts of linguistics that deal with the fundamental structures of language. So, it is not clear that metaphysics can be distinguished from linguistics if metaphysics studies language.

Another difficulty with this view is that neither the study of the fundamental structures of language, nor the study of natural languages, turns out to be as empirical as one might at first think. Languages are composed of signs and the rules whereby those signs may be put together to make sense. But neither the signs nor the rules appear often as data of our experience. What we experience are texts, that is, groups of entities used as signs, selected, arranged, and intended by authors to convey specific meanings to audiences in particular contexts.[98] Languages do not occur anywhere except in texts or as described in texts. A language, therefore, is an abstraction, whose signs and rules depend on texts and are encountered only in texts. We do not experience language.

A third difficulty concerns the fact that metaphysics has traditionally been considered to deal with the world, even though what

---

97. Although for Dummett, metaphysics is the philosophy of thought, he believes we can only approach it through language. *The Logical Basis of Metaphysics*, pp. 3, 15. See also Habermas, *Postmetaphysical Thinking*, pp. 43–4. The rejection of the view that language has priority over thought has a long history. See, for example: Plato, *Cratylus*, 439, p. 473; Russell, "Vagueness," pp. 84–5; and Beck, *Early German Philosophy*, p. 126.
98. Gracia, *A Theory of Textuality*, ch. 1, p. 4.

the world has been conceived to be has varied considerably from philosopher to philosopher. To maintain both that metaphysics studies the world and that metaphysics studies language, one would have to hold that language and the world are one and the same. And, indeed, there are some philosophers who appear to say just that.[99] But this makes no sense, for to study signs and the rules whereby they are put together is quite different from studying tables, chairs, and their relations. It is one thing to study the sign 'cause' and how it functions in discourse, and another to study causes such as the parents who produce a child. The reduction of the object of metaphysics to language does not work.

In short, language, whether understood as the natural languages that exist or understood as the fundamental structures common to all languages, cannot serve as the object of study which distinguishes metaphysics from other disciplines. The distinguishing feature of metaphysics must be found elsewhere.

12. *Texts*

A way to avoid some of the problems that the previous view encounters is to say that the object of metaphysics is texts. After all, texts are empirical entities which are subject to our experience and have concrete features. Of course, an initial difficulty is the very notion of a text, because there seems to be no consensus on what texts are. Indeed, until recently, the notion of a text had received very little attention. But even today, when there is considerable literature on textuality, no agreement has been reached.

There are at least five broad conceptions of texts. According to one, a text is a group of entities used to convey meaning but considered apart from the meaning.[100] Thus, the marks on a piece of paper or the sounds one utters are texts. If P means Q, then P is the text. A second view holds that texts are the meanings of the entities used to convey them.[101] If P means Q, then Q is the text. A third view maintains that a text is the group of entities used to convey meaning

---

99. Heidegger, *Introduction to Metaphysics*, p. 11.

100. Derrida, "Signature Event Context," pp. 172–97; Shillingsburg, *Scholarly Editing in the Computer Age*, p. 49. See also Augustine, *The Teacher*, p. 93–94.

101. This position has been attributed to Gadamer by Wachterhauser in "Interpreting Texts," pp. 442, and 443–45. See also Fish, *Is There a Text in This Class?*, p. vii.

considered in relation to meaning, but to no meaning in particular.[102] Thus, if P means Q, the text is P considered in relation to meaning, but the meaning is not necessarily Q. A fourth view identifies texts with certain acts we perform, the so-called speech acts.[103] According to this view, it is neither P nor Q, nor P considered in relation to some meaning that is the text, but the act or acts I perform when I write or say P. Finally, the last view holds that a text is the group of entities used to convey meaning considered in relation to the particular meaning in question.[104] Thus, if P is used to convey Q, the text is P considered in relation to Q.

Naturally, the understanding of the object of metaphysics will vary considerably, depending on which of these five views one adopts. Because I have discussed the merits of these views elsewhere, and we do not have space in a book on the nature of metaphysics to deal with the intricacies posed by textuality, I shall ignore the views with which I disagree and present the view I favor. This is the fifth view mentioned, except that, even as presented, it needs a bit more filling to make it acceptable. Repeating what I said in the previous section, a text is a group of entities used as signs, selected, arranged, and intended by an author to convey some specific meaning to an audience in a certain context.[105]

The advantages of the view that makes texts, understood thus, the object of metaphysics should be obvious. Apart from the advantages already noted, it is clear that this understanding of metaphysics separates the discipline from other disciplines, for no other discipline makes texts its exclusive purview. It is true that some disciplines study texts, but the texts they study are always of a certain type. Literary criticism, for example, studies literary texts, and so on. But there is no discipline that studies texts *qua* texts.

Another advantage of this view is that, because texts are tied to meanings, the object of metaphysics would be very vast, indeed. So one could not accuse this position of being narrow or parochial. For example, because colors can be related to texts through meanings, they would not be excluded from metaphysics.

---

102. This is a less radical interpretation of Derrida's position; see earlier note 100 for reference. See also Grigely, "The Textual Event," p. 170.
103. McGann, *The Textual Condition*, p. 4. This position is based on the well-known view of Austin in *How To Do Things with Words*, pp. 98 ff.
104. Gracia, *Texts*, p. 47.
105. Gracia, *A Theory of Textuality*, p. 4.

The disadvantages of this position, however, overwhelm its advantages. For instance, if metaphysics studies only what has been said, written, or thought (if one accepts that there can be mental texts), the realm of the possible is completely outside the boundaries of the discipline.

Another problem is that metaphysics would be restricted to the study of a human artifact, for texts are products of human design. But this goes contrary both to much of the theory and to much of the practice of the discipline. Of course, if one were to extend the notion of text to everything which can be the locus of an interpretation, as some contemporary hermeneuticists and postmodernists do, then the difficulty raised by this objection appears prima facie to be avoided, for everything can be the locus of an interpretation.[106] Still, when one probes deeper, one realizes that the identification of texts with everything does not save the position from the difficulty insofar as metaphysics would study everything but only under the aspect of textuality. Hence, even though extensionally metaphysics would study everything, intensionally its field would be quite narrow. And, of course, if it did study everything, then the objection raised earlier against the view of metaphysics as the study of everything would apply.

13. Meaning(s)

Meaning, also, in its sense of linguistic or textual meaning, can be taken as the sole object of metaphysics. And this makes a great deal of sense prima facie, for meaning seems to collect all that we want to know about or do know about. After all, we think and communicate through language, and what empowers linguistic entities is the meaning they have.[107]

Meaning, however, is again a controversial notion about which much disagreement has been expressed throughout the history of philosophy. Most views of meaning fall into one of three categories: views which conceive meaning as reference; views which conceive meaning as ideas; and views which conceive meaning as use.[108] According to the first, the meaning of a sign such as 'Socrates' is

---

106. Miller, "The Critic as Host."

107. Dummett, *The Logical Basis of Metaphysics*, pp. 14–15, 18, 22, 338.

108. There are other views of meaning as well. For example, see Carnap on the meaning of statements in "The Elimination of Metaphysics," pp. 63–5, 76.

Socrates, and the meaning of a sign such as 'cat' is the extension of the term: this cat and that cat and the other cat, and so forth. In the case of sentences such as, 'The cat is on the mat,' the meaning is identified with a fact or with a state of affairs.[109]

According to the ideational view, the meaning of 'Socrates' is the idea or concept of Socrates, and the same goes for the meaning of terms such as 'cat.' In the case of sentences like, 'The cat is on the mat,' which have truth value, the meaning is identified with the proposition meant by the sentence.[110] Of course, as should be expected, there is considerable controversy concerning the status of ideas and propositions, and many philosophers have simply rejected them.[111]

According to the third view, meaning is use. In order to understand this position it is best to refer to the speech-act theory proposed by Austin.[112] According to him, we should distinguish among several acts when we say something like, 'Mary, open the door.' One act is the act of uttering the sentence. This is what he called the "locutionary act." In addition, there is the act that the saying of the sentence is intended to cause. This is the "perlocutionary act." And, in the third place, there is another act one performs in saying the sentence. This is the "illocutionary act." In the example given, the perlocutionary act is trying to get Mary to open the door; the locutionary act is uttering the sounds involved in saying, 'Mary, open the door'; and the illocutionary act is ordering Mary to open the door. Now, in this context, meaning would be the use to which one puts the sentence.

All these views have been criticized harshly and thus are not beyond question. My own position is that the meaning of a text or a sign is what we understand when we understand the text or the sign.[113] The meaning of 'Socrates,' 'cat,' and 'The cat is on the mat' are Socrates, cat, and the cat is on the mat. In all cases, meaning is related to the understanding and to the entity, or entities, used to

---

109. Plato, *Sophist* 237c, p. 980; Augustine, *The Teacher* II, 3, p. 577.
110. Locke, *An Essay Concerning Human Understanding*, Introduction, 8, and Bk. 3, 2, 2, vol. 1, p. 32, and vol. 2, p. 9. Ockham held precisely that the objects of knowledge (i.e., of science) were propositions. "On the Notions of Knowledge and Science" (*Expositio super viii libros Physicorum*, Prologus), pp. 9, and 11.
111. Quine, *The Roots of Reference*, p. 35.
112. Austin, *How To Do Things with Words*, pp. 98 ff.
113. Gracia, *A Theory of Textuality*, ch. 1, p. 18.

convey the meaning. Cat is not a meaning, but cat considered as what I understand when I understand 'cat' is a meaning.

But what is cat, when considered as a meaning? Is it a thing, an idea, or something else? I believe it is a mistake to ask this question and to expect that it will be uniformly answered because meanings vary a great deal. The meaning of 'cat,' for example, is not the same as the meaning of 'the concept cat' or as the meaning of 'Chichi' (Chichi is a cat).

The conception of metaphysics will vary, then, depending on one's theory of meaning. There are objections, however, which affect every theory, in addition to the objections parochial to each theory. The most serious of the former is similar to one of the objections raised against the view that metaphysics studies texts: It unnecessarily limits the scope of metaphysics. Consider the case in which meaning is understood extensionally: then metaphysics would be limited to the study of the extensions of the terms we use, thus excluding ideas, whatever they may be. And, if metaphysics studies ideas, this restricts metaphysics to the study of some sort of thing, excluding from its purview much with which metaphysics has been concerned in its history. Finally, the case with use is similar, for use, again, is a very particular object of study.

Perhaps the most appropriate conception, for the purposes of this view of metaphysics, is the one I proposed, for in that case meaning is understood broadly and, thus, could include all the things mentioned as well as others. Even this is too restrictive, however, in the sense that the meanings in question would be limited by what we have said (or written) and understood, as meanings are necessarily related to understandings and locutions.

The points I have made could be summarized by saying that this position is too narrow, because meaning is always restricted to what we say (or write), insofar as meanings are parasitic to signs and texts. Still, this is not the whole story as will become clear later.

14. Propositions

Propositions are particularly controversial. A frequent understanding of propositions is that they consist of the meanings of sentences which can be true or false. Thus, to a sentence such as 'The cat is on the mat' corresponds the proposition "The cat is on the mat." But this does not tell us enough. For some, these meanings are something in the mind, for others they are something outside the mind. In the latter case, some hold these meanings are facts in the spatiotemporal world and others maintain they are outside the world of space and time. Finally, there are those who reject propositions altogether.[114]

The position that holds that metaphysics studies propositions and propositions are mental can be reduced to one of the positions discussed earlier under the view that metaphysics studies concepts. The position that maintains metaphysics studies propositions and propositions are facts in the world is reducible to the view that metaphysics studies relations. And the position that proposes the object of metaphysics to be propositions considered as outside the spatiotemporal world, is similar to the view that metaphysics studies abstract entities; it is not reducible to it because not all propositions express abstract notions.

Apart from the difficulties which each of these versions of this view has in particular, they all have some common difficulties. One of these is that propositions come in a great variety and these positions do not make clear which of these metaphysics studies.[115] If metaphysics studies all propositions, then it is difficult to see how the discipline can be distinguished from other disciplines considered together as the encyclopedia of all knowledge. But if it does not, then that metaphysics studies propositions is not enough to distinguish it from the disciplines from which it is to be distinguished, for we do not know what distinguishes the propositions metaphysics studies from those it does not.

Another difficulty is that propositions, regardless of how they are interpreted, seem to constitute a very limited object which leaves out much that metaphysics has traditionally studied. For example, one could say that, according to this view, metaphysics does not study physical objects. Of course, to this the supporter of this position could answer in two ways. In one way by saying that metaphysics studies propositions about physical objects and, therefore, does not leave out of consideration what we need to know about those objects. (This assumes that propositions are mental or extra mental but outside the spatiotemporal world of physical objects.)

---

114. Quine, *Word and Object*, § 43, pp. 206–11; Ryle, "Are There Propositions?" p. 37.
115. Ockham acknowledges the problem and points out that it is not the object (propositions) a science studies that distinguishes it from other sciences, but the subjects and predicates of its propositions, which presumably are different for each science. "On the Notion of Knowledge and Science" (*Expositio super viii libros Physicorum*, Prologus), p. 15.

And, in another way, by noting that propositions are facts in the world and, therefore, metaphysics studies physical facts insofar as metaphysics studies propositions.

Finally, one could argue that the only way to avoid the limitations which this view seems to impose on the object of metaphysics is to adopt a position according to which everything seems to be propositional, that is, that the world is exclusively composed of propositions or propositional-like entities. This is certainly a view which has been held, but it is a controversial one.

15. *Presuppositions / First Principle(s)*

Some metaphysicians have claimed that the object of metaphysics consists of absolute, primary, or fundamental presuppositions. This kind of presupposition is to be contrasted with relative, secondary, or derivative presuppositions. The difference between the two is that the first are so basic that every, or nearly every, statement one makes or belief one holds depends on them, that is why they are often called "first principles." By contrast, relative presuppositions are such that only certain statements one makes or beliefs one has depend on them. The principle of noncontradiction, $\sim(P.\sim P)$, is an example of the first; the belief that I own a house is presupposed by the question, How much does the house you own cost?

Aristotle himself spoke of first principles, although sometimes he had in mind epistemological or logical principles such as the principle of noncontradiction[116] and at other times first or primary causes (e.g., God).[117] We have discussed the second in the sections on God and ultimate causes above. Here we turn to the first, which was popularized as the primary object of metaphysics in early modern philosophy[118] and has remained a favorite of some philosophers ever since.[119]

There are, as well, other characteristics associated with absolute presuppositions when these are taken as first principles.

---

116. Aristotle, *Metaphysics* 1005b17, p. 736.
117. Ibid., 1026a30, 1069b1, pp. 779, 872. For examples of those who hold both, see McKeon, *Introduction to Aristotle*, p. xviii, and Copleston, *A History of Philosophy, Vol. I: Greece and Rome*, p. 288.
118. Baumgarten, *Metaphysica*, § 1, p. 1.
119. For different versions of this position, see: Aristotle, *Metaphysics* 1005b15, p. 736; Collingwood, *An Essay on Metaphysics*, p. 31; Whitehead, *Process and Reality*, pp. 18, 25; Broad, "Critical and Speculative Philosophy," pp. 84, 90.

Some philosophers claim they are self-evident,[120] for example, and others argue they are never propounded or stated.[121] These views, however, are based on certain theoretical commitments that cannot be taken for granted, and so it seems more appropriate to use a more theoretically neutral approach. Regardless of the particular characteristics one may associate with absolute presuppositions, however, it is true that most people are unaware of most, and perhaps even all, of the absolute presuppositions on which what they say is based. Indeed, it is the work of the scientist and philosopher to make these presuppositions explicit.

There are at least two ways of understanding absolute presuppositions. According to one, absolute presuppositions are thoughts or mental entities and, therefore, historical. That they are historical means that they are subject to time and belong to some person or other. Consider, for example, the principle of noncontradiction, $\sim(P.\sim P)$. In this view, this principle is a presupposition found in someone's mind when he or she holds anything, say Q, which presupposes that it is not possible for P to be both true and false.

In another way, absolute presuppositions are timeless propositions which stand in a logical relation of priority (however that is understood) to most other propositions. If someone, then, holds one of these other propositions, the absolute presuppositions stand in a logical relation of priority to it. In this sense, $\sim(P.\sim P)$ for example, is not something in anyone's mind, but rather a proposition which is presupposed by some other proposition, such as Q, whether someone does in fact hold Q or not. This means that absolute presuppositions are not historical insofar as they are not subject to time and are not mental insofar as they are not located in anyone's mind.

These two understandings of presuppositions yield two different understandings of metaphysics. According to the first, metaphysics turns out to be a kind of history, for its object is the absolute presuppositions someone had at some point in history.[122] Metaphysical claims, then, turn out to have the form: "P is an absolute presupposition of what X said, believed, held, or even asked, at t."[123] P, then, would not be asserted, but merely reported and no truth value would

---

120. Scotus, "Concerning Human Knowledge" (*Opus oxoniense* 1, 3, 4), pp. 106–7.
121. Collingwood, *An Essay on Metaphysics*, pp. 32–3.
122. Ibid., pp. 52, 58.
123. For a different formula, see ibid., p. 55.

be attached to it. Truth value would only apply to the historical statement concerning who entertained *P* when.

This view of metaphysics is contrary to what practically every metaphysician has claimed or done.[124] Indeed, one would be hard pressed to come up with a metaphysician who would say that absolute presuppositions have no truth value. And most metaphysicians would argue, correctly in my view, that what makes an absolute presupposition such is not that it does not have truth value, but that it is assumed to be true. This is a serious objection against this position, for it challenges its own historical accuracy: Metaphysics has never been a historical science.[125]

Apart from this objection, one can also argue that this view turns out to do exactly what it says it does not do. In claiming that *P* is an absolute presupposition of what *X* holds, say *Q*, it makes a logical claim about the relation between *P* and *Q* which is neither temporal nor historical. Of course, the metaphysician also holds that *X* said *Q* and that *P* is an absolute presupposition of what *X* said, but this is not all the metaphysician claims. Perhaps the point can be brought out by looking at the following sentences:

1. *P* is an absolute presupposition of what *X* said (or thought), namely, *Q*, at *t*.

2. *P* is an absolute presupposition of *Q*.

3. *X* said (or thought) *Q* at *t*.

I believe that sentence 1 is complex and can be analyzed roughly into 2 and 3. Sentence 2 makes a claim about the relation between *P* and *Q* apart from whether *X* said, or thought, *Q*, holds *P*, or has *P* among her thoughts. And 3 makes a claim precisely about the fact that *X* said, or thought, *Q* at *t*. Now, the truth value of 1 depends on the truth value of both 2 and 3. If 2 is false, 1 is false; and if 3 is false, 1 is false. And if both 2 and 3 are true, 1 is true. This means

---

124. Collingwood disagrees with this statement in ibid., p. 54. And I must grant that Aristotle himself, when writing about these principles did not say they were true, but only that they were the ones of which we could have most certainty. *Metaphysics* 1005b6–25, pp. 736–7.

125. For Aristotle, history cannot be a proper science, strictly speaking, because it deals with individuals and scientific knowledge is of the universal. *Poetics* 1451b5, p. 1464. Metaphysics, on the other hand, is the epitome of a science.

that 1 is not exclusively historical, as those who hold this position claim. It also means that metaphysics cannot be a purely historical enterprise.

In order for 1 to be purely historical, it would have to be something like the following:

4. *X* said (or thought) that *P* is an absolute presupposition of what *X* said (or thought), namely, *Q*, at *t*.

But clearly, 1 and 4 do not say the same thing. Moreover, those who have defended this view do not think 4 is the sort of claim made by metaphysicians; they hold metaphysical claims are of the sort 1 is.[126] Now let me turn to the second understanding of metaphysics as the study of timeless propositions which stand in a logical relation of priority to most or all other propositions. This view does not have to deal with the second difficulty which affected the other view. The first one affects it to the extent that many metaphysicians have claimed to be doing something else. Moreover, what metaphysicians in fact do and have done includes more than the study of absolute presuppositions. Indeed, metaphysicians seem to be concerned not just with principles, such as the principle of noncontradiction, but with such things as color. Hence, I do not believe the view that metaphysics studies absolute presuppositions and only absolute presuppositions, even if one understands these nonhistorically, is a viable position.

16. End(s)

According to this position, metaphysics studies ends. As Aristotle puts it, metaphysics is "the science which knows to what end each thing must be done."[127] Now, an end can be understood in various ways. In one way, it is a good, the object of desire for which everything else is done.[128] In an Aristotelian framework this turns out to be one kind of cause: the final cause. And because Aristotle holds there is a final cause of everything else, namely, God, it turns out that metaphysics studies God.[129] We have, then, four different descriptions of the object of metaphysics based on the notion of end: (1) that for

---

126. Collingwood, *An Essay on Metaphysics*, p. 55.
127. Aristotle, *Metaphysics* 982b5, p. 692.
128. Aristotle, ibid., 982b5, p. 692, and *Nicomachean Ethics* 1094a2, p. 935.
129. Aristotle, *Metaphysics* 982b10, p. 692.

which everything else is done, (2) the good, (3) the final cause, and (4) God. Aristotle seems to have believed that these four descriptions are not only not incompatible, but that they also describe the same thing and mean the same thing. If that is the case, and what they describe is God, then metaphysics amounts to theology, a position we have discussed earlier. If the formulations are not equivalent, however, it turns out we have three other views to contend with, and all three encounter difficulties.

If the object of metaphysics is identified with "that for which everything else is done" and the doing is by humans—something Aristotle would reject—then metaphysics is restricted to the study of the end of human action. But that, of course, would be too restrictive and would also tie metaphysics too closely to practical disciplines. If the object of metaphysics is identified with the good, then metaphysics amounts to a kind of axiology. And, again, this would appear to be too restrictive. Finally, if the object of metaphysics is identified with final causes, then metaphysics again becomes very narrow in scope. Indeed, it would not even include the study of causes other than final causes. In short, this view of the object of metaphysics does no justice to the breadth displayed by the history of the discipline.

17. *Most General Predicates*

Another possibility is to conceive metaphysics as the study of the most general predicates of being.[130] Put thus, this formulation results unclear because the term 'predicate' can be taken in various ways. For example, some philosophers speak of predicates as linguistic terms, so that the predicate cat in the sentence, 'Chichi is a cat' is nothing but the word 'cat' in the sentence. For others, however, predicates are concepts through which we understand what the subject of a sentence is claimed to be. In this sense, the predicate cat is the concept cat through which we understand Chichi. Still in another way, a predicate is taken as some feature or characteristic of the things of which it is predicated. So, in the sentence we have been using, cat is a feature which the sentence claims characterizes cats. Of course, there are many other ways in which predicates have been and are understood by philosophers, but these three ways go back a long haul. We find them implicit in much that Aristotle says, for example.[131]

---

130. Baumgarten uses this formula to refer to ontology, which for him is a part of metaphysics. *Metaphysica*, § 4, p. 2.
131. Aristotle, *Categories* 1a17–1b9, pp. 7–8.

The three understandings of predicates mentioned yield three different conceptions of metaphysics as: the study of the most general terms; the study of the most general concepts; and the study of the most general features. The first would convert metaphysics into a part of linguistics, the second into a part of logic, and the third into a part of natural science. But each of these views has similar problems: it is too narrow. By restricting the object of metaphysics to terms, concepts, or features, all three leave out much that metaphysicians have traditionally studied. Indeed, if metaphysics studies only predicable terms, what discipline is concerned with features and concepts? If metaphysics studies only predicable concepts, what discipline studies terms and the features of things? Finally, if metaphysics studies only predicable features, what discipline studies terms and concepts?

But this is not all. There is an even more fundamental problem, for metaphysics has always been concerned with the less general as well as with the most general. For example, it is common place to find discussions of color and even of particular colors, such as red and white, in metaphysical treatises. So, even if we were to accept that metaphysics studies predicates—apart from whether predicates are conceived as linguistic terms, concepts, or features of things—it would certainly be a mistake to say that it studies only the most general predicates. I shall have more to say about this in chapter 7.

18. Combinations

Instead of selecting one entity or kind of entity as the object metaphysics studies, we could simply combine two or more of these and see if they work better together. For example, we could go along with some of Aristotle's statements and say that the object metaphysics studies is being *qua* being and its properties.[132] But this position, like many of the others which would claim to combine many of the views we have discussed, amounts to one of the discussed views; in this particular case, the conception of metaphysics as the study of transcendentals. Indeed, an analysis of these possible combinations yields disappointing results, for in all cases we end up by reducing metaphysics to a cluster of particular disciplines, and this is as unsatisfactory as reducing it to the cluster of all disciplines.

---

132. Ibid., 1003a20, p. 731.

CHAPTER FOUR

Method

Among the various objects we have examined, we have not been able to find one that can function as the object of metaphysics and supply us with the set of conditions that distinguishes the discipline from other disciplines, including philosophy. We must, then, turn to the way in which metaphysics studies its object to see if that contains the distinguishing mark of the discipline. Even if we do not find it in the way metaphysics studies its object or reaches its conclusions, the discussion of various methods should help us determine how it is that metaphysics proceeds and, thus, provide us with a greater understanding of it. I refer to the way metaphysics studies its object as the method of metaphysics or the metaphysical method.

It is usual to find that metaphysicians favor one method over another and that, frequently, they distinguish metaphysics from other disciplines precisely because of the method it employs.[1] There are many different characterizations of method, but the following are particularly pertinent in this context: authoritative/nonauthoritative, a priori/a posteriori, inductive/deductive, discursive/intuitive, descriptive/prescriptive, analytic/elucidative/synthetic, experimental/observational, common sense/uncommon sense, historical/nonhistorical, phenomenological, and dialectical.

---

1. This is perhaps what Plato had in mind when he suggests, in *Republic* 346a, p. 595, that arts differ by their powers or functions. See also Averroes, *On the Harmony of Religion and Philosophy*, p. 49.

A. Authoritative / Nonauthoritative

An authoritative method is one that uses authority or refers to authority as the only, the primary, or the most important basis on which to establish views about an object under study. In contrast, a nonauthoritative method is one which neither relies on nor refers to authority to reach its conclusions. If authoritative and nonauthoritative methods are understood thus, there have been very few authors who have in fact argued that metaphysics is authoritative. The few who have, consider God to be the object of metaphysics and revelation to be the best way of attaining knowledge of God.[2] Hence, they argue, it is by the authority of revelation that metaphysics should proceed. The way to develop a correct view about God is to begin with what he has revealed to us, for that is the most certain way to get at what he is. Conclusions of arguments based on other evidence may be true, and the arguments themselves may be valid and based on true premises, but the degree of certainty and accuracy we have, by using what God has wished to tell us about himself, cannot be compared with the degree of certainty we can have based on other sorts of evidence.

In general, however, most metaphysicians have pointed out that the appeal to authority has little or no place in metaphysics or, for that matter, in any other secular discipline of learning.[3] Disciplines of learning are concerned with knowledge, and authority yields only opinion. This does not mean that we should not rely on proper authorities when we are learning or using what we have learned. We cannot all be physicists, chemists, engineers, lawyers, or physicians. We must rely on what experts tell us about their respective fields of expertise. Scientists regularly accept the conclusions of other scientists in areas where this is necessary for the advancement of their own work. However, this reliance on authority is based on two foundations: The first is the reputation of the person in question as authoritative, that is, as knowledgeable in her field; the second is that the views of the person in question are open to scrutiny and subject

---

2. Bonaventure, *Collationes in Hexaëmeron*, Vision III, Discussion VII, pp. 212–22.

3. Aquinas, *Summa theologiae* I, 1, 8, pp. 13–14; but note that for Aquinas the sciences are ordered hierarchically and some take their principles from the conclusions of other sciences. Ibid., I, 1, 3, p. 7, and *Commentary on the "De Trinitate" of Boethius* 5, 1, ad 5, p. 15.

to testing or confirmation in cases where this is necessary or recommended. Therefore, the use of an authority ultimately rests not on authority but in the provability of the views the authority has put forward. This is very different from the procedure followed in a field like revealed theology, where the ultimate arbiter of truth is a statement from a person or group of persons whose views are regarded as indisputable, and whose authority rests not on proof, but on the fact that they are who they are or hold the office they hold.

Regardless of which view one adopts, the problem with trying to distinguish metaphysics on the basis of whether it proceeds authoritatively or nonauthoritatively is that it is effective in neither case. It is ineffective if it proceeds authoritatively, because then it cannot be distinguished from other disciplines which rely on authoritative procedures, such as revealed theology. On the other hand, if it proceeds nonauthoritatively, it is ineffective because it cannot be distinguished from other disciplines which seek support in nonauthoritative procedures, such as the natural sciences.

B. A Priori / A Posteriori

At first, the a priori/a posteriori method appears more promising to distinguish metaphysics from other disciplines. Indeed, many philosophers have argued that one distinguishing feature of metaphysics is that it is a priori, whereas other disciplines are not.[4] There are, however, two problems with this view. First, there are disciplines, such as mathematics and geometry, which are a priori.[5] So, a prioricity by itself cannot be a distinguishing mark for metaphysics. Second, the a priori/a posteriori distinction is not an uncontroversial one and, as a result, it is not clear that saying that metaphysics is a priori can help us understand its distinctive character. Let me take up the notions of a priori and a posteriori for a moment to determine if, and how, they may apply to metaphysics.

As a part of philosophy, metaphysics is a view about an object or group of objects. Metaphysics can also be considered an activity, a set

---

4. Suárez, *Disputatio metaphysica* 1, 3, 1, vol. 25, p. 22; Kant, *Prolegomena*, § 1, p. 13.
5. Kant is aware of the similarities between metaphysics and mathematics and tries to distinguish the two disciplines in *Prolegomena*, § 2, pp. 15–19.

of rules, or a capacity, but I shall ignore these distinctions here in order to simplify the discussion. To make things easier, moreover, let us say that this view is expressed by propositions which are established according to some method. And by method let us understand the way in which these propositions, which we might call "conclusions," are established. The method, then, requires that certain rules be followed in order to reach these conclusions.

Now, one way of understanding the a priori/a posteriori distinction is to have it apply to a method, that is, to the procedure whereby conclusions are reached. In this sense, an a priori method might be described as one in which the rules prescribe that conclusions be inferred from premises which are not based on observation, that is, premises whose truth is not established through observation. By contrast, an a posteriori method might be described as one in which the rules prescribe that conclusions be inferred from premises which are based on observation. Consider the following argument:

1. All humans are two-legged beings.
   All two-legged beings are mortal.
   Therefore, all humans are mortal.

The method on the basis of which the conclusion of this argument is established appears to be a priori, for no one has yet observed the death of all two-legged beings or the two-leggedness of all humans, even if it is an observable fact that some humans are two-legged.[6] But consider the following argument:

2. This human is a two-legged being.
   That human is a two-legged being.
   Therefore, all humans are two-legged beings.

In this argument, the conclusion is established on the basis of observation, for the premises of the argument refer to observable data. Therefore, the method used must be regarded as a posteriori.

There are, however, problems with this way of distinguishing a priori from a posteriori methods, for the examples we considered seem to lead us into a dilemma: If argument 2 is a posteriori, then so

---

6. This is probably the reason why Aquinas considered propositions such as "Man is rational" to be self-evident (*Summa theologiae* I, 2, 1, p. 19), and Duns Scotus claimed we can have certainty of generalizations (*Opus oxoniense* I, 3, 4), pp. 141–143. For the background to Scotus's discussion, see Aristotle, *Metaphysics* 1027a8–29, p. 781.

is argument 1. The reason for this claim is that the conclusion of argument 2 is used as a premise of argument 1. Indeed, if the bases on which the conclusion of 2 is established are observations, then argument 1 must be a posteriori also, insofar as its conclusion would ultimately be established on the basis, at least in part, of the premises of argument 2, which premises are empirical. If this is correct, then it does not look as if the distinction a priori/a posteriori is helpful in the understanding of any method, let alone that of metaphysics.

Of course, one could argue that this objection is ineffective, because the conclusion of argument 2 does not follow from the premises of the argument. Indeed, one could argue that the conclusion does not follow from any sort of observation, for no individual observation can support the kind of generalization made in the conclusion—because for it to follow, we would have to have observed all human beings—, and therefore the conclusion of 2 is established a priori, if at all.

This response, however, is ultimately irrelevant. Whether or not the conclusion of 2 follows from the premises of the argument will not affect the fact that the argument claims it does, and this is what characterizes the argument as a posteriori. It does not signify that the conclusion does not follow or that the evidence presented in the argument is inadequate; what signifies is that the conclusion purports to follow from premises which record observations. The response confuses the kind of inference drawn in the argument with the value of the argument, just as some confuse soundness and validity in a deductive argument with the deductive character of the argument. Indeed, if soundness and validity were necessary conditions of deductive argumentation, then no deductive argument could be unsound or invalid, and this makes no sense.[7] In short, the objection against this way of distinguishing a priori and a posteriori stands.

There are other ways of understanding this distinction, however. Let us say that a method is a posteriori if it includes a rule according to which the views to be established by the discipline which uses the method would be expressed only by propositions which are verifiable by observation. Examples of propositions verifiable by observation would be the following:

1. Chichi has a black coat.

2. That table seats eight.

7. But some of it made sense to Aristotle, for whom syllogisms are always valid. *Prior Analytics*, 25b32–26a13, p. 68.

Examples of propositions not verifiable by observation would be the following:

    3. A whole is greater than any of its parts.

    4. $2 + 2 = 4$

The truth of propositions 1 and 2 is established through observation. I verify that the cat Chichi has a black coat by looking at Chichi and seeing whether in fact she does or does not have a black coat. By contrast, the truth of propositions 3 and 4 is established through the consideration of the concepts in question or, to put the matter semantically, through the consideration of the meanings of the terms used. I verify that a whole is greater than any of its parts by considering the concepts of whole and part and the relation established in the proposition between these two concepts. I could not verify this proposition on the basis of observation, because I do not have access to all wholes and all parts.

    Note that I have been speaking about method, a way of establishing certain propositional claims and their truth values. To distinguish metaphysics in terms of the method it uses is not to distinguish it on the basis of a distinction between analytic and synthetic propositions. It is not the character of the propositions or what makes them true or false that is at stake here, but the way in which we come to establish that they are true or false. The distinction a priori/a posteriori, as we have been using it, concerns the way in which we claim to know that a proposition is true.[8] As such, this distinction is epistemic and methodological; it concerns our knowledge and the procedure we use to establish it. The distinction analytic/synthetic concerns the causes of a property of propositions, namely, their truth value.[9] As such, it is an ontological distinction; it concerns the way things are. Let me illustrate this point. Consider two of the propositions listed earlier:

    2. That table seats eight.

    3. A whole is greater than any of its parts.

Considered apart from the way we claim to know they are true, if indeed they are so, these propositions are neither a priori nor a pos-

---

8. Kripke, *Naming and Necessity*, p. 34, although Kripke speaks of "truths."
9. Ibid., p. 39.

teriori. They are a priori or a posteriori only insofar as they are considered in relation to the way in which we claim to know them. It is
the procedure of establishing how we know their truth value that
makes them a priori or a posteriori. This is what I mean by saying
that the a priori/a posteriori distinction is epistemic and methodological; it concerns how we come to know that the table seats eight
and a whole is greater than any of its parts.

The classification of these propositions as analytic or synthetic
has nothing to do with the method through which we claim to know
their truth value. It has to do rather with the causes of their truth
value. "That table seats eight" is true if and only if that table seats
eight. "A whole is greater than any of its parts" is true if and only if
a whole is greater than any of its parts. In the first case, the proposition is true in virtue of a fact in the world; in the second case, the
proposition is true in virtue of the concepts it uses. In neither case
does it matter how we come to know the proposition is true—it does
not matter for example, whether I came to know that the table seats
eight because an angel revealed it to me, or because I saw that the
table seats eight, or because someone told me the table seats eight,
and so on. What matters is that the table seats eight. And the same
applies to the second proposition. Analyticity and syntheticity have
to do with the causes of the truth value of propositions. A prioricity
and a posterioricity, as I have spoken of them here, have to do with
the way we come to know the truth value of propositions.

Where we are concerned with method, then, it is irrelevant to
speak of analytic or synthetic propositions; it is pertinent only that
the propositions are established a priori or a posteriori. Whether all
propositions which are established a priori are analytic and all
propositions which are established a posteriori are synthetic is a
matter of debate among philosophers and one that I cannot address
adequately here and need not settle for my argument. I shall come
back to analytic and synthetic propositions in chapter 6.

One point I must address, however, is the claim that the a priori
/a posteriori distinction breaks down because the a priori method
turns out to be a posteriori after all. The argument in support of this
claim consists in pointing out that in order to verify any proposition,
we must know the meaning of the terms of the sentence or sentences
that express it, and that is possible only through observation. Thus,
the a priori method includes an a posteriori component. Consider the
proposition "2 + 2 = 4" expressed by the sentence '2 + 2 = 4.' According to the view presented earlier, this proposition is not verifiable by observation, but simply on the basis of the analysis of the

concepts that compose it. But the analysis of those concepts presupposes the understanding that '2' means 2, '+' means +, and so on, and this knowledge is acquired through experience.

My answer to this objection is that it rests on a confusion between two questions: How do I come to know that the proposition "2 + 2 = 4" is true? and, How do I come to know that the proposition " '2 + 2 = 4' means two plus two equals four" is true? The truth of the first proposition is established independently of experience (even if, in order to establish it one must have established the truth of the second proposition for one of the languages in which the first proposition may be expressed), whereas the truth of the second proposition may be established only on the basis of observation. Thus, we can dismiss this objection summarily.

Another objection is the reverse of the one just mentioned. It argues that the a priori/a posteriori distinction breaks down because, even in the case of propositions which appear to be known a posteriori, a priori knowledge is used. Consider the proposition: "That table seats eight." Such a proposition presupposes notions of table, sitting, and eight. But these are universal notions not available in experience, insofar as all we experience is individual. Therefore, we must come to these notions independently of experience, and the knowledge that the table seats eight is not purely a posteriori.

Once again, the objection is rooted in a confusion. In this case, the confusion is between the claim about the proposition and the concepts used in the proposition which makes the claim. The claim concerns an individual fact—the number of people who can sit at a table—and we come to know it through experience, either because we perceive it or because someone tells us about it. The concepts used may be universal, but that does not alter the individuality of the fact.

In short, the distinction between an a priori and an a posteriori method seems reasonable, but it is not useful in effectively setting metaphysics apart from other disciplines. Indeed, metaphysics seems to use both a priori and a posteriori techniques to establish its conclusions. Metaphysics is not purely a priori because, in its attempt to study its object, metaphysics considers the way we speak and think about that object as well as the way that object is present in our experience. From the time of Plato, metaphysicians have been searching for the proper definitions of such things as substance, for example, and, in order to find them, they have considered not only the nature of substances, but also the way we speak and think about them. The method of metaphysics, then, cannot be exclusively characterized as a priori. But, even if it could, this would not be sufficient to set metaphysics apart from other disciplines, for there are other disciplines which claim methodological a prioricity, such as mathematics and geometry.

Naturally, if contrary to the view that the method of metaphysics is a priori, one were to hold that it is a posteriori,[10] then certainly the method cannot be used to establish the uniqueness of metaphysics, for most sciences are a posteriori. A different factor must be found for this purpose.

C. Inductive / Deductive

In the discussion of a priori and a posteriori method, we touched on the notions of inductive and deductive. These notions are also controversial. Some philosophers argue that no clear distinction can be made between the two, and, even among those philosophers who believe a clear distinction can be made between them, there is no consensus as to the way to draw it. I shall stay away from these controversies and provide three common ways of distinguishing between inductive and deductive which may help us understand how these methods have been used to characterize metaphysics, even though what I say should not be taken as implying I endorse any one of these or that I reject other ways of distinguishing them. Indeed, my discussion should not even be taken as endorsing the view there is a clear distinction between them.

According to one way, a method is inductive if it consists of arguments whose conclusions are claimed to follow only with a degree of probability. In contrast, a method is deductive if it consists of arguments whose conclusions are claimed to follow with absolute necessity.[11] It is, then, the nature of the claim as to how conclusions follow that defines the method, rather than any relation between the

---

10. Whitehead, *Process and Reality*, pp. 6–8. Meinong held that metaphysics is a posteriori because it deals with what exists, whereas "the science of objects" is a priori. "The Theory of Objects," p. 109. For Collingwood, metaphysics is a posteriori because it is historical. *An Essay on Metaphysics*, p. 49.
11. Copi, *Introduction to Logic*, pp. 51–4. See also Williams, "Metaphysical Arguments," pp. 42 ff., for a different view.

conclusions and the premises of the arguments or the nature of the premises and the conclusions.

The following are examples of the application of an inductive method:

1. This swan is white.
   That swan is white.
   Probably, all swans are white.

2. All women are mortal beings.
   All mortal beings are spatiotemporal entities.
   Probably, all women are spatiotemporal entities.

By contrast, the deductive method uses arguments like the following:

3. This swan is white.
   That swan is white.
   Therefore, all swans are white.

4. All women are mortal beings.
   All mortal beings are spatiotemporal entities.
   Therefore, all women are spatiotemporal entities.

Now, metaphysicians have generally made strong claims of certainty about their discipline and some have in fact claimed the highest certainty possible, namely, necessity.[12] This seems to entail that, for them, the method of metaphysics must be deductive in the mentioned sense. But the deductive method must be based on generalizations of some kind in order to be effective, and generalizations are always based on a limited number of experiences,[13] so it would be foolish to claim necessity for such generalizations. Hence, the method of metaphysics cannot be purely deductive in the sense we have discussed.[14] Indeed, some metaphysicians have claimed pre-

---

12. Hamlyn, *Metaphysics*, p. 36.
13. Aristotle, *Metaphysics* 981a–b, pp. 689–91, and *Posterior Analytics* 100a1–14, p. 185.
14. Collingwood comes to this conclusion because he rejects any relations of implication between the solutions to metaphysical problems. *An Essay on Metaphysics*, p. 65.

cisely that the method of metaphysics is inductive, because the conclusions metaphysics reaches are only tentative.[15]

Another common way of distinguishing deductive from inductive is to say that a method is inductive when it uses arguments which proceed from premises whose subjects are individuals, to conclusions whose subjects are classes of individuals, and this regardless of the force of the claim made in the conclusion about the inference. Hence, the following two arguments are inductive:

5. This swan is white.
    That swan is white.
    Probably, all swans are white.

6. This swan is white.
    That swan is white.
    Therefore, all swans are white.

In contrast, a method is deductive if it uses arguments which proceed from at least some premises whose subjects are classes of individuals to conclusions whose subjects are individuals, and this again, regardless of the force of the claim made in the conclusion about the inference, although in this kind of argument it would be foolish to claim anything but necessity.[16] Hence, the following argument is deductive:

7. This bird is a swan.
    All swans are white.
    Therefore, this bird is white.

To understand the distinction between inductive and deductive methods in this way, however, does not help us much. The main reason for this is that metaphysics is not different from most disciplines in that it uses arguments in which individuals are mentioned and arguments in which individuals are not mentioned.[17]

---

15. Whitehead, *Process and Reality*, pp. 6, 12, 15. Some philosophers, however, have claimed the method of metaphysics is neither deductive nor inductive. Williams, "Metaphysical Arguments," p. 51.

16. Aristotle, *Nicomachean Ethics* 1139b26, p. 1027.

17. Some philosophers, however, claim that metaphysics is only concerned with universals, although the most common position is that this is not just characteristic of metaphysics but of all science. Aristotle, *Posterior Analytics* 75b21–36, pp. 122–123, and *Metaphysics* 1027a19–21, p. 781.

One may adopt a third way of distinguishing inductive from deductive arguments. Inductive arguments are those in which the conclusions are more general than the premises, and deductive arguments are those in which they are less general. This way of establishing the distinction accommodates arguments of the sort we have discussed, but also makes room for the following argument, which is deductive:

8. All swans are birds.
   All birds are animals.
   Therefore, all swans are animals.

Again, there have been metaphysicians who have claimed that metaphysics uses only a deductive method understood in the last two senses of deductive presented,[18] and there have been metaphysicians who have claimed the opposite, namely, that the method of metaphysics is inductive.[19] The problem with these positions, however, is that they do not reflect what metaphysicians, including those who hold these views, do. For metaphysics uses arguments of both kinds.[20]

Apart from the objections that can be raised against the attempt to distinguish metaphysics on the basis of particular understandings of the deductive and inductive methods, there is a general objection that applies regardless of which understandings of these are chosen. It is quite obvious that, even if metaphysics were strictly deductive, inductive, or a combination of both in method, this would not distinguish it from other disciplines within and without philosophy.[21] For example, how would it distinguish it from mathematics and physics?

It makes sense to say that metaphysics proceeds both deductively and inductively because, when it makes claims about the relationship among concepts, it most likely claims the kind of necessity that characterizes deductive reasoning, but when it bases its conclu-

---

18. McTaggart, *The Nature of Existence*, pp. 38–53.
19. Whitehead, *Process and Reality*, pp. 8, 14–16.
20. In *Nicomachean Ethics* 1139b30, p. 1027, Aristotle restricts science to the deductive aspect of the process of knowledge and, thus, would seem to have endorsed the view that metaphysics is deductive. But later in the same book (1141a17, pp. 1027–28), he makes clear that Wisdom (another name of metaphysics), includes both intuition (induction) and science (deduction).
21. Grice, Pears, and Strawson, "Metaphysics," p. 5. For various arguments against the deductive character of metaphysics, see Hampshire, "Metaphysical Systems."

sions on experience, the claims it makes involve only probability. Moreover, metaphysics uses arguments whose premises and conclusions have both less general and more general subjects, and mixes them in various ways. Therefore, metaphysics cannot be said to be exclusively deductive or inductive.

D. Discursive / Intuitive

Another methodological distinction that could be useful in understanding metaphysics, and perhaps in distinguishing it from other disciplines, is the distinction between discursive and intuitive.[22] A method may be characterized as discursive if it employs arguments.[23] Arguments are sets of propositions in which one or more propositions are claimed to follow from other propositions. Consider two of the arguments given earlier:

1. All humans are two-legged beings.
   All two-legged beings are mortal.
   Therefore, all humans are mortal.

2. This human is two-legged.
   That human is two-legged.
   Therefore, all humans are two-legged.

Logicians often distinguish between these two arguments in various ways, but for my purposes the differences between the two are immaterial. Nor is it important whether the propositions which are claimed to follow from other propositions in these or other arguments do in fact follow. Nor is the mode in which they follow—necessarily, or with a certain degree of probability—important. It is important for us that, in both arguments, there is a proposition that is claimed to follow from other propositions. This is characteristic of arguments and, therefore, of a discursive method.

---

22. Discursive and anamnestic, for Habermas. *Postmetaphysical Thinking*, p. 31.
23. For Aquinas there is another requirement of a discursive method: it must be based on sense perception. *Commentary on the "De Trinitate" of Boethius* 6, 1, p. 57.

In contrast, a method may be characterized as intuitive if the propositions which it seeks to establish are claimed to follow not from other propositions, but from some things which are not propositions. When, for example, I claim that a particular object is red, and I do not express the reason for my knowing that fact in a proposition or propositions, I have established the claim intuitively. We grasp it intuitively in a sudden, non-argumentative way.[24] Intuitions are flashes of insight or empirical apprehensions. Of course, I can turn an intuitive method into a discursive one if I proceed to give reasons expressed propositionally, but it is not necessary to do so.

Is the metaphysical method, then, discursive, intuitive, or both? It would be difficult to argue that it is one of these to the exclusion of the other, for metaphysicians have traditionally used arguments, but they also make claims supported directly by intuition.[25] But if metaphysics uses both methods, then it does not appear to be different from many—perhaps all—other disciplines. For other disciplines also make claims sometimes based on intuitions and sometimes based on reasons expressed in propositions. Hence, the distinction between the discursive and intuitive methods does not help in distinguishing metaphysics from other disciplines.

E. Descriptive / Prescriptive

Does metaphysics proceed by describing, prescribing, or both?[26] A descriptive method is one which proceeds by telling us how something is. A prescriptive method is one which proceeds by telling us how something should be. If this is so, one may wonder how any discipline could possibly be prescriptive except for those which have to do with establishing rules for human conduct. Surely, the aim of physics is not to tell us how the physical world should be but rather to tell us how it is. And the same would have to be said about chemistry, astronomy, and other disciplines that do not deal with human conduct. By contrast, when we come to disciplines which deal with

---

24. Ibid., pp. 62–3.
25. Williams, "Metaphysical Arguments," pp. 39–41.
26. According to Strawson, it is by description. *Individuals*, p. 9; "Analysis Science, and Metaphysics," pp. 318–20; *Analysis and Metaphysics*, p. 57. According to Henrich, it is revisionary, that is, what I call "prescriptive." *Konzepte*, p. 122.

human conduct, matters are different. Ethics and politics, for example, do not aim merely to describe how human beings behave—that is done in psychology and sociology—but to prescribe the ways they should behave.

Upon closer scrutiny, however, the picture we have painted appears simplistic. Consider physics again. It is true that physics aims to describe the way the physical world works, but in doing so it indirectly establishes certain parameters of conduct. In applying physics, engineering prescribes certain standards. It tells us that if we want to build a bridge that does not collapse under a certain stress, we need to use such and such materials and put them together in such and such a way. One could argue, of course, that engineering, or the application of physics, is not really physics and therefore that physics is not prescriptive at all, but rather purely descriptive.

I believe this argument is sound in the case of physics, although it is not so in the case of some other sciences. Medicine and psychology, for example, aim not only to describe the way the human body and mind work, but also to prescribe ways of correcting what is considered aberrant behavior or functions. Moreover, there is one way in which even physics may be considered to be prescriptive without violating the fact that it seeks to describe the physical world and not to change it. Physics is prescriptive insofar as it seeks to change, for the sake of correction, the way we think about the world. Physics tells us that the world is composed of atoms, for example, even though we do not see them and they are not part of our ordinary way of conceiving the world. By describing to us that the world is composed of atoms, it also prescribes the way we should think about the world, namely, in terms of atoms. And what has been said about physics can be applied in every discipline. It is certainly so in astronomy, as Galileo's case illustrates. Most science, indeed, has to do with changing the way we think, by showing that what we think does not stand up to scrutiny in terms of empirical evidence or rational coherence. Discoveries are more accurate descriptions of the way the world is, but they are intended by those who make them to replace less accurate descriptions and, in this sense, to prescribe the way we should think.

I am not arguing that all descriptive propositions contain a prescriptive dimension. Although this is possible in principle, I am unpersuaded and, in any case, not prepared to defend that position here. The position I wish to defend argues only that scientific, descriptive propositions have a prescriptive dimension. This dimension is not a by-product of their content. What they say does not imply prescription—I am not, therefore, deriving an ought from an is. The prescriptive dimension results from their character as scientific propositions which aim to present an accurate description of the world and to replace any inaccurate ones.[27] One way to express what I mean is in terms of speech-act theory, by saying that one of the illocutionary acts which scientific propositions share is the act of prescribing the way we should think about whatever is being described.

But does this apply to metaphysics as well? Is metaphysics descriptive, prescriptive, or both? If metaphysics is like physics, then clearly it is descriptive insofar as it describes its object, and it is prescriptive insofar as it prescribes the way we should think and speak about it. This assumes, however, two things: First, that metaphysics, in its descriptive mode, describes something other than the way we think or speak; second, that it is possible for metaphysics to describe the object it studies. But both of these assumptions have been challenged in the history of Western philosophy. Kant, for example, challenged the second by arguing that metaphysics is naturally intended to ask certain questions to which it cannot give answers.[28] And Strawson challenged the first by arguing that metaphysics describes the way we think about the world rather than the world itself. Indeed, at the time he first presented this view, Strawson considered it a mistake to attempt to revise the way we think about the world. This attempt he called "revisionary metaphysics."[29]

It should be pointed out that the conclusion that metaphysics should exclude revision of the way we think does not follow from the view that metaphysics cannot answer questions about the object it studies. Such revision could be accomplished on the basis of criteria of rational coherence, for example, independently of any access to its object. Subject *S* may be told by the metaphysician that she cannot

---

27. Strawson's descriptive metaphysics, then, is prescriptive even if it describes the ways we think or can think, because it is presented as the proper way of describing the ways we think or can think. *Individuals*, p. 9.

28. Kant, *Critique of Pure Reason*, p. 7.

29. Strawson, *Individuals*, p. 9. Collingwood also must be understood as holding that metaphysics is descriptive insofar as, according to him, it is the historical study of the presuppositions of science (a science is "a body of systematic or orderly thinking about a determinate matter," p. 4) at any given period. *An Essay on Metaphysics* pp. 33, 47, 49, 54, 55. See also Whitehead, *Process and Reality*, pp. 4, 7–8, 19.

hold both that P and $\sim P$, even if he cannot tell her whether she should hold that P or $\sim P$ because he knows that P or $\sim P$.

Conversely, it does not follow from the view that the business of metaphysics is to describe how we think, that metaphysics cannot also describe an object which is not our thought. One can follow Strawson without following Kant, even though most who adopt Strawson's viewpoint also adopt Kant's. It would be unreasonable to insist that metaphysics only describes what we think, when it can also describe the objects about which we think and therefore correct, if need be, the way we think about those objects. So, only by rejecting both assumptions mentioned earlier, is it reasonable to hold that metaphysics describes what we think and excludes the description of objects independent of our thoughts.

Even under these conditions, is this a reasonable expectation? I argue that it is not for two reasons.[30] In the first place, what we think is not at all clear, evident, and uncontroversial. Descriptivist metaphysicians disagree not only with prescriptivist metaphysicians, but also with other descriptivists; they engage in discussion and argument with the aim of changing their minds. But in doing so they implicitly grant that their own procedure is not purely descriptive. Rather, it implies different viewpoints or ways of thinking about our thought, some of which are incorrect and need to be changed. Hence, descriptive metaphysics turns out to be prescriptive and thus revisionary, even if the revisions in question are not based on knowledge of the world outside our thoughts.[31] Indeed, Strawson's description of metaphysics is itself revisionary to the extent it aims to correct the incorrect ways in which many metaphysicians think about metaphysics.

A second reason against the view that metaphysics is purely descriptive of the way we think is that this view misses the point that thought, and the language used to express it, are also part of the world. Therefore, if we were to take seriously the above objection concerning the indescribability or unknowability of chairs and colors, or, to put it more precisely, of chairs-in-themselves and colors-in-themselves, independently of experience or language, we would have to conclude that the difficulty applies also to our thoughts, experiences, and language. There is really no fundamental difference, insofar as they are considered objects of knowledge, between a chair-in-itself

---

30. For other reasons, see Hamlyn, *Metaphysics*, pp. 4–5.
31. Grice, Pears, and Strawson, "Metaphysics," p. 21; Quinton, in "Final Discussion," pp. 146, and 147.

and a thought-in-itself, or between a color-in-itself and a linguistic-expression-in-itself.

Those who disagree with this assessment will no doubt argue that there is a difference between things-in-themselves and phenomena, insofar as we have privileged access to phenomena. One's thought has a special status with respect to oneself, quite different from the status of a chair, for example. But, again, this objection misses the point. In order to consider phenomena, it is necessary to objectify them, as we do with things-in-themselves. Phenomena, therefore, acquire at least some, if not all, of the more fundamental characteristics of things-in-themselves. As objects of thought, they cease to have the privileged status required to differentiate them from so-called things-in-themselves.

In short, then, metaphysics is both descriptive and prescriptive. It is descriptive of the object it studies, whatever that object may be, and it is prescriptive insofar as that description seeks to correct our views about that object. From this it follows that we cannot expect to distinguish metaphysics from other disciplines merely based on the fact that its method is different from theirs. There is in metaphysics, as in physics and other disciplines, a descriptive as well as a prescriptive methodological component, even if, unlike such disciplines as psychology and ethics, its prescriptive element concerns only thought and not external action.

F. Analytic / Elucidative / Synthetic

At least since Plato, philosophers have explicitly considered the analytic method. In the *Theaetetus*, Plato criticizes it sharply, but that has not deterred subsequent philosophers from finding it useful.[32] Indeed, several important philosophers of the early twentieth century contended that analysis was the proper method of philoso-

---

32. Plato, *Theaetetus* 202ff., pp. 908ff.
33. Moore, Russell, Collingwood, and Ryle, among many others, advocated the method of analysis, although what they meant by analysis differs in important ways. Cf. Moore, "A Reply to My Critics," p. 663; Russell, *Logic and Knowledge*, p. 192; Collingwood, *An Essay on Metaphysics*, pp. 22, 24, 38–45; Ryle, "Systematically Misleading Expressions," p. 36. Antecedents of the analytic method can be found, for example, in Aquinas (*Commentary on the "De Trinitate" of Boethius* 6, 1, pp. 62–4), and Kant (*Prolegomena*, § 5, p. 23, n. 4.).

phy[33] and some went so far as to say that metaphysics is nothing more than a method of logical analysis.[34] Although different philosophers differ as to the nature of the analytic method, the object to which it applies, and the significance of the conclusions which one may reach through it, there are some elements common to the method that seem to run through most of the philosophies of those who claim to use it.

The basic idea is, perhaps, that analysis involves replacing something, the *analysandum*, with something else, the *analysans*, and that the *analysans* is composed of elements which are simpler than the *analysandum*. Moreover, it is also important to realize that the *analysans* and *analysandum* are equivalent, so that there is no significant property of the *analysandum* which the *analysans* does not have, and vice versa. This equivalence is ontological, however, for epistemically it is easier to understand the *analysans* than the *analysandum*.[35]

Those who view analysis as the proper method of metaphysics argue that the aim of this method in metaphysics is to get to the most fundamental elements of reality, being, concepts, experience, or language (depending on the author in question), and they conceive these elements as themselves not subject to further analysis. The task of metaphysics, then, is that of breaking down complexes into ultimate constituents.[36] If the analysis is of language, then it concerns terms such as 'bachelor' and their relation to other terms, such as 'human' and 'man.' If the analysis is of concepts, then it involves the break down of concepts such as bachelor into other concepts, such as human and man. If the analysis is of realities or beings, such as physical objects, then it involves their basic components, say atoms. If the analysis is of empirical experience, such as the perception red square, then it has to do with the perceptual elements that make up the experience, such as the perception of red, and so on.

Described in this way, the method of analysis could very well serve to distinguish metaphysics from disciplines other than philosophy, but it does not look as if analysis could distinguish metaphysics within philosophy from other branches of philosophy. Indeed, many of those who favor the method of analysis do not restrict the method to metaphysics but extend it to all philosophy and

---

34. Carnap, "The Elimination of Metaphysics," p. 77.
35. Moore, "A Reply to My Critics," p. 663.
36. For a linguistic approach, see Moore in "A Reply to My Critics." Russell proposed a more metaphysical approach in *Logic and Knowledge*.

some even to all disciplines.[37] This, then, is the first objection against using this method as a distinguishing mark of metaphysics.

The second objection has to do with various criticisms which have been leveled against the method itself, questioning its viability and effectiveness. Among these one stands out. Of what benefit is a method which is supposed to produce enlightenment through analysis and yet sees as its end the point where further analysis is impossible? If there is no further analysis, enlightenment would appear impossible. This is, in fact, one of the criticisms which Plato brings against it in the *Theaetetus*.[38] He argues: If knowledge consists in justified true belief and the justification consists in analysis, then justification is never possible and neither is knowledge, because the elements with which an analysis ends are not themselves subject to analysis.

Another criticism of the method of analysis is that it involves circularity. In this view, all analysis leads eventually to circularity, for the *analysans* of the most general categories includes reference to those very categories.[39] A well-known example used in these contexts is being, for all analyses eventually lead to being, and any analysis of being will always include being in it. As the most general category, so the argument goes, there is no further category or categories to which being could be reduced.[40]

These objections have led some philosophers to argue that analysis cannot be a proper method for metaphysics and they replace it with what has come to be called "elucidation."[41] Elucidation, in contrast with analysis, does not seek to reduce categories into other categories but rather to relate them. This method grants that the system of categories in terms of which we think about reality is circular, but it circumvents the paradox which defeats analysis by redefining enlightenment in terms of connection rather than reduction. The task of the metaphysician is to reveal the varied and com-

---

37. Collingwood, *An Essay on Metaphysics*, pp. 22–3. Some philosophers in fact exchange the terms 'philosophy' and 'metaphysics.' Cf. Popper, "Metaphysics and Criticizability."
38. Plato, *Theaetetus* 209, p. 918.
39. Strawson, *Analysis and Metaphysics*, p. 18. Of course, one can also argue that analysis also involves falsification, but this is not so easily defended for all cases. Cf. Strawson, "Analysis, Science, and Metaphysics," p. 313.
40. Aristotle, *Metaphysics* 998b22, p. 723.
41. Strawson, *Analysis and Metaphysics*, p. 18.

plex connections among categories in the system of categories we use to think, not to reduce them to a set of irreducible categories.

For the reasons given, it makes sense to argue not only that analysis cannot be, by itself, the sole method of metaphysics, but also that elucidation is another method of metaphysics. Moreover, there is empirical evidence to justify these claims insofar as an examination of the method used by most metaphysicians reveals that they do much more than analyze. Here it is important to note that, although metaphysicians engage in methodological procedures which do not involve analysis, they also engage in analysis. Indeed, analysis reveals one of the many relations among the categories through which we think: the relation of more complex categories to more simple ones in terms of which they can be taken or to which the first ones can be reduced.

Part of what the metaphysician might want to do is to show, for example, that the category substance is reducible to other categories. Therefore, it is a mistake to believe that analysis and elucidation are completely different methods, perhaps even contrary ones. Analysis may be one of the things one does when one is engaged in elucidation. But there are others as well. Elucidation may be seen as a search for the connections among categories, yet such a search can include putting categories together either by drawing similarities among them or by consolidating them into more encompassing ones. In this sense, elucidation involves synthesis, which is just the reverse of analysis.

The question we must ask now is whether elucidation, with all the sub-methodologies it may entail, is a sufficiently discriminating method to set metaphysics apart from other disciplines. The answer seems to be negative, for the method of most disciplines involves precisely establishing connections among various categories. True, in some sciences these connections are, primarily or even exclusively, causal connections. For example, physics might be primarily interested in establishing causal connections between, say, mass, force, and velocity. And chemistry might be primarily interested in establishing causal connections between heat and combustion. But that does not deny the fact that causal connections are relations of a sort and, therefore, fall within the province of elucidation.

Those who see elucidation as the proper method of metaphysics, and wish to distinguish metaphysics from other disciplines precisely on the basis of this method, might argue that sciences do not in fact use elucidation insofar as they are concerned with things and their features, rather than concepts. Physics studies the relations between

mass, force, and velocity, whereas metaphysics studies the relations
between the concepts of mass, force, and velocity. But this distinction
does not help, for then it is not the method that distinguishes metaphysics from other disciplines, but the object to which the method applies. To smuggle that object into the picture by requiring that
elucidation be concerned with concepts alone, or for that matter with
language, does not change the fact that it is the object that would determine both the method and the difference between metaphysics
and other disciplines.

In short, neither the method of analysis, nor the method of elucidation, seems to be effective in distinguishing metaphysics from
other disciplines, even though metaphysics appears to use both.
Moreover, it is clear that metaphysics uses synthesis as well, when
it puts categories together, and thus it is similar to other disciplines
of learning which do so as well.

G. Experimental / Observational

One of the most common ways in which modern science is distinguished from other disciplines is through the method of experimentation. Indeed, this method is used not only to distinguish
modern science from nonempirical disciplines, but even to distinguish it from empirical disciplines which use observation but do not
conduct controlled experiments. Thus, modern science is contrasted
with Aristotelian science and some social sciences, as well as with
nonempirical sciences like mathematics and disciplines like philosophy. Hence, if it turned out that metaphysics were nonexperimental in method, this would be a way of distinguishing it from those
disciplines that are experimental.

Of course, even under those conditions, a nonexperimental
method would not be sufficient to set metaphysics apart from all
other disciplines, for there are some other disciplines that are not experimental. For the purposes of identifying the specific difference of
metaphysics, its nonexperimental character will not do. All the
same, if we could establish that metaphysics is nonexperimental in
method, we would have a further grasp on its nature.

Is metaphysics nonexperimental? The answer to this question is
not as simple as it first appears. It is clear, from what we have seen
thus far, that metaphysics involves empirical observation to some
extent, but does it go beyond observation to engage in experimentation? Well, yes and no. Metaphysics does not manipulate situations

so as to test theories on the basis of outcome. Unlike physicists and chemists, metaphysicians do not set up laboratories where experiments are designed and carried out. To this extent, it is obvious that metaphysics is nonexperimental and, therefore, differs from sciences like physics and chemistry. But there is another sense in which metaphysics does design experiments to test hypotheses. These are the so-called mental experiments. They are imaginary cases whose object is generally to illustrate the feasibility of a theory by looking at its implications. Most of these mental experiments are intended to illustrate the consistency of a theory or to establish its inconsistency. Unlike scientific experiments, then, they have nothing to do with the physical world or factual feasibility; rather, they concern logical possibility. They involve imaginary situations in which the concepts under scrutiny are seen to function in ways which may confirm or undermine a certain view.

If experimentation is restricted to the realm of the physical and factual, then metaphysics is clearly not experimental. But, if a more general notion of experimentation is used, which applies to the realm of the mental and logical, then metaphysics may be considered to use experiments. In neither case, however, can we find a distinguishing feature of the discipline in this methodological peculiarity, for there are other disciplines which share the same methodological characteristics.

H. Common Sense / Uncommon Sense

The view that the philosophical method in general and the method of metaphysics in particular should be based on common sense has a long tradition. Some Aristotelians claim, indeed, that this is precisely what characterizes the method used by Aristotle.[42] And there is the tradition of Scottish realists which found its most distinguished exponent in the non-Scottish G. E. Moore.[43] The nature of this method, however, is not always clear. There are at least three positions with respect to the use of common sense in philosophy or metaphysics. One holds that all philosophy should begin with the examination of the commonsensical view of the world. Considered thus, common sense is the origin of philosophy, for all philosophy begins

---

42. Veatch, *Aristotle*, p. 12.
43. Moore, "A Defense of Common Sense."

with the examination of our ordinary beliefs about the world. Another view holds that common sense is a strong criterion of philosophical truth in such a way that all philosophical propositions must be found in the ordinary commonsensical view of the world. Consequently, if a philosophical proposition is not found among the propositions that compose such a view, the proposition is to be regarded as either nonsensical or false. Finally, there is a view that holds that common sense is a weak criterion of philosophical truth in such a way that: (1) if a philosophical proposition is part of the commonsensical view of the world it is true;[44] (2) if a philosophical proposition contradicts any proposition which is part of the commonsensical view of the world, it is false;[45] and (3) if a philosophical proposition is not part of the commonsensical view of the world, but does not contradict common sense, it may be true.[46]

Philosophers have not been shy about criticizing common sense. Apart from the difficulties involved in coming up with a precise definition of common sense, there are at least three objections one can bring out against the view that metaphysics can be distinguished from other disciplines because it uses the method of common sense. The first objects that the conclusions of metaphysics are apodictic and therefore could not be based on opinion.[47] This is a powerful objection but it rests on the assumption that metaphysics is indeed apodictic, and that seems unwarranted. The conclusions of metaphysics, just as the conclusions of most other human inquiries, are contingent on the vicissitudes of human knowledge. This objection, therefore, does not carry much weight.

The second objection is more serious because it takes much less for granted. It argues that common sense does not consist in a complete methodology. It is rather a regulative principle which accompanies all sorts of other methodological principles. Hence, common sense by itself does not exhaust the method of metaphysics and therefore it cannot be said that, *qua* method, it distinguishes the discipline from other disciplines.

---

44. This is as far as Aristotle seems to have gone. See the philosophical lexicon in *Metaphysics* 1013aff., pp. 752ff., where he often considers the way we speak in his clarification of various notions.
45. This seems to be Veatch's position. *Aristotle*, p. 12.
46. Moore seems to hold all three parts of this view. "In Defense of Common Sense," pp. 44–5; see also *Some Main Problems of Philosophy*, pp. 2, 16, 18.
47. Kant, *Prolegomena*, § 5, p. 24, and "Solution," p. 118.

If someone retorts that common sense could still be considered as the distinguishing principle of metaphysical methodology and, therefore, serve to separate the discipline from other disciplines, one can provide a last objection. This is that the method of common sense is regulative and should be part of any method. For we should change the way we commonly think about the world only when we have compelling reasons to do so, and this is precisely what common sense prescribes. If this is the case, then common sense cannot be idiosyncratic to metaphysics.[48]

Now, just as some metaphysicians have thought the proper method of metaphysics essentially involves common sense, there have been some who either explicitly or implicitly favor a method which can only be described as uncommon sense. This method involves the use of language in disturbing and shocking ways to force us to see similarities and differences which in everyday experience escape us.[49] A metaphysical proposition, then, is a kind of illuminating falsehood, a paradox which serves to point our attention to something we had previously missed. In this sense, the task of metaphysics is precisely to go against what is dictated by common sense; it is to undermine what is commonly accepted as well as the common ways in which we speak and think.

There is some truth to this view insofar as, indeed, some of the greatest metaphysicians have gone against or at least questioned, established beliefs and have put forth views which at the time were often considered different, odd, and even radical, and only later became accepted, if indeed they ever did. But do metaphysical views have to be false? Are not the hidden differences and similarities discovered through metaphysics true, at least some times? And does not this fact explain why these apparently shocking views become accepted precisely because they are better than what was had before? And what if, after all, part of our common-sense view of the world is true?

Even if we were to modify this position and propose that metaphysical statements do not have to be false and do not always have to contradict common sense, still, the method of uncommon sense seems too narrow to accommodate what most metaphysicians do. It is true that part of the job of metaphysicians is to challenge the

---

48. For a different attack on common sense, see Habermas, *Postmetaphysical Thinking*, pp. 38–9.
49. Wisdom, "Philosophical Perplexity," pp. 104, 109–10.

conceptual status quo, but that is not all they do and certainly not something that distinguishes their method from that of other disciplines. Metaphysicians challenge the conceptual status quo, but they also take from it those elements which seem to them to be true. Moreover, if the goal of this position is to emphasize the need for a critical spirit in metaphysics, then the same should be said of other disciplines. It is not just metaphysics that needs to be critical; all intellectual disciplines must be constantly on their guard against intellectual complacency and ideological dogmatism. The search for knowledge must always be critical, whether in metaphysics or in chemistry. For those reasons, the use of what I have called the "method of uncommon sense" cannot be distinctive of metaphysics.

I. Historical / Nonhistorical

Most metaphysicians have considered metaphysics a nonhistorical discipline. Indeed, Aristotle thought of metaphysics as the first among sciences and in a sense paradigmatic for them, whereas he conferred a somewhat dubious scientific status to history.[50] The reason is that, for him, science is always of the universal, and history deals with individuals. Of course, if metaphysics is nonhistorical, and most sciences are nonhistorical, then the nonhistoricity of metaphysics cannot play a role in distinguishing it from other disciplines. I know of no one who has tried to find the uniqueness of metaphysics in such a widely shared feature.

With the arrival of historicism, however, some metaphysicians have argued that metaphysics is indeed a historical discipline. Metaphysical statements aim to describe the past and metaphysics is nothing other than the history of metaphysics.[51] Metaphysicians carry out their task *qua* metaphysicians by telling us what other previous metaphysicians thought or said and by bringing to light the presuppositions that led them to the conclusions they reached. So metaphysics is the history of metaphysics and its method, like any other historical method, involves the recovery of the past. This entails examining historical sources—texts mostly—and rethinking what past metaphysicians thought. We must relive the problems past metaphysicians discussed and we must put ourselves in their

50. Aristotle, *Poetics* 1451b1–7, pp. 1463–64.
51. Collingwood, *An Essay on Metaphysics*, p. 58.

shoes as it were. Metaphysics is history, but it is a peculiar kind of history, for it is the history of metaphysical thought and metaphysical thought has to do with the formulations and presuppositions of everything we say or think.

Supporters of this conception of metaphysics and its method see value in it because of its empirical basis. Metaphysics, just like the empirical sciences, works with sources to which we have access in experience, even if the conclusions it reaches go well beyond experience. Moreover, uncovering the presuppositions at work in our predecessors helps us uncover the presuppositions at work for us and thus allows us to free ourselves from the shackles of tradition and culture.[52]

Even the cursory description of this view reveals that it is inadequate to sustain the uniqueness of metaphysics. In the first place, it is clear that metaphysics cannot be distinguished from other histories except by reference to its object—what other metaphysicians thought of the fundamental presuppositions that underlie the thought of a particular philosopher or metaphysician. And this makes this view either dependent on the nature of the object in question, circular, or both.

In addition, as we saw in the discussion of presuppositions/first principles in the last chapter, there are serious problems with the claim that metaphysics is a historical enterprise. For these reasons, then, we must conclude that this position fails to establish the distinct character of metaphysics in terms of method.

J. Phenomenological

The phenomenological method was not developed as a metaphysical method; nevertheless, it was motivated precisely by considerations similar to those which had prompted metaphysicians to develop different methodologies. As proposed by its founder, Husserl, its goal was to put philosophy back on a scientific course.[53] Its core is constituted by what is called "phenomenological reduction." This involves two steps. The first is the systematic and radical bracketing (*epoché*) of our basic assumptions about the status of what is given in consciousness.[54] If we are conscious of a tree, we are supposed to bracket our inclination to think of the tree as a physical, extramen-

---

52. Taylor, "Philosophy and Its History," p. 21.
53. Husserl, "Phenomenology," p. 118.
54. Ibid., pp. 121–2, 125.

tal object, for example. Likewise, we must resist the inclination to conceive it as a mental phenomenon of some kind. We should simply take what is given to us in consciousness as it is given, without adding to it ontological or "objectifying" commitments of any kind. In the *epoché*, an experience remains as it is; for example, an experience of this house remains isolated from any objectifying judgment which can be made about it.

The second step of the method is the description of the given. This is supposed to be an ontologically neutral description in which the given is presented precisely as given. Instead of supplying what is not given, the status of the given as object, for example, we are supposed to describe what we are conscious of as we are conscious of it. This description extends both to what is experienced (the noematic) and the experiencing (the noetic) of it.

The aim of the phenomenological method is the a priori development of formulas which express the essences or possible forms of what we are given in consciousness and the invariable structure of consciousness itself. Thus, the essence of tree, apart from all assumptions built around it, is established on the firm ground supplied by experience.

Obviously, this is certainly a method metaphysics could and perhaps should use.[55] Moreover, it is not out of the question that this method could distinguish the discipline from other disciplines. Yet, there are difficulties with these claims. In the first place, it looks as if at least some of the peculiarity of the method derives not from the method itself, but from the object to which the method is applied. After all, the unbiased examination of data is supposed to be something common to all scientific pursuits. It is only because this unbiased examination is applied to consciousness that the philosophy of consciousness, which is nothing but a new version of metaphysics, can be distinguished from other disciplines.

There are, moreover, questions concerning the viability of the method itself. For example, how are we assured that the essences we reach through the method are in fact essences of what we experience rather than essences of what appears to us? Is a tree what is given to us in consciousness or something else? Have we really escaped the realm of the mental? Naturally, much has been said about these matters and I cannot even present, let alone discuss adequately, the

---

55. Among those who argue for its use is Seifert, *Essere e persona*, pp. 406–7.

many difficulties which have been raised concerning this view in the limited space I have. For us, it suffices to see that there are difficulties with the phenomenological method and, even apart from the difficulties, it is not clear this can be used to set metaphysics apart from other disciplines. Indeed, even if its combination of both empirical and a priori aspects were sufficient to distinguish it from purely empirical sciences and purely a priori sciences, it is not clear how it could be distinguished from other branches of philosophy.

K. Dialectical

There are at least two ways of understanding the view which holds that the method of metaphysics is dialectical. In one way it means that metaphysics uses dialogue: Metaphysicians must engage in dialogue either with each other or at least with the ideas proposed by others when they practice the discipline. In this sense, metaphysics must follow the Socratic method; it is not a discipline that can be pursued independently of others and their viewpoints.[56] In another way, to say that the method of metaphysics is dialectical is to claim that it follows certain laws of thought, certain patterns that lead inexorably to certain ends.[57]

Both of these positions are controversial. The first runs into trouble with the very notion of dialogue, for it is not clear what it involves. Is the claim that metaphysicians can only do metaphysics when engaged in oral or written dialogue with other metaphysicians? This rules out most metaphysical treatises, including Aristotle's. Or is the notion of dialogue used broadly so that the requirement is satisfied merely by the consideration of the views of others? This, again, is unsatisfactory as I have pointed out elsewhere, for dialogue requires the possibility of the parties involved in the dialogue changing their positions.[58] Besides, why can metaphysicians not consider views which occur to them and which have never been held or even will be held by anyone? Clearly, the notion of dialogue is not only unclear but it is in one sense too narrow to describe the method used by metaphysicians. But not only that, in another sense it is too broad, for dialogue is used

---

56. Veatch, in *Swimming against the Current*, pp. 1–12, argues that dialogue is a necessary condition of all philosophical investigation.
57. Hegel, *The Science of Logic*, pp. 147 ff.
58. Gracia, *Philosophy and Its History*, pp. 153–4.

in all sorts of other contexts besides metaphysics and, therefore, could never serve to distinguish the discipline from the other human enterprises that use dialogue. In particular, it does not help to distinguish metaphysics from other branches of philosophy, for it is philosophy in fact whose method is often described as involving or requiring dialogue.

The other way of understanding the dialectical nature of the metaphysical method is not more successful. According to it, the metaphysician must, and in fact does always, follow certain preestablished patterns. These patterns are what supporters of this position call "the dialectic" and consist in a logic of development and progress. How this logic of development and progress is analyzed varies from author to author, but the best known example is the one proposed by Hegel. According to him, philosophy, like everything else, moves in a threefold pattern beginning with a stage called "thesis," followed by a stage that negates it called "antithesis," and finally reaching an ultimate stage called "synthesis." The synthesis is both the end of a dialectical process and the beginning of another in which the synthesis of the old process functions as a thesis of the new.

Two problems with this view undermine it. The first is rather obvious: It relies on the assumption that metaphysics always develops according to a preestablished dialectical pattern, and that is far from settled. Indeed, the claim that metaphysics, like everything else, follows a dialectical pattern is highly speculative and relies on a particular metaphysical view. To use such a speculative claim to support some other claim is methodologically unsound, for one would have to accept an entire metaphysical interpretation of the world in order to accept this view about the nature of metaphysics.

More serious than this objection, however, is that the dialectical method, according to those who grasp it, applies not only to metaphysics, but to everything. Therefore, if the method used by metaphysics is to distinguish the discipline from other human enterprises, the difference must be found in something other than the dialectic. Indeed, if this method is a reflection of the way reality works, all disciplines concerned with reality must use it. Logic itself, considered as the art of reasoning, is the most evident exponent of the method. So, it makes no sense to argue metaphysics is unique because of its use. If there is anything unique about metaphysics, it would rather have to do with something else, perhaps the fact that metaphysics applies the method at a level of generality, or to a degree of extension, that is not found in any other discipline. But this is a different view of the matter.

CHAPTER FIVE

Aim

Apart from the object and the method, one may look for the source of what is peculiar to metaphysics in its aim.[1] The examination of possible objects and methods of metaphysics and the failure to find in them, considered separately or in combination, the *differentia* of the discipline, has prepared the way and revealed the need for a discussion of its aim. What is the aim of metaphysics, then, and can we distinguish metaphysics from other disciplines based on the aim it pursues?

Metaphysicians have not been shy about identifying the aim of metaphysics. So many aims have been identified in the history of philosophy that their adequate discussion would fill one thick volume, and perhaps more than one. I discuss briefly only some of these which I consider particularly important. I gather them into five groups: theoretical, practical, ideological, aesthetic, and critical.

A. Theoretical

Perhaps the first explicitly stated aim of metaphysics was the theoretical.[2] We find it in Aristotle, when he identifies that aim as knowledge. Knowledge is conceived as an accurate representation

---

1. This is one possible reading of Plato's statement in *Republic* 346, p. 595, that arts differ by the benefit that is peculiar to themselves.
2. Aristotle, *Metaphysics* 981b, 982b28, pp. 690, 692, and *Nicomachean Ethics* 1141b1–25, pp. 1028–29.

of the thing known in the knower, whence the expression 'speculative science,' from *speculum*, mirror. Since Aristotle, this view has been expressed in many different ways. Some speak of understanding or clarifying concepts, others of discovering truth, and still others of identifying the assumptions and presuppositions on which knowledge rests, but in all cases the aim amounts to some kind of knowledge.[3]

This theoretical aim has been frequently contrasted with the practical aims of other disciplines, such as engineering and medicine, where there is some result of the knowledge sought. In this sense, it is not difficult to distinguish metaphysics from those disciplines whose aim is to accomplish something other than mere knowledge.[4] These disciplines are regarded as instrumental. The theoretical aim is also frequently contrasted with that of disciplines intended to guide action, such as ethics, economics, or politics.[5]

Finally, the theoretical aim is also contrasted with the aims of some instrumental disciplines, like logic, whose primary function seems to be to facilitate the aims of other disciplines. For what is generally called "logic" today, that is, the study of reasoning, is supposed to serve as an instrument of the philosopher and particularly of the metaphysician.[6]

Yet, disciplines other than metaphysics are not all either practical or instrumental, a fact which rules out distinguishing them from metaphysics on the basis of their aim. Indeed, some of those who identify the aim of metaphysics as theoretical recognize this fact.[7] Thus, the view that metaphysics is to be distinguished from other disciplines in that it is theoretical is unpersuasive.

---

3. Avicenna, *Metaphysica* 1, p. 11; Aquinas, *Commentary on the "De Trinitate" of Boethius* 5, 1, pp. 6, 13; Randall, *Nature and Historical Experience*, p. 136; Collingwood, *An Essay on Metaphysics*, pp. 22–3; Broad, "Critical and Speculative Philosophy," pp. 88, 90.

4. Aristotle, *Metaphysics* 981b, p. 690, and *Nicomachean Ethics* 1141a20–1141b10, p. 1028.

5. Aristotle, *Nicomachean Ethics* 1040a25–1040b7, p. 1026; Aquinas, *Commentary on the "De Trinitate" of Boethius* 5, 1, pp. 6–7.

6. Boethius, *In "Isagogen" Porphyrii commenta*, 2nd ed., p. 142.

7. Aristotle, *Metaphysics* 1026a17, p. 779; Boethius, *On the Trinity* II, p. 8. This is one of the reasons why some reject that metaphysics is theoretical in any way. Metaphysics, they believe, is not at all like science. Adorno, *Against Epistemology*, pp. 41–2.

B. Practical

A discipline of learning has a practical aim if its aim is not knowledge for its own sake, but knowledge for the sake of accomplishing something else which is wanted or needed.[8] Practical disciplines are further distinguished into instrumental and practical properly speaking, depending on whether their aim is to serve as a tool of some other discipline (e.g., logic),[9] or to guide human action (e.g., ethics).[10] Note that, as in those disciplines which have a theoretical aim, practical disciplines, whether instrumental or properly practical, are concerned with the acquisition of knowledge. The difference between the two is that, for practical disciplines, such knowledge has to be put to use.

Some philosophers hold, however, that there are no purely theoretical disciplines because there is no knowledge for its own sake; all knowledge is for the sake of some other aim which responds to particular wants or needs. The aims in question vary, but at least four should be mentioned in connection with metaphysics. Those who follow Wittgenstein see the aim of all philosophy as the promotion of what might be called "conceptual health."[11] Metaphysical problems are the result of linguistic muddles, that is, the ineffective use of language. It is the function of philosophers to clear up these muddles and restore us to a state of health, where we use language in such a way that metaphysical muddles do not arise.[12]

A second group of philosophers under this category see metaphysics as an instrument of action. For pragmatists, knowledge is simply the means to action, sometimes necessary for it and at other times not, but always related to action. The aim of metaphysics, as of all other disciplines, is to facilitate action; what matters are results.[13]

A third group takes its cue from Heidegger. They see the aim of metaphysics and philosophy as the restoration of human beings to a

---

8. Aristotle, *Metaphysics* 981b15–22, p. 690.
9. Boethius, *In "Isagogen" Porphyrii commenta*, 2nd ed., pp. 140–2; Meinong, "The Theory of Objects," p. 93.
10. Aristotle, *Nicomachean Ethics* 1140a25–30, 1141b22, pp. 1026, 1029. Boethius, *In "Isagogen" Porphyrii commenta*, 2nd ed., pp. 140–2.
11. Wittgenstein, *Philosophical Investigations*, § 255, p. 91.
12. Those who adopt views similar to this usually avoid talking about metaphysics altogether; they prefer to speak about "philosophy" instead. Cf. Ryle, "Systematically Misleading Expressions," p. 35.
13. Whitehead, *Process and Reality*, pp. 8, 17, 19.

state of what they call "being-there." In Heidegger's own words: "That [state] always includes our [i.e., man's] own future being-there in the totality of the history allotted to us—to the domain of being which it was originally incumbent on man to open up for himself."[14] This is, then, a historical task concerning the state of human beings.

Finally, there are those more recent philosophers who practice what they call "hermeneutics." According to them, the aim of any discourse, including metaphysical discourse, is to promote dialogue, which they understand as more discourse.[15] If one asks further what the aim of discourse is, they sometimes respond that it is edification.[16]

From what has been said, it follows that those who view the aim of metaphysics as therapeutic, those who view it as hermeneutical, and those who view it as a restoration to a former state can easily distinguish metaphysics from disciplines outside philosophy. Neither the sciences nor the arts see themselves in these terms. The difficulty comes in when an attempt is made to distinguish metaphysics within philosophy, for there does not seem to be any difference of aim between it and other branches of philosophy. For pragmatists the difficulty is more serious, for they see all knowledge as practical and, therefore, the difference between metaphysics and other disciplines must be found elsewhere.

C. Ideological

The aim of a discipline is ideological just when it is preestablished by considerations foreign to the discipline and its natural applications. The ideological aim should not be confused with the practical uses mentioned under the previous category. One can do metaphysics for the sake of conceptual health, the efficient functioning of society, or the development of dialogue, and not be ideological. The reason is that these aims may be concordant with the nature of the discipline. Metaphysics may be in fact a therapeutic, pragmatic, or hermeneutic discipline. The use of mathematics and physics by engineers is not ideological.

---

14. Heidegger, *An Introduction to Metaphysics*, p. 34.
15. Or, as Rorty puts it, a conversation. *Philosophy and the Mirror of Nature*, pp. 389, 394.
16. Ibid., p. 377. See also Habermas, *Postmetaphysical Thinking*, p. 35.

There are at least three ideological aims for metaphysics that should be mentioned: (1) the defense of a view which is not the result of the practice of the discipline; (2) the bringing about of change in an individual person or a group; and (3) the empowerment of an individual person or a group so that the individual person or the group in question can dominate other individual persons or groups. Many religious leaders see metaphysics as serving the aim of achieving salvation, but I am not referring here to the use of metaphysics in general for the understanding of a particular faith or its clarification. That is the sort of use to which medieval theologians put all philosophy. For them, philosophy, including metaphysics, became the servant of theology. What I have in mind is a more radical position in which metaphysics is used to defend any view. This, too, was present in the Middle Ages, for philosophy and metaphysics were used to argue for Christianity and against other religious faiths. Philosophy and metaphysics, then, were used in accordance with the perceived needs of the views in question. Note that there are similarities and differences between this use of metaphysics and the use the Greek Sophists made of philosophy. In the case of the latter, the use of philosophy was intended for personal advancement; in the former, the use of metaphysics was intended for the defense of what was believed to be the truth. The Sophists did not believe in any truth, whereas those who used metaphysics for apologetic aims in the Middle Ages did, and this is an important difference. But there are similarities, for neither the Sophists nor the medieval apologists were concerned with the aims of philosophy or metaphysics considered apart from the non-metaphysical aims they intended to pursue.

Many of the social philosophies which arose in the nineteenth century also made and continue to make an ideological use of metaphysics and philosophy in general, for their aim is to achieve certain goals in society irrespective of whatever goals the discipline may define for itself. The use Marxism makes of ideas to bring about social change is a paradigmatic example of ideological use. The goal is predetermined: the establishment of communism. Metaphysics and philosophy, then, become tools, instruments to be used only insofar as they help to achieve the goal.

Ideological use has also had as a goal empowerment and domination. This is the kind of use of philosophy which Plato attributed to the Sophists—in their case it was a matter of individual empowerment and domination by knowing how to manipulate and influence people through the rhetorical use of philosophical arguments. But there are also examples of ideological uses which target groups or governments as seats of power. The ideological use of positivism in Mexico during the dictatorship of Porfirio Díaz, for example, is a clear example of this phenomenon. Porfirio Díaz and a group of intellectuals of the period used positivist ideas to maintain order in society so that they could retain control of the state.[17] A more blatant use of philosophy for political purposes has seldom occurred in human history.

Even a cursory glance will reveal that an ideological aim is not sufficient to distinguish metaphysics from other disciplines, whether within or without philosophy. Ideological use can be extended to any discipline and there is nothing peculiar about metaphysics that makes ideology idiosyncratic to it. True, philosophy in general lends itself to ideological use. This has been well known from the time of the Sophists. Plato, for example, complained bitterly about what he considered to be the misuse of philosophy and philosophical techniques for personal advancement.[18] This is probably the reason why some philosophers have viewed philosophy as necessarily ideological. But ideological use is not peculiar to metaphysics. Law, for example, is frequently used ideologically.

Apart from the fact that ideological use cannot serve to distinguish metaphysics from other disciplines, there are also objections to the ideological use of metaphysics in itself. Most of these are well recorded in the history of philosophy. Perhaps most significant is the fundamental incompatibility between the aim involved in the acquisition of knowledge and ideological aims. Such aims seem to be contrary to each other. Consider, for example, the aim of personal advancement. It is quite possible, indeed it is to be expected, that the pursuit of personal advancement will entail behavior which goes contrary to what is expected of a metaphysician. It is expected, for instance, that the metaphysician will make rigorous use of logical techniques and will not regard as proven something for which she has no proof. Yet, it may be in one's best interest to use fallacious reasoning to convince those who lack knowledge of logical techniques. There is, then, a potential for conflict in the behavior required by ideological and nonideological goals which undermines the view of metaphysics as an ideological discipline.[19]

---

17. Zea, *Positivism in Mexico*, p. 221.
18. Plato, *Apology* 36c, p. 17.
19. Perhaps it is Strawson's concern about ideology, after all, that provides a motivation for his descriptive metaphysics. *Analysis and Metaphysics*, p. 16

D. Aesthetic

Metaphysics may also be conceived as having what might be called an "aesthetic aim."[20] In this sense, metaphysics would seek to create an aesthetic object, to provide some kind of aesthetic experience, or both. Some philosophers have spoken of metaphysics or metaphysical systems as having much in common with poetry and art. Metaphysics, according to them, shares the same goals as these, and these goals are achieved both through an activity and the product of that activity. The aim of both the contemplation and production of metaphysical systems is to produce an aesthetic experience.[21]

Understood thus, it is clear that metaphysics could be distinguished from some other disciplines on the basis of its aim, although some of those who argue in favor of an aesthetic goal for metaphysics often argue also for an aesthetic goal for most other disciplines which do not have an immediate practical aim. We often hear, for example, of the aesthetic dimensions and goals of certain sciences such as mathematics. But, even if one were to restrict the aesthetic goal to only a few disciplines, still that would make it impossible to use an aesthetic goal as the distinguishing mark of metaphysics.

The view that metaphysics' primary or fundamental goal is aesthetic may very well be misguided. The best support for this objection is to be found in the very claims that metaphysicians make. Metaphysicians make truth-value claims and often state explicit goals, for what they do as metaphysicians, which have nothing to do with creativity or aesthetic experience. One could argue, of course, that (1) they do not really know what they are doing, or (2) in addition to what they think they are doing they are accomplishing something else. The first argument will not do unless there were very good reasons to suppose that most metaphysicians are simply mistaken. But on what basis could one argue that? If what metaphysicians do and say is to be taken as evidence for the understanding of metaphysics, just as what physicists do and say is to be taken as a

---

20. Sometimes this is put in terms of pleasure (Aristotle, *Nicomachean Ethics* 1177a23, p. 1104) and sometimes a comparison is drawn between metaphysics and poetry (Heidegger, *An Introduction to Metaphysics*, p. 21).
21. Vasconcelos, *Tratado de metafísica*, pp. 391 ff., 478. Some logical positivists point out that even this benign interpretation of metaphysics is mistaken. Ayer, *Language, Truth, and Logic*, p. 44.

basis for the understanding of physics, then we cannot just dismiss it. To do so would be to adopt a nonempirical method of procedure and that would open the doors to whimsical philosophy.

On the other hand, that metaphysicians may accomplish aesthetic results in addition to those they intend to accomplish does not support the view that the aesthetic results are the primary or fundamental goals of the discipline. If, anything, these aesthetic goals would have to be considered secondary or accidental and, as such, could not be associated with metaphysics in a fundamental way. And this brings us back to the point that an aesthetic aim cannot serve to distinguish metaphysics from other disciplines.

F. Critical

Some philosophers have argued that the aim of philosophy, and even of metaphysics, is primarily critical.[22] What is meant by this differs considerably from philosopher to philosopher. For some, the criticism refers to the assumptions and presuppositions on which the lived-world rests.[23] For others, the criticism is addressed to science, for science describes only a limited aspect of our experience and it is the task of metaphysics to maintain awareness of other aspects of it.[24] Still, others argue that it is the attempt to refute theories given in answer to problems.[25] But these various views share some common elements. Perhaps the most characteristic is that it is not the function of metaphysics to develop theories or build conceptual structures and models of reality. Rather, the function of metaphysics is to criticize, attack, and dismantle theories and conceptual structures others have erected in the past. Metaphysics aims to tear down rather than to build.

There are many reasons for this conception of the discipline, and different periods of the history of philosophy have favored different ones. For example, one of the most recent views along this line is

---

22. Kant, *Prolegomena*, "Solution," p. 111.
23. Habermas, *Postmetaphysical Thinking*, p. 50.
24. Broad, "Critical and Speculative Philosophy," pp. 98–9. See also Whitehead, *Process and Reality*, p. 15. Habermas argues against this way of understanding the critical nature of philosophy in *Postmetaphysical Thinking*, pp. 48–51.
25. Popper, "Metaphysics and Criticizability," pp. 214–17, although he finds this to be a common element between metaphysics and science.

that metaphysics, and indeed philosophy in general, must be critical because theories are instruments of oppression whose use is self-serving. Theories are dogmatic and exclusionary by nature; they leave out the experiences of other people, and they impose the parameters according to which one must think and act. What makes them particularly virulent is that they are created by a powerful minority, by an elite which has usurped power and thus uses them to impose its views of the world on others. Through the use of theories and their identification with the truth, these elites are capable of dominating others and perpetuating their power and prominent position in society.[26]

The solution to this situation is to realize the dangerous nature of theories. Accordingly, some argue the aim of metaphysics must be the critical examination of theories to show their limited value and their connection to the interests of dominating groups. Others go even further. For many postmodernists and deconstructionists, the aim of metaphysics, if it is to survive in any way, must be the destruction of theory and theory building. In essence, metaphysics ceases to be metaphysics as traditionally conceived.

An older, less radical understanding of the critical nature of metaphysics and its aim sees the justification for this conception in the fact that there are limitations on what metaphysics can yield. Again the field is divided here. For some, such as the logical positivists, these limitations are based on the nonempirical nature of the discipline and the impossibility of arriving at any sensible conclusions apart from experience. Metaphysics must give up its grandiose aims of determining the so-called ultimate nature of reality. The only disciplines that reveal to us the way things are, are the empirical sciences because they are based on experience and can make accurate predictions.[27]

A less radical, more Kantian viewpoint, also holds that metaphysics has to abandon its dogmatic posture because it can never ascertain the truth of the conclusions it reaches. Metaphysics is always groping in the dark and can never reach conclusions which will prove stable.[28] But that does not mean that metaphysics must give

---

26. Rosen, "The Limits of Interpretation," p. 214; Foucault, "Prison Talk"; and Foucault, "Nietzsche, Freud, Marx," p. 65.
27. Ayer, *Language, Truth, and Logic*, ch. 1, p. 50; Carnap, "The Elimination of Metaphysics," p. 60.
28. Heidegger makes this point in terms of the inconclusiveness of the question of being. *An Introduction to Metaphysics*, pp. 9, 17.

up trying to build models of the ways things are. Kant is certain it cannot stop.[29] Yet those models must be taken as just that, as models constructed by reason in an ongoing critical process which has no end.[30]

One can easily drag out many arguments against the viewpoint that the aim of metaphysics is solely critical. Perhaps the most obvious is that criticism requires something to be criticized. If the aim of metaphysics is merely to criticize and to tear down, once every theory has been criticized and torn down, what is there left to do? One cannot have destruction without something to destroy, and one cannot have criticism without something to criticize.

Now, it is possible to argue that metaphysicians need not function as builders of what metaphysicians are supposed to destroy; others are responsible for the building. But this is rather a disingenuous response, which makes perhaps only a verbal point. It is like saying that we need not call those who build conceptual structures metaphysicians but that, all the same, someone has to be in charge of building such structures.

There is another, more subtle argument, however. Criticism is either internal or external. Internal criticism assumes the principles under which the theory at issue has been formulated. To criticize in this way is actually to accept a theory about the formulation of the theory in question. The critic who proceeds in this way is not acting purely as a critic, insofar as, in order to criticize, he or she must accept some theoretical principles, and this seems to vitiate the procedure and the position. Internal criticism cannot be pure criticism. But if the criticism is external, then it is clear that the critic must adopt also some point of view, some theoretical stance not only concerning the method of criticism, but even perhaps about the substance of the theory in question.

By way of example, suppose I wanted to criticize Aristotle's view that sublunary substances are composed of matter and form. Internally, I could criticize Aristotle by pointing out that he is inconsistent. But to do this, I have to assume, if only methodologically, that Aristotle holds something else in some other part of his philosophical works. And this is, of course, an assumption based on a theoretical stance concerning the relation of Aristotle to his writings, his intentions, and so forth. Moreover, I also have to assume certain

---

29. Kant, *Prolegomena*, § 57, p. 102, and "Solution," p. 116.
30. Ibid., §§ 58, 44, pp. 106–107, 80.

rules of logic, such as the principle of noncontradiction, and are not these theories?

Now let us suppose that my criticism is going to be external. I plan to criticize Aristotle from the point of view of an idealist who believes that there is no such thing as matter, but that sublunary substances are simply bundles of immaterial forms. To do this, I must begin by pointing out that it makes sense to conceive the world in immaterial terms and that is precisely the reason the Aristotelian hylomorphic theory does not work. I must adopt a viewpoint. Furthermore, I must accept certain principles about how to judge the theories and these principles and, of course, part of a theory about epistemic acceptability. For example, I might proceed by pointing out that any theory must accord with my experience and that idealism satisfies this requirement, whereas Aristotelian hylomorphism does not.

The point is simply that criticism is always contingent on some theoretical assumptions. Now, skeptics reject this argument. For them, certainty is not possible and their task, as philosophers, is precisely to show that what other philosophers believe to be founded on firm ground is actually unfounded. But, how can they show that the views of other philosophers are unfounded without committing themselves to any view? They claim their commitment to the principles under which they criticize others is only methodological. They accept certain assumptions only because those whom they aim to criticize accept them, not because they themselves are committed to their truth. In short, all criticisms of other positions they make are internal and, precisely because their aim is to undermine the positions in question, they cannot be considered to have committed themselves to any of the principles under which the positions rest.

The skeptics are wrong for, as I indicated earlier, the game cannot be played this way. Indeed, if the principles under which a position is criticized are held only methodologically, then the conclusion which is supposed to refute the position has only a methodological force, and no refutation has taken place. Aristotle established this point many centuries ago: In order to refute, one must grant, and if one does not want to grant anything, then one must remain silent.[31]

This does not mean that metaphysics does not have a critical component and that it must be dogmatic. Clearly, dogmatism is

---

31. Aristotle, *Prior Analytics* 66b5, p. 97; Aquinas, *Summa theologiae* I, 1, 8, p. 14.

undesirable. If we have learned anything from the history of metaphysics, it is that there are no theories which are immune from criticism. But we have also learned that some theories are better than others. This alone should be sufficient to show not only that the aim of the discipline cannot be purely critical, but also that criticism is very important, for the relative value of different theories can only be brought to light under careful scrutiny. Criticism, then, is essential in metaphysics, but it is essential precisely because the discipline aims to formulate theories which are better than other theories.

From what we have seen, metaphysics may have several aims. Some of these can be considered fundamental, whereas others cannot. In either case, however, it is clear that the aim by itself cannot serve to distinguish metaphysics from other disciplines.

CHAPTER SIX

Propositions

Apart from the attempts to distinguish metaphysics from other disciplines on the bases of its object, method, and aim, there is another attempt which has antecedents in the Middle Ages, but only becomes part of the mainstream in early modern philosophy. I should qualify this statement by saying that many of those who adopt this approach do not intend to exclude other ways of distinguishing the discipline, and that others are concerned with the elimination of the discipline altogether rather than with its distinction from other disciplines.

This approach distinguishes metaphysics in terms of the kind of knowledge metaphysics is. This is usually explained in terms of the type of proposition (or statement, judgment, or sentence, depending on the philosopher) that metaphysics discusses or the type of proposition in which metaphysical views are expressed.

Five positions may be distinguished within this approach. The first claims that the subjects and predicates of metaphysical propositions are different from the subjects and predicates of propositions belonging to other disciplines. The rest find the uniqueness of metaphysical propositions in their being analytic and a priori, synthetic and a posteriori, synthetic and a priori, or meaningless.

A. Different Subjects and Predicates

According to this view, metaphysics, like any other kind of knowledge which can be expressed in propositions, may be distinguished from other kinds of knowledge in terms of the subjects and predicates of the propositions that compose it.[1] Thus, in the case of metaphysics, the subjects of those propositions might be things like God, being, substance, being *qua* being, and so on, and the predicates might be such as eternal, indefinable, and so on. A metaphysical proposition such as, "God is eternal," differs from a proposition in medicine such as, "Aspirin is effective against headaches." And, of course, it is the fact that metaphysics is composed of propositions like the first and medicine is composed of propositions like the second that separates metaphysics from medicine. Moreover, this applies to all sciences and knowledge. The set of propositions of each discipline will be different from the set of propositions that compose every other discipline because the subjects of the propositions and their predicates will be different.

Naturally, if in fact it turns out that the set of propositions that composes each discipline is unique, then this is an effective way of distinguishing each discipline from all others. But, we may ask, why are these statements unique? In principle there is no reason why the propositions that compose each discipline need be different from the propositions that compose other disciplines, and unless we can identify a reason why it is so, this position merely postpones the solution to the problem at hand.

The only way in which this position can solve this problem is by explaining why the subjects and predicates of the propositions of particular disciplines, such as metaphysics, are different from the subjects and predicates of the propositions of other disciplines. And the only answer that makes sense is that the objects for which those subjects stand and the characteristics that characterize those objects, and which are expressed by predicates, are different. So, this position reduces to the position that metaphysics is distinguished from other disciplines by the object or objects it studies. But we have already explained why this way of distinguishing metaphysics is not effective.

B. Analytic A Priori

This position holds that metaphysics is characterized and distinguished from other disciplines in that it is composed of analytic a priori propositions. In order to explain this position, we must explain briefly what is meant by analytic a priori propositions. Unfortu-

---

1. Ockham, "On the Notion of Science and Knowledge" (*Expositio super viii libros Physicorum*, Prologus), p. 15.

nately, there is no universally accepted way of describing these propositions in the history of philosophy. In the Middle Ages, these propositions correspond roughly to what were called "self-evident propositions." Thomas Aquinas described them as propositions in which "the predicate is included in the essence of the subject."[2] Kant, who spoke of judgments rather than propositions, considered a judgment analytic when it "expresses nothing in the predicate but what has been already actually thought in the concept of the subject, though not so distinctly or with the same full consciousness."[3] A current standard way of describing analytic propositions is to say that a proposition is analytic if and only if it is true in virtue of what it says; or, to put it in a more popular form, a proposition is analytic solely in virtue of the meaning of its terms. "The whole is greater than any of its parts" is analytic because it is true in virtue of what it says, namely, that the whole is greater than any of its parts; its truth is based simply on the concepts contained within the proposition. All these formulations have problems. A more technically precise formulation states that propositions are analytic if they "are true solely by virtue of their logical form."[4] Thus, the proposition "Socrates is not both a Greek and not a Greek" is analytic because it has the form $\sim(P.\sim P)$ and all propositions with that form are true. Sometimes this is expressed by saying that the denial of an analytic proposition entails a contradiction.

Of course, there is no reason why one could not have analytically false propositions, but in order to allow for these, the definition of an analytic proposition must be changed to something like this: A proposition is analytic if and only if its truth value is determined by what it says, or by its logical form, and so on.[5] In this way, we can say that the proposition "Squares are not squares" is analytically false.

Now, generally it is accepted that the a prioricity of propositions depends on the way we arrive at them. A priori propositions are propositions to whose knowledge we arrive independently of empirical experience. In this sense, a prioricity is a feature of propositions that depends on method, for it is the way we get at them that determines whether they are a priori or not. A proposition like "$A = A$" is

---

2. Aquinas, *Summa theologiae* 1, 2, 1, p. 19.
3. Kant, *Prolegomena*, § 2, p. 14.
4. Carnap, "The Elimination of Metaphysics," p. 76.
5. Ibid.

a priori because presumably we know it is true independently of our empirical experience. Now, I have already discussed the problems that the notion of a prioricity raises in chapter 3 and, therefore, I shall not repeat them here. But it is important to keep in mind that the attempt to distinguish metaphysics in terms of analytic a priori propositions does not involve only the character of the propositions contained in it but also involves an element of method.

The problems with this position are of three sorts. First, it is not clear that all metaphysical propositions are both analytic and a priori. Propositions such as, "God exists," or "The universe is finite," for example, do not seem to be on the same footing as propositions such as, "The whole is greater than any of its parts," and "$A = A$." Moreover, even if one granted that the conclusions one reaches in metaphysics are always expressed by analytic a priori propositions, not all metaphysical propositions are conclusions of arguments. At least some premises of arguments used to reach metaphysical conclusions are not themselves conclusions of arguments. And not everyone agrees that all the premises of arguments used in metaphysics can be said to be analytic and a priori. Only if one were to adopt a view such as that of Leibniz, could one justify this position.[6] But Leibniz's view is certainly controversial and would make the intelligibility and viability of the discipline depend on highly contested ground.

Even if this objection were not taken seriously, this view has to face two other problems. First, the fact that there are other disciplines that are generally considered to be composed of analytic a priori propositions, such as mathematics and geometry. And, of course, the question arises as to what distinguishes metaphysics from these.

Second, there is the controversial character of the notion of analyticity itself. We saw already that philosophers have devised various ways of explaining it, but that is not all. Some philosophers question the very distinction between analytic and synthetic propositions for a variety of reasons. For example, they argue that the distinction requires the use of such nonempirical, non-behavioral notions as proposition and concept.[7] The relevant point for us is not whether these philosophers are right or not, but rather that the basis on which metaphysics is to be distinguished is too controversial to serve its purpose. It would be better to establish the distinction of the discipline on less contested foundations.

---

6. Leibniz, *Philosophical Papers and Letters*, pp. 268–9.
7. For Quine, the very notion of proposition is to be rejected. *Word and Object*, pp. 206–11.

C. Synthetic A Posteriori

This view holds that metaphysics is distinguished from other disciplines because it is composed of synthetic a posteriori propositions. This is not a position that has been openly espoused by many, but many philosophers have in fact held that metaphysical propositions are synthetic and a posteriori.[8] A synthetic proposition is one whose truth value is not determined by what it says, that is, by the meaning of its terms, or alternatively, by its logical form.[9] The proposition, "The cat is on the mat," is synthetic because its truth value is determined not by what it says, namely, that the cat is on the mat, but by the fact that the cat is on the mat or that it is not on the mat. The concept of cat does not include the concept of being or not being on the mat. A proposition is a posteriori when it is arrived at through empirical experience. The proposition, "The cat is on the mat," is a posteriori because I know it is true from empirical experience alone. A synthetic a posteriori proposition, then, is one whose truth value is not determined by the concepts it uses, and the knowledge we have of it is not based on empirical experience.

The problems with the position that metaphysics contains only synthetic a posteriori propositions and that this is what distinguishes the discipline are similar in some ways to the problems which affected the previously discussed position. For one, it has to account for the controversial notion of a posteriori, the counterpart of a priori. Then, too, this view cannot easily distinguish metaphysics from certain other disciplines. Indeed, some adherents of this position acknowledge that this view turns metaphysics into a branch of history, which they then go on to distinguish from other disciplines on the basis of the object it studies. Yet metaphysics would be confused not only with history, but with most other disciplines, insofar as most of them use synthetic a posteriori propositions.

D. Synthetic A Priori

If neither analytic a priori nor synthetic a posteriori propositions are by themselves sufficient to distinguish metaphysics, one may want to argue, with Kant, that it is synthetic a priori propositions (or

---

8. Collingwood's view that metaphysical statements are historical clearly entails it. *An Essay on Metaphysics*, p. 49.
9. For Kant's formulation, see *Prolegomena*, § 2, p. 14. Often this kind of proposition is called "empirical." Carnap, "The Elimination of Metaphysics," p. 76.

judgments, for him).[10] A synthetic a priori proposition is one that is known independently of experience and yet its truth does not depend exclusively upon the concepts from which it is composed. Kant was aware that metaphysics had also been regarded as containing analytic propositions (judgments, for him) such as, "Substance is that which only exists as subject." But he held that these analytic propositions, although pertaining to metaphysics, were not properly speaking metaphysical. They belonged rather to what he called "philosophia definitiva," a propaedeutic part, or perhaps we should say, preamble, to metaphysics proper. The aim of these propositions was to make clear various distinctions among our concepts. On the other hand, metaphysics, properly speaking, contained only synthetic a priori judgments.[11] Examples of these judgments are: "The world had a beginning," "God exists," and "The soul is immortal."

The great advantage of this position is that it can effectively distinguish metaphysics from other disciplines, for it does not seem that any other discipline involves synthetic a priori propositions. Of course, Kant encountered a bit of trouble in that, contrary to general opinion, he thought that the propositions of mathematics also were synthetic a priori. So he had to find a further difference between mathematics and metaphysics.[12] However, because this view of mathematics is not widely accepted today, one can avoid this difficulty altogether and claim that only metaphysics has synthetic a priori propositions.

The main difficulty with this position is precisely the notion of a synthetic a priori proposition. Indeed, most philosophers would claim that the propositions Kant regarded as synthetic a priori are either synthetic a posteriori, analytic a priori, or meaningless, so that there are not in fact any propositions that are synthetic a priori. The notion of a synthetic a priori proposition is not only controversial but frequently challenged. For this reason it makes no sense to use it to distinguish metaphysics from other disciplines as long as it is possible to establish the distinction in other terms, more acceptable to the majority of philosophers and even to those who reject the notion of a synthetic a priori proposition. I will, therefore, omit discussion of the merits or demerits of this position, although I should remind the reader that the very distinction between a priori and a posteriori I argued, in chapter 3, to be problematic.

---

10. Kant, *Prolegomena*, § 2, pp. 18–9.
11. Ibid.
12. Ibid., pp. 15–18.

E. Meaningless Regarded as Meaningful

Those who have defended the positions so far discussed concerning metaphysical propositions have generally had as their aim to explain metaphysics and, thus, establish it firmly as a discipline. Others, however, are not so well intentioned. The logical positivists did distinguish metaphysical statements from the statements of other disciplines, but their aim was to do away with metaphysics rather than to establish it on firm ground.[13] They claimed that metaphysical statements lack cognitive meaning and express only an attitude toward life. In this sense, they are no different from statements made in lyrical poetry. The difference comes from the fact that those who make them, in contrast with those who compose lyrical poetry, treat them as if they had cognitive meaning. Metaphysical statements are meaningless because they are neither empirical, that is, statements which make claims about what we experience, nor analytic, that is, statements that make claims about the relation among concepts (or logical form).[14]

On the basis of the kind of statements metaphysicians make and the way these statements are regarded by them, it is possible to distinguish metaphysics from other disciplines. The empirical sciences consist of meaningful statements of the empirical sort. Sciences like mathematics and geometry consist of meaningful statements of the analytic sort. And poetry consists of emotionally expressive statements, but those who make them take the statements as such. It is only the metaphysician who pretends to make cognitive claims which are in fact not cognitive.

Several objections may be raised against this view. In the first place, one can argue that metaphysical statements are not meaningless. Indeed, the verificationist criterion of propositional meaning used by logical positivists to show that metaphysical statements are meaningless is now generally regarded as unacceptable, for the formulation of that very principle in a statement is either analytic, and then vacuous, or synthetic, and then limited. Metaphysical statements are meaningful insofar as the truth conditions of those statements can be identified apart from whether those conditions do or do not involve empirical verification or logical form.

---

13. Ayer, *Language, Truth and Logic*, pp. 33 ff.
14. Carnap, "The Elimination of Metaphysics," p. 76.

Obviously, this formulation of this objection cannot be regarded as conclusive against the logical-positivist view of metaphysical statements. To make the case, much more would have to be added, and this is not the proper place for it. For our purposes, it is sufficient to indicate the difficulties involved in the logical-positivist thesis and, therefore, its prima facie inadequacy as a basis for the distinction of metaphysics.

Another objection along similar lines would be a rejection of the logical-positivist way of distinguishing metaphysics by pointing out that accepting it would result, indeed, as the logical positivists explicitly claimed, in the elimination of metaphysics. And that is hardly an appropriate way of distinguishing it. The enterprise of distinguishing metaphysics has a place only within a context in which the peculiarities of the discipline, rather than its elimination, are explored.

Again, this objection is not conclusive, but it points to a consideration that must be taken into account. There is, however, one way to show that the logical-positivist attempt to distinguish metaphysics is not effective. For it is not just metaphysicians who make senseless statements they regard as sensible. The insane, the mentally incompetent, and those unskilled in a particular language often do so as well. Therefore, metaphysics could not be distinguished simply in virtue of the meaningless of its statements and the way those who make them regard them.

In short, then, the character of the propositions used in metaphysics does not effectively account for the distinction of the discipline. Indeed, some philosophers have gone so far as to claim that metaphysical statements are not different in any way from any other statement, so that any statement can be metaphysical.[15] But this is going too far. As we shall see, metaphysical claims can be distinguished from other claims, although not all statements (or propositions, judgments, or sentences) found in metaphysical discussions are distinguishable from those found in other disciplinary discussions. Still, it is not the character of the statements themselves that distinguishes metaphysics, but the object metaphysics studies coupled with the specific aim it pursues. And these are also the reasons that explain the peculiarities of metaphysical claims.

---

15. Warnock, in "Final Discussion," p. 153.

CHAPTER SEVEN

Definition

Philosophy, I claimed in chapter 2, is either: (1) a view of the world, or any of its parts, which seeks to be accurate, consistent, comprehensive, and supported by sound evidence; (2) the activity whereby such a view is developed; (3) the rules which are to be followed in the formulation of such a view; or, finally, (4) the ability to develop such a view. As a view, the aim of philosophy is to reflect an understanding of its object. As an activity, the aim of philosophy is to produce a view which will in turn reflect an understanding of its object. As a set of rules, the aim of philosophy is to prescribe the way to go about developing a view as described in 1. And, as an ability, the aim of philosophy is to make possible to develop 1, to engage in 2, or to follow 3. In all cases, it is a necessary condition of philosophy that a view meet the stipulated conditions, and, insofar as metaphysics is a branch of philosophy, what is a necessary condition of philosophy is also a necessary condition of metaphysics. Therefore, it is a necessary condition of metaphysics to be a view which meets the stipulated conditions.

To say this, however, is not to say anything that can set metaphysics apart from other branches of philosophy or to make clear exactly how it differs from nonphilosophical disciplines. This condition is too general to help us in the quest for the *differentia* which sets metaphysics apart. Moreover, this condition cannot be made to fit our needs by regarding metaphysics as having a narrower scope than other disciplines, for we saw earlier that metaphysics seems to be concerned with everything. The method of metaphysics, taken by itself, did not

seem to help us either, for again metaphysics seems to share methodological procedures with many other disciplines. The same applies to
the aim considered by itself, for the general aim of metaphysics does
not seem to be different from that of other disciplines. Finally, the
character of metaphysical propositions was not fruitful in distinguishing metaphysics because other disciplines use similar propositions or
because what is supposed to distinguish metaphysical propositions
from other propositions presupposes excessively controversial theses
concerning the nature of those propositions. Evidently, we must look
for the specific character of metaphysics elsewhere.

I believe the specificity of metaphysics can be found in both the
object it studies and what it specifically seeks to establish about that
object. The method, considered by itself or in conjunction with the object or aim of metaphysics, does not seem to play a defining role in this
matter; it seems rather more like a result of the character of the discipline than a determining factor in that character. This is, in fact, contrary to what some philosophers have argued and to what I expected
when I first set out to think about the nature of metaphysics. Indeed,
it seems reasonable to suppose that the distinguishing characteristic
of metaphysics as a discipline of learning, be found in its method. Yet,
it turns out not to be so. Those early philosophers, who claimed a
strong relation between metaphysics and its object, were closer to a
satisfactory position than early-modern methodologists, who tried to
define the discipline in terms of how it deals with its object.

The view I wish to defend here has two parts. Its first part identifies metaphysics with that part of philosophy that studies categories.[1] Categories come in a great variety and in different degrees of
generality. Among the most general we can find categories such as
being, thing, feature, relation, quality, universal, individual, essence, possible existence, class, entity, and so on. Among the least
general we find categories such as human, cat, table, red, three-foot
long, woman, god, stupid, book, language, and sister. In between we
find all sorts of categories, such as animal, mammal, mineral, plant,
furniture, building, science, and color. Yet, this tells us very little
about categories, so I must say something more about what categories are if my proposal is to be taken seriously.

Unfortunately, this is not easy, for categories have been one of
the most contentious topics of philosophical discussion since Aris-

---

1. For an antecedent, see Whitehead, *Process and Reality*, p. 12. Moore
spoke of kinds rather than categories in *Some Main Problems of Philosophy*, pp. 1–2. See also Brentano, *Theory of Categories*.

totle first used the term. The Greek term Aristotle used for category meant predicate and, indeed, for him categories were kinds of predicates, the most general kinds of predicates.[2] In *Categories*, Aristotle uses the term technically to refer to substance, quantity, quality, relation, place, time, position, state, action, and affection,[3] although he also speaks of less general predicates, such as white, half, and last year. Aristotle's categories are not, strictly speaking, the predicates we use when we speak in ordinary language; rather, they are the most general predicates that can be used. Thus, white and here are not categories, but quality and place are. To repeat, then, the Aristotelian categories may be taken as the most general predicates which can be predicated; they are the most general kinds into which the predicates we use in ordinary discourse may be classified.

Predicability, then, is not a sufficient condition of categoricity; but nonpredicability is a sufficient disqualification. For Aristotle, it is the individual that is not predicable. Examples of individuals are this horse and a certain point of grammar present in a knower.[4] The first is what Aristotle calls a "primary substance," and he defines it as that which is neither predicable of nor present in a subject.[5] The second is, like a primary substance, nonpredicable, but it can be present in a subject. Both are individual and neither is predicable.

That Aristotle used to refer to categories with the Greek term which corresponds roughly to the term 'predicate' in English, does not mean that he understood categories to be merely linguistic terms or words. This is why I have not placed what Aristotle regards as predicates within single quotation marks. There is ample evidence within Aristotle's text itself suggesting that, for him, categories are not just linguistic terms which reflect the fundamental ways in which we speak about things, but also ways in which we think about things and ways in which things are.[6] But none of this is clear in Aristotle, and even if it were clear, it would not necessarily and sufficiently describe what a category is; it would only describe what Aristotle thought it is.

---

2. Elsewhere Aristotle appears to use the term also for kinds of predications and kinds of objects. *Topics* 103b20–27, p. 195.
3. Aristotle, *Categories* 9a27, 11a37, 11b7, *et statim*, pp. 24, 28.
4. Ibid., 1b5, p. 8.
5. Ibid., 2a11, p. 9.
6. See how Aristotle speaks in ibid. And also 1a20, p. 7. Within a few lines Aristotle uses *ta legomena* (things that are said) and *ta onta* (beings). The interpretative tradition that favors a linguistic or logical understanding of the categories goes back to Porphyry, *In Aristotelis Categorias*, p. 56.

We need much more than I have so far said to resolve this question, but that will have to wait until chapter 9, where I discuss various ways in which categories may be conceived. Still, we need a way to refer to categories. One way to do this, would be to follow Aristotle and speak of them as predicates. For us, however, this entails that categories are linguistic entities, for we conceive predicates linguistically, as will be explained presently. Another way is to talk of categories as concepts, but that would commit us at the outset to a form of conceptualism. Or we could speak of categories as extramental entities, which would prima facie commit us to realism. Such commitments, however, should not come at the beginning but rather at the end of an inquiry, as theoretical proposals backed up by argumentation. What we need at this point is a neutral way of speaking about categories that will not commit us to any single view of them. I propose, then, that we refer to *categories* as whatever is expressed by a term or expression, simple or complex, which can be predicated of some other term or expression.[7] This formula allows us to talk about categories without committing us to a particular view of categories, and it leaves open the question of their ontological status and thus of the nominalistic, conceptualistic, or realistic status of metaphysics. Categories are whatever is expressed by predicate terms such as 'human,' 'concept,' and 'word,' be that something real, conceptual, or nominal.

The term 'predicate' itself is used in a variety of ways by philosophers and, therefore, I must make clear how I use it here in order to prevent confusion. Some conceive predicates as properties which are claimed to belong to the subjects of which they are predicated. Others conceive predicates as concepts through which we think about the subjects of which they are predicated. And so on. I shall consider predicates to be linguistic entities which are joined to other linguistic entities, namely, the subjects of the sentences of which they are predicated. Thus, 'black' is a predicate when it is a term which is joined to a subject, say 'ebony,' through a copula. Predicating, then, is the act of putting together linguistic terms in a certain way. The aim of predicating is to make a claim that the conditions specified by the predicate are satisfied by whatever the subject expresses. Thus, the sentence, 'Ebony is black,' makes the claim that the conditions of being black, specified by the predicate 'black,' are satisfied by ebony. And the sentence, 'Socrates is the son of Sophroniscus,' makes the

---

7. Compare this formula with Aristotle's in ibid., 1a25–27, p. 7.

claim that the condition of being the son of Sophroniscus, specified by the predicate 'the son of Sophroniscus,' is satisfied by Socrates. Socrates, moreover, is taken as what the proper name 'Socrates' expresses.

Predicates, then, should not be confused with categories. Categories are what predicates express, not the predicates themselves. Predicates are linguistic entities whose function is to specify the conditions to be satisfied by the entity expressed by the subject. Nor should categories be confused with conditions, for categories need not be conditions of anything. Categories become conditions only when they are expressed by a predicate whose function is to make a claim concerning the relation of a category to something else. Black is a category; 'black' is a predicate when it is found in a sentence such as, 'Ebony is black'; and the category black becomes a condition only when it is expressed by a predicate in a sentence such as, 'Ebony is black.' Conditions are always conditions of something; they are related to something. But categories need not be so.

The other term that needs clarification in the formula I have proposed to refer to categories is 'to express.' I have said that categories are whatever is expressed by predicates. And, I have also spoken of the subjects of sentences as expressing that which is claimed to satisfy the conditions specified by a predicate. A confusion may arise because 'to express' is, like 'to predicate,' used in a variety of ways. Philosophers speak of words, sentences, and the like, as expressing thoughts, ideas, concepts, and propositions. Moreover, it is not ordinary to find the term used in relation to proper names. We do not usually say that 'Socrates' expresses Socrates. Some might say that 'Socrates' expresses a sense or a meaning, such as a definite description, or that it refers to Socrates, but seldom, if ever, that it expresses Socrates. However, I would like to use 'to express' technically in such a way that 'Socrates' expresses Socrates and 'black' expresses black, and this regardless of whether the terms in question function as subjects or predicates. Naturally, a further analysis is required to make clear what Socrates and black are, but that is not pertinent for the present. One last point: I do not take what terms express to be, strictly speaking, their meaning for reasons I shall make clear later.

The formula I have adopted with respect to categories allows us to include within categories such controversial items as nothing, square circle, unicorn, possible, and so on. Moreover, it makes clear that only individual entities are excluded, entities such as this cat, Socrates, Rocinante, or my present knowledge of grammar. These are excluded because they are not expressed by terms or expressions that can be predicated of other terms or expressions. 'This cat,' 'Socrates,' 'Rocinante,' and 'my present knowledge of grammar' cannot be predicated of other terms or expressions and, therefore, what they express are not categories. When these terms appear in third place after a copula (for example, in 'X is Socrates'), they do not function as predicates in a predicative sentence, but as terms in an identity sentence.

Keep in mind that a predicate specifies the conditions which, in a sentence, are claimed to be satisfied by what the subject expresses. The difference between a predicative sentence and an identity sentence is that what is expressed in the grammatical predicate is the same as what is expressed in the grammatical subject in an identity sentence, but it is not the same in a predicative sentence. For this reason, subject and predicate are interchangeable in identity sentences. In predicative sentences the predicate specifies some, and only some, conditions which are supposed to be satisfied by what the subject expresses. Therefore, what the subject and predicate express are not the same thing. In identity sentences, however, the subject and predicate express the same thing. The reason that the exchange of subject and predicate is not possible in certain sentences that appear to be identity sentences is that they are not in fact identity sentences. 'Cicero is Tully,' for example, is not a true identity sentence, as this sentence could be taken to mean that Cicero is called Tully, and being called Tully, of course, is not everything Cicero is. Of course, if 'Socrates,' for example, were a name for a simple or complex predicate—say a definite description like 'the son of Sophroniscus'—then 'Socrates' would be a predicate, but in that case it would not express an individual.

In short, we have a formula which allows us not only to speak about categories, but also to discriminate categories from non-categories, without committing ourselves to a definite view concerning the ontological status of categories. This is all we need at this point.

The understanding of categories I have presented is not intended as a proper definition which specifies a set of necessary and sufficient conditions. It is rather an identifying description which allows us to distinguish between categories and non-categories in practical terms without tying us to a particular view of categories; it merely provides a criterion for us to identify categories. Indeed, this view allows for the possibility that there is no set of necessary and sufficient conditions of categories, or it could allow for the view that categories are after all extramental, conceptual, or nominal. But I shall have more to say about this in chapter 9.

Another point of contention concerning categories is their number. Aristotle never settled on a definite number and it is evident that there are predicates that fall into more than one of the categories he listed, such as 'prior' and 'posterior,' which can apply to time and place, and others which fall into every category he listed, such as 'good' and 'one.'[8] Subsequent philosophers have speculated as to the exact number of the most general categories and, moreover, some have understood these most general categories as irreducible, primarily diverse, and jointly exhaustive.[9] By irreducible, they generally mean that the categories in question cannot be subject to further analysis; there are no more general categories into which they can be broken down. By primarily diverse, they generally mean that they are completely different, having nothing in common; they are regarded as mutually exclusive. By jointly exhaustive they mean that, taken together, they comprise everything. Often it is also said of them that nothing but 'being' (and perhaps the predicates which are coextensive with 'being,' such as, 'one,' 'identical,' and the like) can be predicated of them. In this, they are to be distinguished from other predicates we use. Cats and dogs, for example, have in common that they are mammals, even if dogs do not meow and cats do not bark ('mammal' can be predicated of both 'cat' and 'dog'). Plants and animals have in common that they are living and physical, even if plants lack the capacity to move and animals lack chlorophyll ('living' and 'physical' are predicated of 'plant' and 'animal').

If we were to understand metaphysics exclusively as the study of irreducible, primarily diverse, and jointly exhaustive categories, the task of metaphysics would not only be quite limited, it would also exclude much that metaphysicians have done throughout the history of the discipline. This is a serious flaw, for a satisfactory conception of metaphysics should do justice to those aspects of our

---

8. Ibid., 1b–2a, p. 8; *Topics* 103a–b,190a33–35, 225b5–6, pp. 193–4, 231, and 303; *Metaphysics* 1017a25–27, 1028a12–13, and 1068a8, pp. 760–761, 869, and 783.
9. For Plotinus's criticism of the Aristotelian categories, see *Enneads* VI, 1, 1–24, pp. 443–70. The Stoics reduced the number to four: subject, quality, state, and relation. See von Arnim, *Stoicorum Veterum Fragmenta*, vol. 2, 369. Kant (*Prolegomena*, § 39, p. 70), and Leibniz (*Philosophical Papers and Letters*, pp. 229, 464) also proposed reductions in number. For more recent proposals, see Brentano, *The Theory of Categories*; Grossmann, *The Categorial Structure of the World*; and Lowe, "Ontological Categories and Natural Kinds."

experience of the discipline, and of generally accepted practice, which do not include contradictions. If the notion of category is to be of any use for understanding the object of metaphysics, it must be understood broadly. Of course, this raises a problem similar to that faced by the view of metaphysics which claims it studies everything. Indeed, many of the objections raised against the view that metaphysics is the encyclopedia of all knowledge apply to this position. The reason is that everything said or thought is said or thought in terms of categories as defined above. Hence, if metaphysics studies categories, it turns out metaphysics studies everything.

Thus far, however, I have presented only the first part of my view. In the second part, I maintain that metaphysics studies different categories in different ways because it seeks to establish different things about them. It is not only its object that sets metaphysics apart, but its object taken together with what it specifically seeks to establish about that object. Concerning the most general categories, metaphysics has a threefold aim: First, it seeks to identify the most general categories; second, it seeks to define them if at all possible and, if not, at least to describe them in ways which allow us to recognize them. I do not make definition a requirement because the most general categories may not be definable as there may not be categories in terms of which they may be defined. Third, it seeks to determine the relationships among these categories.[10]

These three tasks, indeed, are part of what metaphysicians have been doing all along. Consider Aristotle. First, he identified what he considered to be the most general categories, which for him were the ones mentioned earlier.[11] Then, he proceeded to define and explain them. He defined substance, for example, by saying that, in its primary sense, it is what is neither predicable of nor present in a subject.[12] Finally, he explained how these categories are related. For example, he noted that primary substance is what exists and everything else depends on it for its existence.[13] But this model of procedure is not unique to Aristotle. It is easily seen to apply to authors such as Kant, Whitehead, Russell, and Wittgenstein, all of whom differed from

---

10. This is not so far, perhaps, from what Moore had in mind in *Some Main Problems of Philosophy*, pp. 23, 24–25, or what Broad was aiming at in "Critical and Speculative Philosophy," p. 99.

11. Aristotle, *Categories* 9a27, p. 24.

12. Ibid., 2a11, p. 9.

13. Ibid., 2b5, p. 9.

Aristotle and from one another as to the identity of the most general categories, their proper understanding, and their relations.

Yet, this is not all that concerns metaphysicians. Metaphysicians are concerned also with less general categories. They speak of color and person, for example. Indeed, they even speak about specific colors such as red, and various kinds of persons, such as human and divine. But they do not ask the same questions about them that they ask about the most general categories. When discussing less general categories, metaphysicians are not concerned, for example, with the identification of the colors to be found in the spectrum, nor are they concerned with the definition of the color red, or the relation of red to yellow. The concern of metaphysics with these less general categories is twofold: First, metaphysics seeks to fit them properly into the most general categories it has already identified, defined (where possible), and related; second, metaphysics seeks to determine how they are related to all the most general categories, including the ones in which they do not fit. Consider the cases of red, human, and language. Metaphysicians will seek, first, to determine within which of the most general categories red, human, and language fit. Is red a quality or a relation, for example? Are humans substances or bundles of features? Are languages features or relations? Second, metaphysicians will ask, for example, whether red is related to substance (substance is a category where red does not fit) as an effect is to a cause, or again whether language is related to substance (substance is a category where language does not fit) as an effect is to a cause? And so on. The questions that metaphysicians ask about less general categories are questions related to the most general conditions of those categories or about how those categories are related to the most general ones.[14]

In accordance with the four senses of philosophy mentioned earlier, we can now establish four different understandings of metaphysics depending on whether we refer to a view, to an activity, to rules, or to an ability:

1. Metaphysics is a philosophical view which seeks: (a) to identify the most general categories; (b) to define the most general

---

14. For a dissenting view, see Grice, Pears, and Strawson, "Metaphysics," p. 7, but compare Strawson's later statement in *Analysis and Metaphysics*, p. 35. According to my view, a great part of what the metaphysician does is to connect and relate categories. Husserl emphasizes the same task in the context of formal ontology in *Logical Investigations*, pp. 816 ff.

categories if at all possible and if not, at least to describe them in ways which allow us to identify them; (c) to determine the relationships among the most general categories; (d) to fit less general categories into the most general ones; and (e) to determine how less general categories are related to all the most general categories, including the ones in which they do not fit.

2. Metaphysics is the activity whereby a view such as the one described in 1 is developed.

3. Metaphysics is a set of rules which are to be followed in the formulation of a view such as the one described in 1.

4. Metaphysics is the ability to produce the view described in 1, to engage in the activity described in 2, or to develop the set of rules mentioned in 3.

Of these, 1 takes precedence over the others because it is presupposed by the others. The activity whereby a view is produced, the rules which guide such production, and the ability which makes such production possible, all presuppose the view. The view is what gives sense to all the others; it is the goal or end, as Aristotle would put it. Therefore, the primary sense of metaphysics is the first, a view of the world or any of its parts which meets the specified conditions. In this sense, metaphysics turns out to be the categorial foundation of all our views, of all our knowledge. As the view of the most general categories and how less general categories are related to them, it is the conceptual foundation of everything else we know.

B. Metaphysics and Other Disciplines

Now we can see how the specific aim of metaphysics differs from that of philosophy and other disciplines. It differs from that of philosophy considered as a whole, because philosophy seeks to develop a comprehensive view about anything whatever. In that sense, the task of philosophy is more broad, including not only that of metaphysics, but also that of other disciplines. Philosophers feed on other sources of information to develop an overall and comprehensive view of the world or any of its parts. By contrast, the aim of metaphysicians is quite restricted; they seek to provide a general categorization and to see how the specific categories found in our experience, or posed by other disciplines, fit within it.

The aim of metaphysics differs from that of other disciplines because metaphysics is not concerned with the identification and definition of less general categories, nor is it interested in determining the relations among those categories. Particular sciences posit triangles and electrons, for example, and they attempt to define them and to explain how they relate to other, specific, entities such as squares and protons. The geometer posits triangles and tells us that a triangle is a geometrical figure with three angles; and the physicist posits electrons and tells us that an electron is one of the constituent elementary particles of an atom and so on. Metaphysicians, by contrast, are not interested in identifying or defining these specific categories, or in determining their relations. Rather, metaphysicians are interested in establishing whether triangles and electrons are substances, qualities, relations, or events, for example, or whether the list of the most general categories should be modified to accommodate discoveries made in other disciplines.

In conclusion, it is in the specific aim and object of metaphysics that we find the *differentia* which distinguishes the discipline from other disciplines and makes a niche for it within philosophy. According to its specific aim, metaphysics is concerned with categorization; according to its object, it is concerned with every category, although with the most general categories in one way and with less general categories in another way. It is a mistake to try to restrict the object of metaphysics to one individual being (e.g., God), a set of individual beings (e.g., God and individual souls), one kind of being (e.g., immaterial being), or even to being *qua* being, for that entails a restriction to certain categories and metaphysics is concerned with every category.

Nor can any method which may help to fulfill the task of metaphysics be disqualified. This is one reason why metaphysics cannot be distinguished from other disciplines in terms of method. It is a mistake to think of metaphysics as purely a priori, for metaphysics draws from experience to form a list of the most general categories into which the world can be divided. Indeed, how could one proceed to categorize if one had nothing to categorize? And what is to be categorized is at least in part what we have been given in experience. To categorize running as an activity, we must first determine what is characteristic of running and this is possible only by taking account of experience. But metaphysics goes beyond experience in the formulation of the very categories according to which experience is organized in a most general way, for there seem to be certain categories which are prerequisites of experience.[15] Some philosophers have claimed, for example, that the subject/object dichotomy is presupposed by experience. But, even apart from categories which seem to be prerequisites of experience, we often determine membership within a category through inspection of the content and implications of concepts considered apart from experience. The product of the multiplication of two numbers, for example, is itself a number. So, it is also a mistake to think of metaphysics as purely a posteriori.

The same can be said about the use of analysis, elucidation, and synthesis. Metaphysics seeks to analyze, elucidate, and synthesize, for indeed analysis is part of elucidation and presupposes synthesis. Moreover, the metaphysical method is both discursive and intuitive. Discursive, because it reaches conclusions which are the result of inferences drawn from premises; intuitive, because it relies on concepts which are derived from experience rather than from propositional expressions of that experience. The metaphysical method is also both descriptive and prescriptive. It is descriptive insofar as it describes the object it studies; and it is prescriptive insofar as a correct description of that object is intended to prescribe the way we should think and speak about it. Likewise, metaphysics uses both inductive and deductive procedures, for it uses arguments whose conclusions are claimed to follow necessarily from their premises and arguments whose conclusions are claimed to follow only with more or less probability. Moreover, metaphysics uses arguments whose conclusions are more general than their premises and arguments whose conclusions are less general than their premises. Metaphysics uses observation and mental experimentations. It both follows and challenges common sense. It is historical insofar as it uses what others have said and experienced, but it is unhistorical insofar as it deals with the past as if it were the present and makes atemporal claims. And metaphysics uses dialogue and the phenomenological method to the degree these are useful in advancing its aim. Even the authoritative method has a place in metaphysics, at least to the extent that metaphysics generally accepts the conclusions of other disciplines in order to reach its own goal. Metaphysics, for example, does not dispute the existence of electrons and black holes; it accepts their existence on the authority of physicists and astronomers who posit them, in order to proceed to the categorization

---

15. Cf. Kant, *Prolegomena*, § 39, p. 71.

of these entities. And the same goes for their definition, which metaphysics takes from physicists and astronomers.

But doesn't this mean, after all, that metaphysics can be distinguished from other disciplines in terms of its method? Consider mathematics. Couldn't we say that, insofar as mathematics is strictly a priori and metaphysics includes an a posteriori dimension, metaphysics can be distinguished from mathematics in terms of method? Likewise, couldn't one argue that revealed theology and metaphysics are distinguished in terms of method, because revealed theology takes its fundamental principles on the authority of revelation, whereas metaphysics does not? Of course, this is true. But my claim is not that metaphysics cannot be distinguished in terms of its method from this or that particular discipline. My claim is that metaphysics does not have an idiosyncratic method which characterizes it and separates it from all other disciplines because no other discipline shares in it. The method of metaphysics is not different from the methods used by other disciplines. Indeed, metaphysics does not differ from them even in the fact that metaphysics combines the methods of other disciplines into an overall method. Even if we were to dispute this last point, it would not follow that what is distinctive about metaphysics is its method, for metaphysics shares its method with some other branches of philosophy.

C. Three Objections

Now we must consider three objections. The first argues that my definition of metaphysics is inadequate, because it is based on a fuzzy distinction between most general and less general categories. The problem is not so much that we cannot always distinguish between two categories in terms of the degree of generality, but that it is not clear which are the most general categories metaphysics seeks to identify, define (where possible), and relate, and which are the less general ones it seeks merely to relate to the most general ones.

The answer to this objection is that, indeed, there is no easy, simple, or clear way to establish which are the most general categories metaphysics studies in one way and the less general ones metaphysics studies in another way. Indeed, it appears that the categories which are taken to be most general and the ones taken to be less general may shift from time to time as particular disciplines develop and claim categories which hitherto had been the province of metaphysics. For example, the pre-Socratic philosophers posed certain categories, such as air and fire as most general categories. But these categories would now have to be considered less general categories according to my scheme, because they are the province of physics, chemistry, and other particular sciences.

To acknowledge that all of the categories metaphysics studies are not easily determined, and that our view of some of them may change from time to time, however, is not to acknowledge that the view of metaphysics proposed here must be abandoned. It is simply to recognize that metaphysics (remember, it is fundamentally a view), like other disciplines, is a human product and, as such, subject to historical development. It is well known that philosophy is the mother of all sciences, but this does not mean that philosophy has ceased to exist because areas it previously studied have become independent of it. Similarly, that particular disciplines may claim categories previously studied by metaphysics does not mean that metaphysics must disappear; it only means that particular metaphysical views, in which those categories were considered most general, have to be modified to make room for the discoveries of other disciplines.

It is important to note that the difficulty of establishing which particular categories metaphysics studies, and the way in which it studies them, does not constitute a serious objection against my view. The reason is that distinctions among disciplines of learning can seldom, if ever, be hard and fast. This is true of all human learning. Can anyone define, clearly and strictly, the limits separating chemistry and physics, for example? There are always areas in which the distinction is clear, but there are areas in which it is not, for human learning is not perfectly compartmentalized and is always in a process of change. Human knowledge is a continuum in which boundaries are not always discernible and, even when discernible, are subject to change.

The last observation brings me back to the point I wish to emphasize. Although there are areas of dispute, that is, categories whose investigation is not clearly determined to fall into the province of metaphysics or some particular discipline, there are areas in which this is not so. No one has ever disputed, as far as I know, that the category of substance, for example, is clearly in the province of metaphysics. So, there are, and there will continue to be, areas of dispute, but that does not entail that the view of metaphysics presented here is flawed.

Second, one may object that the conception of metaphysics I have presented is quite different from that for which most metaphysicians have consistently argued throughout history, namely, that metaphysics is concerned with being and, therefore, that I am violating one of the principles to which I said my account would adhere.

One way to answer this objection is to say that, regardless of what many metaphysicians say, it is a fact that they have been concerned as much with categories such as nonbeing and nothing as with categories of being. Plato, for example, devotes considerable attention to the category of nonbeing in the *Sophist*,[16] and Suárez devotes an entire Disputation to similar categories in the *Metaphysical Disputations*, although he cleverly puts the Disputation dealing with such categories at the end and distinguishes it from all the others.[17] Therefore, to say that metaphysics studies only categories of being is to leave out much that metaphysicians have studied and, in my view, must study; it is to present an incomplete and inaccurate understanding of metaphysics.

Another way to answer this objection is to say that most, if not all, the categories of nonbeing turn out, upon analysis, to be categories of being; it is just that we refer to them in negative terms. Plato was perhaps the first to try to give an analysis of what-is-not in terms of what-is through the notion of difference.[18] In this sense, a category such as non-red is nothing but all colors except for red. And this means that non-red is a category of being rather than a category of nonbeing.

This is all very well, yet it remains the case that not all categories of nonbeing can be analyzed in terms of being and, therefore, there is still a problem. Consider the most obvious case of such a category: nothing. Since nothing connotes the absence of being, it appears nonsensical or even contradictory to say that it is a category of being. So, even if we were to suppose that most categories of nonbeing can be reduced to categories of being, there is at least one which cannot and, therefore, the view I have proposed here cannot be identified with the view according to which metaphysics studies being.

---

16. Plato, *Sophist* 237b ff., pp. 980ff.
17. Suárez, *Disputationes metaphysicae* 54, vol. 26. The order he adopts sets a precedent that was to be followed by a host of metaphysicians in the seventeenth and eighteenth centuries. See, for example, Scheibler, Index to the First Book of *Opus metaphysicum*.
18. Plato, *Sophist* 257b, p. 1003.

A possible answer to this retort is that all categories of nonbeing, including nothing, appear to be parasitic on categories of being. Just as non-red is parasitic on red because it consists in the denial of red, so nothing is the denial of thing, and nonbeing is the denial of being. This means that these categories are studied only in terms of the categories they deny, and in this sense their study is correspondingly parasitic on the study of categories of being. One can argue, then, that the study of nonbeing is in fact the study of being considered under a particular aspect, namely, its negation. Therefore, there is no reason why metaphysics should not study categories of nonbeing, nor is there a reason why such a study should entail that the object of metaphysics has to do with categories other than those of being. This is, of course, not the same as saying that all categories of nonbeing are categories of being, as was argued earlier. Rather, it is to say that categories of nonbeing are studied in relation to being. The first position claims an ontological identity; the second claims a procedural connection.

This last suggestion seems to provide a sensible answer to the objection, but the answer is only provisional, for we have not yet dealt with the fundamental question of the status of categories. This, however, requires considerable discussion and I, therefore, leave it for a later chapter.

A third objection I should consider argues that the view of metaphysics I have presented isolates the discipline from both the world and our experience of the world. Metaphysicians have always been concerned with the world in which we live and with the experiences we have of it. This means that metaphysicians are concerned, after all, with sticks and stones, and because sticks and stones, or the experiences we have of them, are not categories, the object of metaphysics cannot be categories.

The response to this objection has two parts. First, the objection seems to presuppose that categories are either abstract, disembodied entities like Plato's forms, or general concepts, and therefore that they are unrelated to the world or to our experience. But this is not what I take categories to be at all, as I shall argue in chapter 9.

Second, the objection is based on a false inference. It claims that according to my view metaphysics is not concerned with the world and our experience of it because its object is categories. But if this were so, the same would apply to the empirical sciences. The empirical sciences, just like metaphysics, are concerned with categories except that the categories with which they are concerned are less general than some of those with which metaphysics is concerned, and they are not concerned with the relation of these less general categories to the most general ones. Physics is concerned with volume and weight, not with this volume and this weight, and volume and weight are categories. I challenge anyone to find as a conclusion of physics a statement about a non-category, such as this volume or this weight. So, if metaphysics is not concerned with the world and our experience of it because it studies categories, physics, too, for the same reason would not be concerned with the world and our experience of it, which is preposterous.

The mistake which is at the base of the objection arises because those who raise it do not realize that, although all science is concerned with categories of one sort or another, the epistemic bases on which science draws its conclusions are observations of non-categorial members of categories. To know about weight and volume I must examine this and that weight and this and that volume. To know about humans I must examine Socrates, Xanthipe and many other individual humans. To know about color I must examine not just this and that kind of color, but also this individual instance of this or that kind of color. And the way I access these is through experience. But, of course, the scientific inferences I draw once I have examined these individuals are not about them, that is, they are not about this weight, Socrates, or this instance of red, or about my experience of this weight, Socrates, or this instance of red. These inferences are going to be about the categories to which these individuals belong, namely, weight, human, and red.

In short, just like other disciplines of learning, metaphysical views are about categories, so categories are the proper object of the discipline. But these views are based on the consideration of non-categorial members of categories.

D. Taxonomy

I must now make a few brief comments about the principal parts of metaphysics. This is necessary because often particular authors confuse metaphysics with some of its parts, thus unnecessarily restricting the scope of the discipline. The discussion of such a taxonomy, then, prevents confusions which may obscure the nature of metaphysics.

Some of the parts of metaphysics with which it is most frequently confused are ontology, etiology, philosophical anthropology, theology, and the philosophy of language. There are many others, but for the sake of brevity I shall use only these as examples.

Consider those philosophers who identify metaphysics with ontology. Ontology is concerned with the study of the most fundamental categories of being and with the relations among them.[19] This naturally explains the use of the term 'ontology' and suggests that the discipline deals with being, a traditional description of the object of metaphysics. The use of the term 'ontology' to refer to metaphysics appears in early modern philosophy and is still with us.[20] Indeed, many contemporary metaphysicians speak of their discipline as ontology.[21]

Yet, if ontology involves only the subject matter mentioned, it is clear that it excludes much that metaphysicians discuss. For example, much of what is discussed in the philosophy of mind falls outside ontology, for it does not concern the development of the fundamental categories of being and the exploration of the relations among them. It concerns rather the categorization of the mind and the description of its relations to various categories, and this does not seem to be a part of ontology.

Something similar applies to etiology. Etiology is the study of causes. But, although everything can function as a cause in some sense in certain circumstances, there are many aspects of things which have little to do with causality as such or with things functioning as causes.

Theology and philosophical anthropology also turn out to be too narrow. The object of the first is the divinity, leaving out the study of all sorts of categories. And the object of the second is the human being, also an object too narrow to include all that is investigated in metaphysics.

In short, metaphysics should not be confused with other branches of philosophy. But that does not mean that it cannot be properly divided into branches. The best way to perform this division, when the discipline is understood in the way I have proposed, is to do it in terms of the two groups of categories it studies, the most general and the less general. To divide it in those terms means, however, that

---

19. For slightly different formulas, see Grossmann, *The Categorial Structure of the World*, pp. 3, 9; and Strawson, *Analysis and Metaphysics*, p. 30.
20. Wolff used it in the title of his treatise on metaphysics, *Philosophia prima, sive ontologia* (1729), but there are antecedents in Clauberg (*Metaphysica de ente*, p. 283); Goclenius (*Lexicon*, p. 16, under "Abstractio materiae"), and others.
21. See, for example, Grossmann, *The Categorial Structure of the World*, pp. 3–5, and Hamlyn, *Metaphysics*, pp. 8 and 34–37.

just as the line of demarcation between the most general and the less general does not always appear to be clear, so, too, the line of demarcation between the two corresponding branches of metaphysics does not always appear to be sharp.

General metaphysics is that branch of the discipline that concerns itself with the identification and definition (when possible) of the most general categories and with the study of the various relations among them. By contrast, *specific metaphysics* is that branch of the discipline that concerns itself with less general categories.[22] A frequent mistake is to confuse metaphysics proper with one of its two main branches.

Naturally, these two branches of metaphysics can be subdivided further. General metaphysics may be divided, for example, into ontology (the study of being), etiology (the study of cause), and other subfields of investigation. Specific metaphysics, likewise, may be divided into such branches as theology and anthropology. The first tries to fit the category of the divine within the categories identified and defined in general metaphysics and to determine how some of the features which characterize the single member of that category are related to all the most general categories. Anthropology tries to do the same with the specific categories pertinent to human beings,

---

22. The distinction between general and specific metaphysics (or universal and particular metaphysics) was used in the seventeenth century, although there was no consensus as to how to understand it and I know no case in which it was understood as I have suggested here. See Baronius, *Metaphysica generalis* (1654); Calov, *Metaphysica divina* (1636 and 1650); Gutke, *Primae philosophiae* (1618); Rutgers, *Universalis metaphysica* (1619); and Scheibler, *Epitome metaphysicae specialis* (1617) and *Opus metaphysicum* (1617). According to Scheibler, for example, general metaphysics studies "being in common, and its general principles and attributes"; special metaphysics studies "the division of being into substance and accident, and explains what is under these." *Opus metaphysicum*, p. 67. The origin of the distinction is obscure. Beck (*Early German Philosophy*, p. 121) suggests it originated with Cornelius Martini, but Scharlemann (*Thomas Aquinas and John Gerhard*, p. 21), although acknowledging its presence in Cornelius Martini and in Suárez, claims it was in Jacob Martini's *Exercitationes theorematum metaphysicorum* (1604) that it was first emphasized and where it became significant. In recent times, this distinction has been used by neoscholastics to separate "the science of what is negatively immaterial" from "the science of what is positively immaterial." Mercier, *A Manual of Modern Scholastic Philosophy*, p. 410.

such as person. Note that, apart from these metaphysical questions concerned with categorization, there are many other questions, philosophical and nonphilosophical, that can be raised, and prompt views, about God or human beings. Such questions are not the province of metaphysics and the views to which they give rise are not metaphysical views. They are the province of other disciplines. The definition of God, for example, does not fall within the theology which is a part of metaphysics, and the definition of human being does not fall into the anthropology which is a part of metaphysics.

The lines of demarcation among the branches of metaphysics are not always clear. Just as the categories that metaphysics studies are not always clear and their identities and degrees of generality may vary, so the lines that separate the subdisciplines of metaphysics are not always clear and may vary depending on the development of human knowledge in general. Any classification of disciplinary studies, including metaphysics, should be taken only as a model to be used in further study and discussion.

E. The Name of the Discipline

One point remains which concerns the name of the discipline. As is well known, the discipline has been called by several names throughout its history. Among these, 'first philosophy,' 'metaphysics,' 'theology,' and 'wisdom' have been used most frequently.[23] All four names can be traced to Aristotelian texts. The first and the last two were in fact used by Aristotle himself,[24] and the term we have been using in this book, 'metaphysics,' can be traced to Andronicus of Rhodes, who edited the texts we now know as Aristotle's *Metaphysics*.

From what we saw earlier, it is a mistake to call the discipline "theology." But, is any of the remaining terms more appropriate than the others? Each of these terms has advantages and disadvantages. The disadvantages come from the connotations they have acquired during the long history of the discipline.

---

23. There are others as well. Whitehead, Broad, and Hampshire, for example, call it "speculative philosophy." *Process and Reality*, p. 4; "Critical and Speculative Philosophy," p. 96; "Metaphysical Systems," p. 29. For other, less frequently used and now out of fashion terms in connection with metaphysics or its branches, see Wundt, *Die Deutsche Schulmetaphysik des 17. Jahrhunderts*, pp. x–xxvi.
24. Aristotle, *Metaphysics* 1026a24, 1025b1, 981a27, pp. 779, 778, 690.

Those who prefer 'first philosophy' usually want to emphasize the priority that metaphysics has with respect to all other branches of knowledge, but often this priority is mistakenly understood in ontological and epistemological terms.[25] The ontological priority of metaphysics can be taken in at least two senses. First, metaphysics is prior because it studies beings which are ontologically prior, such as God.[26] Second, metaphysics is prior because it ontologically precedes other disciplines—it exists before the others do. The first sense is widespread in the history of philosophy, but does not fit the definition of metaphysics I have proposed. And the second is clearly wrong. Regardless of the way the discipline is understood—as a view, an activity, a set of rules, or an ability—it is not prior in existence to other disciplines.

The epistemological priority of metaphysics can be taken to mean that the study of metaphysics must precede the study of other disciplines, because one must know metaphysics before one can know what other disciplines teach. But this is clearly wrong. Physicists are certainly not required to study metaphysics before they engage in the study of physics.

The priority of the discipline, then, cannot be ontological or epistemological. Indeed, its priority is logical, in the sense that less general views imply more general ones, and metaphysics is the discipline which aims to formulate the most general views.[27] Another way of putting this is to say that less general categories presuppose the most general ones and this discipline is concerned with the most general categories and the relations of less general categories to the most general. This logical relation does not imply ontological or epistemological priority. So much, then, for 'first philosophy.'

The term 'metaphysics' has been used throughout the history of the discipline to emphasize that the discipline is concerned with what is outside our world or what is not material, or that the study of the discipline comes after the study of physics (often called

---

25. Avicenna, *Metaphysica* 1 and 2, pp. 12 and 14; Aristotle also mentions but does not explore temporal priority for obvious reasons in *Metaphysics* 1028a32, p. 783.
26. Aristotle, *Metaphysics* 1050b1–6 and 1028a32, pp. 830 and 783.
27. Aquinas, *Commentary on the "De Trinitate" of Boethius* 5, 1, p. 9. Elsewhere, however, Aquinas states that metaphysics is called "first philosophy" because it studies first substances. See "Preface," *Commentary on the "Metaphysics"*, p. 2. See also Collingwood, *An Essay on Metaphysics*, p. 5.

"natural philosophy"). These connotations go back to ancient and medieval understandings of the term.[28] But, if our proposal is correct, then these interpretations of the discipline are unfortunate, for the discipline does not deal exclusively with what is outside our world or with what is immaterial. Moreover, whether its study is to be carried out after physics has nothing to do with what it studies or how it studies it. The discipline is concerned with all kinds of categories, although it studies them in different ways, depending on whether they are less general or most general. Therefore, the term 'metaphysics,' like the term 'first philosophy,' is not entirely appropriate.

What Aristotle and his commentators mean by 'wisdom' when they apply this term to the discipline is not always clear. It appears that the use of the term is intended to emphasize that this is what the philosopher is searching for: Wisdom is what the lover of wisdom wishes to achieve.[29] As such, this term would be quite consonant with the understanding of the discipline I have proposed, insofar as it could be interpreted as a view about categories and their interrelations. Indeed, elsewhere Aristotle identifies philosophic wisdom with scientific knowledge, combined with intuition, of things that are highest by nature.[30] This, again, could be interpreted to refer to categories, but it could also be referring to the divine. In the latter case, philosophic wisdom would turn out to be theology. At any rate, because the term 'wisdom' does not really signify anything in particular about the object, method, aim, or propositions of the discipline, its utility is questionable. Moreover, it is bound to create confusion with the many other things that have also been called wisdom in the history of human thought. It might be better, then, to dispense with it.

By contrast, both terms, 'first philosophy' and 'metaphysics,' can be of use, provided one understands they refer to the discipline concerned with the most general categories and with the relation of less general categories to those which are most general. The discipline may be called "first philosophy" precisely because it is concerned with what one might call "first," in the sense of most general, cate-

---

28. Aquinas uses the third in *Commentary on the "De Trinitate" of Boethius* 5, 1, pp. 8–9, and 6, 1, p. 64. See also pertinent references in chapter 3 earlier.

29. Aristotle, *Metaphysics* 981b5, 982a15, pp. 690, 691; Collingwood, *An Essay on Metaphysics*, pp. 5 and 10.

30. Aristotle, *Nicomachean Ethics* 1141b3, p. 1028.

gories, and the relation of second, or less general categories to the first categories. And the discipline may be called "metaphysics" because it is concerned with categories which go beyond the ones which are closer to us in the sense of being less general, and with the relation of these less general categories to the most general ones. This, however, is stretching matters quite a bit. For this reason, it would be more appropriate to call the discipline "first philosophy." And, indeed, technically, this has been the name favored by many of those who have carefully thought about this matter.

All the same, the term 'metaphysics' ties the discipline to the title of the first important book in which the discipline is explicitly discussed, Aristotle's *Metaphysics,* and to the first influential systematic treatment of the discipline in the West written after Aristotle's treatise, namely, Suárez's *Metaphysical Disputations.* Moreover, the term 'metaphysics' is widely used, not only in the history of philosophy but also today. So, it would make no sense to dismiss it. Hence, for purely historical and pragmatic reasons, it makes sense to continue calling the discipline "metaphysics," and that is what I shall do here, although in this book the term refers only to the discipline as I have defined it.

F. Some Loose Ends

I have defended the view that metaphysics is the study of categories and I have claimed that this view best fits what most metaphysicians have been doing throughout the history of the discipline. It may not be completely clear, however, what my view entails. For example, I have claimed that one branch of metaphysics is theology and theology is generally understood as being concerned with God. But presumably, God is not a category, so how can I claim metaphysics studies categories?

The answer to this is that the object theology studies is not God, but the category of divinity. Of course, the most widespread view among metaphysicians who practice theology is that the category of divinity can have only one member, so that there can be only one God. If this is so, then clearly in studying the category of divinity, metaphysicians/theologians study only one being in the sense that the category they study has only one member who satisfies all the conditions prescribed by the category. Besides, the formulation of views about categories involves the study of their members and so it is that theologians study God and botanists study plants. The case of God, then, is not a counter example to my view.

Apart from this case, other possible counter examples may be cited. For instance, how can the traditional concerns of metaphysicians to establish ultimate causes and principles, be construed as a study of categories?

Again, the answer is not difficult, for what metaphysicians do when they study ultimate causes is to identify the relations of the category ultimate cause to other categories. To identify the so-called First Cause is simply to study the general category of cause and see how the category of first can be combined with it and be related to other categories such as second cause, effect, and so on. The same can be said about principles. Consider the case of the so-called principle of individuation. The study of the category principle of individuation amounts to the study of how this category is related to other categories, such as spatiotemporal location or bundle of features, which have been proposed as principles of individuation, and such as material object or person, which are supposed to be individual.

Still, one might want to raise the question of existence. Metaphysicians have traditionally been concerned with existence and what exists. But, one might argue, how can this kind of study be conceived as a study of categories? Isn't existence established on the basis of empirical evidence and not on the basis of conceptual analysis?

The response to this objection must begin, first, with an answer to the last question: Yes, existence seems always to be established on the basis of empirical evidence, even though nonexistence can sometimes be inferred on the basis of conceptual analysis alone (e.g., the nonexistence of square circles) and some philosophers have claimed that the existence of at least one being can be established on the basis of conceptual analysis alone.[31] But I have not argued anywhere that the method of metaphysics is exclusively conceptual analysis or that the study of categories entails the exclusive use of the method of conceptual analysis. We learn about categories through acquaintance with members of those categories in experience, although again, this does not rule out that we formulate our views about those categories through the use of conceptual analysis as well.

Second, existence, existing entity, possible entity, merely possible entity, and so on are general categories and as such the metaphysician is entitled to study them and to relate them to other categories, such as cat, individual, the last Dodo bird, and so on. Moreover, metaphysicians are also entitled to talk about whether a

---

31. Anselm, *Proslogium*, ch. 3, pp. 8–9.

particular category has or does not have any members, and so on, based on the evidence they have from experience and conceptual analysis.

My classification of existence as a category no doubt will raise eyebrows. Does this mean that existence is some kind of property? If so, there is a long and respectable tradition of philosophers, from Kant to Quine, who have explicitly rejected this view, and with good reasons. They have argued that existence is not a property of things that exist and, therefore, that the term 'exist' cannot be considered a proper predicate. And I agree, existence is not a property and 'exist' is not, in a technical and narrow sense, a predicate.[32] But I have said nothing that implies they are. My view is that 'exist' is a predicate in ordinary language and as such whatever it expresses, and certainly it must express something because we understand it, is a category. Now, whether that category is or is not like categories which are properties is a matter to be decided in ontology, the branch of metaphysics that studies categories such as existence and being. My definition of metaphysics and my understanding of category leave open the question of the status of existence.

Three other closely related issues may pose difficulties: Do discussions of free will/determinism, knowledge, and ontological priority enter into metaphysics? Many metaphysicians have claimed the first do; some metaphysicians have claimed the second do; and most metaphysicians either engage in discussions of the notion of ontological priority or have used such a notion in their discussions.[33] If they are right, how can I account for these views in my conception of metaphysics?

The first subject matter is not difficult to fit into metaphysics as I have conceived it. What is usually discussed in metaphysical analyses of free will and determinism is whether the will of persons is free or determined when persons act. Within my conception of metaphysics, the study of this issue would involve a study of the relations of the categories free, will, person, and determined, as well as any others that are directly or indirectly related to these provided at least some of these are among the most general categories. It is not the task of the metaphysician to establish whether President Clinton's veto of a particular bill passed by Congress was a free or

---

32. See, for example, Kant, *Critique of Pure Reason*, A225, B273, and A598–599, B626–627, pp. 243 and 504–505.

33. Gorman, *Ontological Priority*.

determined act. But it may be the job of the metaphysician to establish whether the categories of free and will can be put together with the category person. Naturally, this is an oversimplification of the issue, but I hope it serves to illustrate my point.

With respect to knowledge, the situation is more complicated. How can I say that knowledge can be a category studied in metaphysics when knowledge seems to be the province of epistemology?

It is one thing to study the conditions under which knowledge may occur and another to study the category knowledge. The study of the conditions under which knowledge can occur is the province of epistemology. And, indeed, the very understanding of what knowledge is, that is the formulation of its proper definition, also falls within epistemology. It pertains to epistemology not only to establish under what conditions I can know that P but also whether knowledge is, say, justified true belief. The categorization involved is specialized.

For metaphysicians, on the other hand, the questions are different. Metaphysicians want to know whether knowledge is one of the most general categories and, if it is not, how knowledge fits within the most general categories and is related to them. Is knowledge individual or universal, physical or nonphysical, a quality or an event, and so on, if indeed these categories are the most general ones?

With respect to ontological priority, the answer is not difficult. Ontological priority is a category because we predicate 'ontologically prior' and its correlate, 'ontologically posterior,' of all sorts of things. As a category, then, ontological priority is studied in metaphysics. We must determine whether it is one of the most general categories and, if it is, we must describe it and establish its relationships to other most general categories. And if it is not one of the most general categories, we must establish how it fits into the most general categories and determine how it is related to them. Naturally, if ontological priority is one of the most general categories, then it is part of the metaphysician's task to establish how less general categories are related to it, which is, in effect, to use ontological priority in the construction of a view of how all categories stand in relation to each other.

Finally, we come to an objection which is perhaps the most in tune with much contemporary philosophy. It could be formulated in terms of modernity by arguing that my view is a thoroughly modern one and thus, like all views based on the assumptions of modernity developed by the Enlightenment, it fails to take account of the precarious character of our knowledge. Modernity assumes that our views can be final, rigid, objective, and theoretical.[34] The fact is that no knowledge we can have is final, the ways in which we parcel the world are imprecise, the objectification of the world is misleading, and our conceptions are dependent on praxis rather than the reverse. A conception of metaphysics such as I have proposed falls right into the modernist program. This is why it is either impossible[35] or must be supplemented with something else.[36]

This objection is based on the assumption that all categories are final, rigid, objective, and theoretical. But this assumption is unwarranted. There is nothing in the notion of category, as we shall see in chapter 9, that requires it to have the mentioned conditions. To force these conditions on it is more of the kind of reductionism which is responsible for much confusion in metaphysics and against which I shall argue in chapter 9. There are some categories that have the characteristics mentioned, but there may be others that do not and one cannot know this until one has examined them. Moreover, even if all categories had such characteristics, our experience of them, by contrast, is always limited, perspectival, and historical. This objection fails to take into account the distinction between categories and our views, that is between categories and what we know about categories. We may hold a view, say a certain proposition, which is true or necessary, but this does not mean that our knowledge of the proposition is certain. Truth and necessity are features of propositions; certainty is a feature of how we hold propositions. Therefore, it is possible to have various degrees of certainty with respect to a proposition which is true or necessary. As many philosophers have pointed out, it is questionable whether we can hold any proposition with absolute certainty.[37] As humans, we should not expect to have views which transcend our condition. Our knowledge is necessarily conditioned by who we are, when, and in which circumstances. There is always a distinction between the truth of a view we hold and the certainty with which we hold it.

Our job as metaphysicians, then, is never complete, even when the views we hold are in fact true, for our certainty concerning those views and our grasp of them is conditioned and even tenuous. There is no end to metaphysics because the understanding that humans

---

34. Habermas, *Postmetaphysical Thinking*, pp. 36, 50–1.
35. Ibid.
36. Desmond, "Being, Determination, and Dialectic," p. 763.
37. Broad, "Critical and Speculative Philosophy," pp. 88–89.

can have of categories is always incomplete and partial and must be reestablished by every age, culture, and individual person.[38] Metaphysics is an ongoing and never-ending enterprise, with no claims to finality. Human experience is too limited to allow us to claim anything else.

The view of metaphysics I have proposed, then, is not modern in the bad sense the term has acquired in certain contemporary philosophical circles. Nor is it logocentric in the sense that it neglects the role of practice in theory building or ignores the practical origin of our views of the world. Indeed, it is for metaphysics to determine the relation of categories such as practical to categories such as view, theoretical, and metaphysical, opening the door to various oppositions concerning these relations and, thus, avoiding the charge that it condemns metaphysics to an unwarranted logocentrism.

The same could be said against the charge of totalizing. Yes, metaphysics seeks to develop a complete view, to fit the categories found in our experience into a whole that makes sense, but this whole, this total picture if you will, must always be regarded as limited and partial. It is not a totality but a mere attempt at a totality. Metaphysics does not have to be totalizing.[39] Metaphysics can be the study of categories and still be engaged in a continuous process of questioning.

In short, I hope to have made a convincing case that my conception of metaphysics accommodates most of the studies in which metaphysicians have engaged throughout the history of the discipline. Beyond some general remarks about method, however, I have not explored the question of how metaphysicians are able to access the object they study and thus formulate their views. Undoubtedly, this is an important question concerning the discipline, but one that is best left to epistemology. For us, a more pertinent issue concerns the status of categories. Before I turn to it, however, I would like to say something about reduction. The reason for what might appear to be a detour is that it is a misguided attempt at reduction that leads to various mistaken views of categories and of the nature of metaphysics.

---

38. Ibid., p. 97, although Broad goes too far in saying that we have no grounds for preferring one metaphysical system over another.
39. Habermas disagrees in *Postmetaphysical Thinking*, pp. 34–39.

CHAPTER EIGHT

Reduction

In chapter 9, I claim that it is an attempt at reduction which is largely responsible for the misguided positions I describe as realism, conceptualism, and nominalism in metaphysics. Before I lay out the claim in detail, then, it should be useful to clarify the notion of reduction and to point out the aims pursued by those who use it in metaphysics.

Although there has been considerable discussion of reductionism in this century, the discussion has tended to gravitate toward certain contexts to the exclusion of others. For example, considerable attention has been devoted to the empiricist attempt to reduce physical objects to phenomena, or, to put it differently, to the translation of statements about physical objects into statements about mental phenomena. Likewise, there has been substantial discussion of attempts to reduce the mind to the body (or vice versa), logical principles to psychological laws, moral principles to social customs, qualities to quantities, theoretical entities to observable entities, and so on, although these efforts have not gone unchallenged.[1] There are certain areas of metaphysics, semantics, and axiology, however, where reductionism often plays a role but that role has not been examined to any great extent.[2]

---

1. For approaches which have been characterized as reductionist, see: Loar, *Mind and Meaning*, and Parfit, *Reasons and Person*. For explicit challenges to reductionism, see: McGinn, *The Subjective View*; Davidson, "Mental Events"; and Blackburn, "Moral Realism."
2. Strawson is one of the exceptions. *Analysis and Metaphysics*, pp. 17–28, 45–47.

There is not always, moreover, a clear understanding of reduction. Indeed, often there are both conflicting implicit and explicit views which vitiate its discussions, creating confusion and ambiguity. Therefore, my aim in this chapter is to clarify the notion of reduction, in order to pave the way for its use in the chapter that follows. My main point there will be that the reductionist tendency in metaphysics has unfortunate implications that, ironically, defeats the purposes for which it is used. The impact of what I say concerning reduction is epistemological, even though much of what I say has to do with metaphysics and logic.

Although discussions of reductionism tend to be technical, this discussion will not be. The use of technical terminology in discussions of reductionism is advantageous within narrow disciplinary parameters, such as the philosophy of science and the philosophy of mind. But a similar procedure cannot be followed when the discussion extends beyond the narrow confines of a subdiscipline or area of study. Because this book deals with metaphysics considered in general, I have tried to refrain from the use of jargon parochial to particular branches of philosophy.

I. The Intension of 'Reduction'

In trying to understand reduction, we do not receive much help from etymology. The term 'reduction' comes from the Latin *reductio*, which meant a teaching or bringing back, a restoring. The verbal form *reduco* had similar meanings, although in later Latin its use was extended and included the sense of producing some shape, quality, condition, and so on. But none of this is very helpful in understanding reduction. For further help we can turn to ordinary language. And here the initial problem we encounter is the enormous variety of uses of the verb 'to reduce.' When these various uses are examined, however, it appears that they fall into the following formal structures:

1. to reduce X

2. to reduce X of Y

3. to reduce X to Y

Examples of all three are easy to come by. Consider 1. We speak of reducing forest fires, hydrocarbons, life, smog, weight, disease, and so on. Similarly with 2, we speak of reducing the price of vegetables, the number of colds we get per year, the size of our waists, the density of paint, and so on. And, as frequently, with regard to 3, we say we reduce several questions to one, chaos to order, nature to laws, days to hours, ionic copper to metallic copper, a man to tears, and a woman to poverty, among many others.

Upon closer examination, however, it appears that the formal structures of 1 and 2 may be actually the same. Indeed, 1 looks like an elliptical version of 2, for all the examples given of it may be expanded without change in meaning into the form of 2; and the examples of 2 may be expressed elliptically, without the loss of meaning, into the form of 1. It is the same to reduce forest fires, hydrocarbons, life, smog, weight, and disease, as to reduce the number of forest fires and hydrocarbons, the amount of life and smog, the pounds one weighs, and the number of diseases humans suffer. In like manner, it is the same to reduce the price of vegetables, the number of colds we get per year, the size of our waists, and the density of paint as to reduce the vegetables, the colds we get a year, our waists, and the paint. There are cases in which a particular expression might sound odd or unclear. This may be the case, for example, with the expression 'to reduce the paint.'[3] But, taken in context, the expression would be understandable. All of this supports the view that 1 is an elliptical version of 2. Therefore, we may conclude that the actual formal structures in which 'to reduce' is used are in fact two rather than three, namely:

2. to reduce X of Y

3. to reduce X to Y

Further examination reveals, however, that 2 may itself be an elliptical version of 3. For reducing the price of vegetables is nothing but in fact to reduce one price to another; reducing the number of colds is to reduce one number to another; reducing the size of our waists is to reduce one size to another; and so on. So, in fact, although at the outset it appeared as if there were three different formal structures which statements expressing reduction could take, upon analysis it turns out that there is only one:

3. to reduce X to Y

---

3. Indeed, the expression appears odd in English, but is quite ordinary in Spanish, for example.

Now, because 'to reduce' is a verb that expresses an action, reduction appears always to imply an agent. But one may question whether in fact it does, for 'to reduce' is frequently used passively in the following ways:

4. X is reduced

5. X of Y is reduced

6. X is reduced to Y

These expressions, unlike the ones we have been examining thus far, do not seem to presuppose an agent. Could not one argue, for example, that X is reduced by itself, that X of Y is reduced by itself, or that X is reduced to Y by itself, or alternatively, that the reductions in question are the result of processes which involve no agents? Consider the case of purely natural processes in which the size of an epidemic is reduced due to causes which do not involve agents. And the same could be said about the reduction of the number of rain showers that fall in an area in a year, or the reduction of a certain metal to another.

There is also an active use of the verb 'to reduce' which does not seem to presuppose an agent. Consider the statement, 'Water reduces to hydrogen and oxygen.' The formal structure in question is as follows:

7. X reduces to Y

This active use of the verb and the passive uses mentioned earlier indicate that reduction does not presuppose an agent in all cases. If one wished to defend the view that, in spite of this evidence, reduction always presupposes an agent, one would have to show that these expressions can and must be translated into other expressions which indicate the existence of an agent or they do not indicate cases of true reduction. Thus, one might argue that 'X reduces to Y' does not express a case of reduction but should be translated as 'X is composed of Y,' for example. And one might argue that the passive uses mentioned, again, should be translated into statements which do not indicate reduction. For example, 'Wine is reduced to vinegar' means simply that wine has changed into vinegar.

In short, the thrust of this response is to point out that the ordinary uses of 'to reduce' entail various notions, some of which are either not appropriate or detract from the effort to formulate a clear, consistent, and unambiguous notion of reduction as involving agents. If my task in this book were to come up with an effective theoretical formulation of reduction, and I wanted to defend the view that reduction presupposes an agent, then I would have to meet those challenges. But this book is not about reduction in general; it concerns only the use of reduction in metaphysics. And, insofar as metaphysics as we know it is carried out by humans, and reduction in it is a result of human activity, I need not engage in a protracted discussion of whether all reduction involves agents, for clearly, reduction in metaphysics presupposes an agent.

I shall call the agent responsible for the act of reducing, the "reductive agent" or "agent of reduction." I shall call that on which the reductive agent acts, the "reductive subject" or "subject of reduction." And I shall call that toward which the reduction aims, the "reductive object" or "object of reduction."

Even though reductive statements share a basic formal structure, there are important differences among them. This is evident from the various examples provided earlier in passing. The examples given involved the reduction of:

1. several questions to one

2. chaos to order

3. nature to laws

4. days to hours

5. ionic copper to metallic copper

6. a man to tears

7. a woman to poverty

To these we could add the following, some of which have also been mentioned:

8. time to space

9. jargon to plain language

10. an argument to standard syllogistic form

11. certain things to their former shape

12. a building to rubble

13. civilization to barbarism

14. person to explaining the situation

15. water to wine

It should be obvious from even a cursory examination of this list that many more, and different, examples could be added. But the ones provided should suffice for my limited purpose, which is to illustrate certain subcategories of the formal structure 'to reduce X to Y.' The first of these subcategories is one in which Y is the effect of a cause acting upon X which results in a change. Cases 2, 5, 6, 7, 11, 12, 13, 14, and 15 fall into this subcategory. For example, case 2, the reduction of chaos to order, involves a cause which acts on chaos to bring about order. This is the sort of thing Plato's *Demiurge* does when he imposes the forms on primeval matter. Another obvious case is 12, namely, the reduction of a building to rubble. In this instance, something such as a wrecking ball, acts as a cause that changes the building into rubble. Cases 13 and 15 can be analyzed in the same way. But there are some differences worth noting with 5, 6, 7, 11, and 14. The main difference with 5 and 11 is that the change brought about by the cause does not affect the reductive subject but only certain features of it. To reduce certain things to their former shape (case 11) is to effect a change in their features—there is no change of X to Y. Likewise, when I reduce ionic copper to metallic copper, I still have copper; what has changed are some features of the copper.

Cases 6, 7, and 14 are also different. In these cases, again, there is no change of the subject of reduction or in the features. In cases 6 and 7 the changes are of states. That a man is reduced to tears (case 6), means that he has been changed from a state in which he is not crying to one in which he is. And the reduction of a woman to poverty (case 7), is a change from a state of nonpoverty to one of poverty. Case 14 is also different insofar as the change concerns the initiation of an action rather than a change of features or states. That a person is reduced to explaining a situation means that something causes the person to engage in the action of explaining. But neither the person, nor her features or states, are changed.

From this analysis it does not follow that there are no other kinds of what I will from now on call "causal reduction." Indeed, one could easily think of cases in which this kind of reduction applies to relations, times, and so on. I have restricted myself to the kinds and examples provided for the sake of brevity and because the discussion of additional kinds and examples would not have contributed further to the clarification of the issues raised in this book.

The most important thing to note in the cases of reduction examined is that in all of them there is some kind of change. Something changes into something else. In some cases the subject of reduction is changed into the object of reduction; in other cases the change applies to the features and states of the subject of reduction; and still in other cases it involves the initiation of actions. In all cases something that was there ceases to be what it was in order to make room for something else, is transformed into something else, or an action is initiated.

By contrast, cases 1, 3, 4, 8, 9, and 10 seem to be on a different footing altogether. The reduction in these cases does not entail changes of the sort mentioned. Rather, these cases seem to involve the production of something distinct from the reductive subject, its features, states, or actions. Consider example 1, the reduction of several questions to one. This reduction does not involve a change in the questions, but rather the formulation of a new question which is regarded as equivalent to the set of original questions in some respects and is also considered more useful or better in others. Something similar may be said about 10, the reduction of an argument to standard syllogistic form. For the original formulation of the argument is not altered even though a new formulation of it, which follows standard syllogistic form, is used in its stead. Case 9, the reduction of jargon to plain language, and case 4, the reduction of days to hours, involve the production of translations of a sort. In case 9, the reduction consists in the production of a linguistic formula equivalent in meaning to the reductive subject but which has certain advantages over it, such as accessibility to a greater audience, clarity, elegance, and so on. The reduction of days to hours involves the translation of certain temporal measure, namely, days, into an equivalent temporal measure, that is, hours. We have, then, two systems of measuring or counting and the use of one in place of the other. Case 3, the reduction of nature to laws, entails the use of certain relations in the understanding of nature. This reduction does not involve a change in nature, but the formulation of certain principles which help us understand the way nature works.

None of these cases poses serious difficulties of interpretation. Case 8, however, does. The main difference between it and the other cases examined is that the other cases are all cases of ordinary-language use, whereas the expression 'to reduce time to space' is technical, an instance of scientific parlance. As such, its meaning is a matter of theoretical stipulation. This case in fact is of the same sort as those found in the philosophical literature in which authors speak of a reduction of mind to matter, qualities to quantities, thoughts to sensations, and so on. For the moment let us set it aside.

Let me summarize what we have learned concerning reduction from ordinary-language use and its analysis. We have found that there are two general kinds of reduction. In one, a change occurs in the reductive subject, its features, or states, or there is the initiation of an action. In the other, nothing like this is the case. Instead, we have the production of a reductive object distinct from the reductive subject. In both cases, the resulting object—whether it be a changed reductive subject or an entirely new entity—takes the place of the reductive subject for particular purposes. In cases where the reductive subject is changed, this is clear, for there is no longer that subject as it was. But even in cases where the reductive subject is not changed, the reductive object takes its place for the purposes which motivated the reduction in the first place. For example, when several questions are reduced to one, it is the one question that is put to use. Likewise, when jargon is reduced to plain language, or an argument is reduced to standard syllogistic form, it is the plain language and the argument in syllogistic form that are used.

Two points seem to follow from these remarks. The first is that reduction always entails some kind of replacement.[4] In the case of causal reduction the replacement is absolute in the sense that the reductive subject is treated as if it had ceased to be what it was and had become something else: water becomes wine, chaos becomes order, and so on. In the case of the second type of reduction, the replacement is relative because the reductive subject is treated as if it continued to be what it was, but some other object takes its place in certain contexts. For the assessment of validity, for example, the argument in standard syllogistic form takes the place of the original formulation of the argument. Likewise, hours, rather than days, might be used in contexts where measuring in terms of hours is more convenient than measuring in terms of days.

A second point suggested by what has been said is that reduction always entails some kind of evaluation in which the reductive subject is judged less valuable in some sense, or for some purpose, than the reductive object.[5] This is clear in the second kind of reduction. For the

---

4. Cf. Feyerabend, *Realism, Rationalism and Scientific Method*, pp. 44–5.
5. Charles and Lennon put this in terms of "privileging." *Reduction Explanation, and Realism*, p. 5.

assessment of validity, it is *better* to use arguments in standard syllogistic form than arguments which have not been put in that form. The choice of an hour as temporal measure rather than a day indicates the *preference* of one over the other for particular reasons. And the same point can be made with respect to causal reduction. The reduction of water to wine implies a comparative evaluation of water and wine in the context in which the reduction takes place.

Apart from replacement and the kind of evaluation we have discussed, reduction might appear at first always to involve decrease.[6] That it involves decrease in some cases is quite obvious. In case 1, several questions are reduced to one, for example. But even a superficial consideration of the other cases cited earlier reveals that decrease is not always, indeed not even frequently, involved in reduction. The reduction of days to hours, for example, involves increase rather than decrease in number. The same could be said of case 12, where a building is reduced to rubble, for rubble seems to be a plurality of sorts and thus more than one building. And one often speaks of "reducing something to its components," which seems to imply a change from one to many. Moreover, most of the cases cited earlier involve neither decrease nor increase. In case 5, the reduction of ionic copper to metallic copper, and in case 15, the reduction of water to wine, there appears to be no question of increase or decrease. And the same may be said about many of the other cases of reduction discussed.

The classical formulation of one common kind of reduction used by philosophers of science claims that reduction always involves a derivation of one theory from another.[7] This is generally recognized today as too narrow an interpretation of reduction. Some reduction does not entail derivation.[8] There are cases in which reduction involves the replacement of a theory by another which cannot be derived from it because the replaced theory is considered to be completely wrong. For derivation to take place the replaced theory must be regarded as being right in some sense. If it were regarded as completely wrong, then there would be an exchange and the elimination of one theory rather than a deduction

---

6. Ibid., p. 2.
7. Nagel, *The Structure of Science*, pp. 339, 352. See also Oppenheim and Putnam, "The Unity of Science as a Working Hypothesis."
8. Dupré, *The Disorder of Things*, p. 98. See also Smith, "Modest Reductions and the Unity of Science," p. 32, and Feyerabend, *Realism, Rationalism and Scientific Method*, pp. 55 ff.

of one from the other.[9] Consider the case in which physicalism is reduced to phenomenalism and vice versa. These two views are incompatible with each other and, therefore, one could hardly claim that one can be derived from the other.

In short, reduction involves both ontology and axiology. It involves ontology insofar as all reduction involves a replacement of something by something else; it involves axiology because the replacement is based on an evaluation of what is more effective or appropriate in achieving a goal whose accomplishment is desired; that is, value claims are made on behalf of one kind of entity (e.g., matter) as opposed to another (e.g., mind). This does not mean, however, that reduction applies only in ontology and axiology. Reduction involves ontology and axiology but it may be applied in at least five different areas, depending on the nature of the reductive subject. In ontology, reductive subjects are things, entities, beings, or realities. Thus, we say that a thing or a being is replaced by something else. This reduction is ontological because it concerns the way the world is and not the way we think, speak, or value it. In epistemology by contrast, the reductive subject is knowledge. Thus, we say that the knowledge we have about this or that is to be replaced by the knowledge of something else. This reduction is epistemological and not ontological insofar as it concerns the knowledge we have of the world rather than the way the world is.

Some present-day philosophers might claim that this kind of distinction is either unintelligible or worthless. It is unintelligible because the only thing we can know is what is given in experience and, thus, it makes no sense to speak of entities apart from what we know about them. Indeed, even if one were to grant that this is not so, and thus that it makes sense to speak of a world independent of our experience, the distinction would be worthless, for we have access to that world only through experience.

My response to these arguments is that claims about a world independent of our experience are different from claims about the experience we have of the world. Consequently, we must understand the difference between these claims in order to assess their truth value. I have more to say about this later.

---

9. But not everyone agrees. See Charles and Lennon, *Reduction, Explanation, and Realism*, p. 12. The classical conception of reduction is in fact narrower than it should be. For Nagel, for example, reduction is always a kind of explanation of one theory in terms of another, whence the requirement of derivability. *The Structure of Science*, pp. 337, 338.

In logic, reduction applies to concepts and thus concerns neither the way the world is, nor the knowledge we have of it. In this case, again, there might be some protests from those who do not distinguish between logic and ontology or between logic and epistemology.[10] To those who reduce concepts to the way we think of things, one could give an answer similar to the one which was given to those who wish to obliterate the distinction between ontology and epistemology. Whether the concept of a thing is no more than what we think of the thing or not, is a matter of debate among philosophers. Thus, whether we take one or the other view of this matter, a distinction between the two should be kept for methodological reasons if nothing else. With respect to the other matter, the answer may not be so easy, for even those who wish to distinguish between ontology and logic accept that logic is a reflection of ontology: The concept of a thing reveals in fact what the thing is.[11]

In linguistics, the reductive subject is language or parts of language. Thus, we speak of reducing linguistic expressions to some other expressions. The claim, then, is about linguistic entities rather than realities found in the world, our knowledge of these realities, or the concepts of these realities. Of course, one could say that language is part of the world and, therefore, that linguistic reduction is no more than a kind of ontological reduction. I have no quarrel with this view. But the important differences between language and the world may justify regarding linguistics as something separate from ontology and, therefore, regarding linguistic reduction as a separate category from ontological reduction.

Finally, in axiology, reduction applies to values. And again, there may be some who wish to subsume this category under one of the others listed, but to do so entails more than just a statement to that effect, for values seem to occupy a different level in our experience from the levels already mentioned. Thus, a justification of such a move would be in order.

We can summarize what has been said in the following formulas:

Reduction in ontology:	Entity X is reducible to entity Y.
Reduction in epistemology:	Knowledge of X is reducible to knowledge of Y.
Reduction in logic:	Concept X is reducible to concept Y.

---

10. Cf. Quine, *Word and Object*, § 33, p. 161
11. Or at least this is what it is expected to do. Strawson, "Reply to Jorge J. E. Gracia," pp. 113–14.

Reduction in linguistics: Expression 'X' is reducible to expression 'Y.'

Reduction in axiology: Value X is reducible to value Y.

All these formulas are interpreted versions of the general claim that "X is reducible to Y." But it is important to distinguish them because these various kinds of reductions do not apply under the same conditions. In ontology, for example, the reduction claimed applies to beings, whereas in epistemology it applies to knowledge, and so on. These various kinds of reduction are not only distinct, but they do not follow from each other necessarily. It may be the case, for example, that an entity, say a table, is reducible to its components, say its legs, and so on. But it does not follow from this that knowledge of the table is reducible to knowledge of its components or vice versa. Someone may have knowledge of the components of a table and yet have no knowledge of the table.

Of course, this may not always apply. One could argue that when one concept C is reducible to another concept C', the things to which C refers are also reducible to C'. For example, one could claim that the concept of brother is reducible to the concepts of male and sibling taken together precisely because a brother is nothing but a male sibling. But this may not always be so.[12] In short, we need to keep in mind that ontological, epistemological, logical, linguistic, and axiological reductions are not necessarily equivalent and, therefore, that claims of such reductions need not be equivalent. These various kinds of reduction are related in various and complex ways which need to be kept in mind if claims about different kinds of reduction are not to be confused.

Still, this is not enough; there is something else at play here that needs clarification. When philosophers speak of reduction, they often speak of it as applying to theories. They say that reduction is a relation between explanatory theories.[13] Now, a theory is a human construct, a conceptual construct if you will, expressed in language. And if this is so, it would appear that both the reductive object and the reductive subject are, after all, conceptual or linguistic entities. If a theory is what we say or think about X, then reduction involves the replacement of one way of speaking or thinking about X by another way of speaking or thinking about X. In short, contrary to what I

---

12. Strawson, "Analysis, Science, and Metaphysics," p. 313.
13. Charles and Lennon, *Reduction, Explanation, and Realism*, p. 3; Nagel, *The Structure of Science*, p. 338.

have claimed, reduction seems to apply only to concepts (or thoughts) and linguistic entities. So, which view is correct? Both, for these views refer to different things.

It is true that, in all reduction carried out by humans in an area involving human knowledge, there must be either linguistic or conceptual replacement, for theories are ways in which we think and they are expressed in language. But these theories can be about different things and thus the claims they make are not always about the ways we think or the ways we speak. When philosophers replace physicalist language by phenomenalist language, for example, their claim is not about language, but about the nature of the world; they claim the world is phenomenal rather than physical in nature or the world is composed of phenomena rather than physical objects. Hence, one can say that all reduction involving human knowledge entails conceptual or linguistic replacement and at the same time hold that the reduction in question refers to entities, knowledge, or value.

At the beginning I made clear that these different kinds of reduction depended on the character of the reductive subject. In ontology, the reductive subject is an entity; in epistemology it is knowledge; in logic it is a concept; in linguistics it is an expression; and in axiology it is a value. In the examples, however, I proceeded as if in fact the reductive objects were always of the same kind as the reductive subjects: In ontology, entities; in epistemology, knowledge; in logic, concepts; in linguistics, expressions; and in axiology, values. But the character of the reductive subjects and the objects are not always the same. Indeed, in philosophy perhaps the most common reductions are precisely those that involve subjects and objects of different characters: entities are reduced to concepts; values to entities, and so on.[14] It is important to keep this in mind, especially when we apply what we have learned here to the topic of this book.

II. Aims of Reduction

Because I am speaking primarily of reductions that are products of human agents who pursue goals, it is appropriate to ask about the aims of reduction. Why is it that human agents engage in reduction?

---

14. For example, Strawson accuses Quine of reducing "commitments to entities" to "canonical notation." *Analysis and Metaphysics*, p. 45.

To ask about the aims of human agents in a philosophical context is always risky for at least two reasons. The first is that this kind of inquiry would seem to be more a province of psychology than of philosophy. The second reason it is risky is that human aims can be so varied and idiosyncratic that no matter how many are identified, there is always the possibility that another could be found. Why bother looking for any, then?

My concern, however, is not with psychological motives, but with what might be called "philosophical" aims, and the range of those aims is not as varied and idiosyncratic as psychological motives. According to a position defended earlier, at least in one important sense philosophy is a certain view that one takes of something or other. As such, then, a philosophical aim must be understood as the aim of producing, developing, and supporting such a view. So, if reduction is used in philosophy, its aim must be to help produce, develop, and support such a view. Therefore, it turns out that the aim of reduction is fundamentally epistemic. The aims of reduction in philosophical contexts generally have to do with our views and the support for them, that is, with knowledge. This, however, is the most general philosophical aim. If one looks closer at cases of reduction, it is not difficult to see more specific ones. There are at least five of these which stand out.

The first is perhaps the most obvious: The Principle of Parsimony, often known as "Ockham's Razor," is a well-known rule in the history of philosophy and in general is applied to all human explanations. The simpler and more economical explanation, the one that involves the least number of entities and complications, is always the one that should be favored, provided it accounts for the same facts.[15] Indeed, this principle is embedded in the nature of explanations because explanations involve, at least in part, making plain what is not so, and this process depends on simplification and in replacing a large number of items by a lesser number, so that the picture one has is clearer and more understandable. Naturally, reduction is helpful here, for much reduction involves the replacement of a greater number by a lesser number.

The aim of simplification and economy is methodological, but there are other aims based on other considerations. Much reduction is aimed at bringing consistency into a view or system of thought by eliminating those factors which threaten such consistency.[16] Like-

---

15. Some times this has been put in terms other than simplicity. Charles and Lennon, *Reduction, Explanation, and Realism*, p. 1.
16. Parfit, *Reasons and Persons*, pp. 210, 240.

wise, a desire to have a proper foundation in experience leads some
to a reduction which allows the replacement of nonobservable elements by observable ones.[17] The fourth factor is bringing out the constituents of a thing. This is guided by the belief that a good
explanation or understanding consists in telling us about the elements that make up something.[18] Thus, to explain or understand X
is to produce a description of Xs components.[19]

Finally, we must not forget ideological factors. By this I mean
considerations which have to do with the defense of certain views or
positions to which a prior commitment has been made.[20] I call these
factors "ideological" because they do not have to do with the understanding, development, or explanation of a view, but with the defense of a view whose value is no longer questioned.

From what has been said, it is clear that the use of much reduction in philosophy is claimed to be justified, apart from ideological
considerations, on the basis of four well-known principles: the Principle of Parsimony, the Principle of Acquaintance, the Principle of Non-
Contradiction, and the Principle of Analysis. It is not my business in
this book to defend particular formulations of these principles, but it
should help to give some idea of what they propose. The following formulations may serve that purpose:

Principle of Parsimony:	In the development of theories, explanatory entities should not be multiplied beyond necessity.
Principle of Acquaintance:	The terms used in theoretical descriptions should refer to entities with which one is directly acquainted.
Principle of Non-Contradiction:	No theory is acceptable which includes or implies a contradiction.
Principle of Analysis:	Knowledge of X is best achieved through knowledge of Xs components.

17. Allaire, "Bare Particulars," n. 2; Hochberg, "Ontology and Acquain-
    tance," p. 53.
18. Dupré, *The Disorder of Things*, p. 88.
19. Moore, "A Reply to My Critics," p. 663; Russell, *Logic and Knowledge*, p.
    192. If the analysis is linguistic, then it involves translation. Strawson,
    "Analysis, Science, and Metaphysics," p. 312.
20. Charles and Lennon, *Reduction, Explanation, and Realism*, p. 6.

These four principles are widely accepted not only by philosophers, but also by practitioners of other disciplines of learning. Their
acceptance, however, is generally qualified. Rather than absolute
rules of procedure, they are usually taken as desiderata which, in context, may not be rigorously applied. Indeed, philosophers are well
aware of their limitations. Nor should it be overlooked that their value
has been assessed differently by different philosophers and that not
all of these principles are regarded as being on the same footing.

Consider the Principle of Parsimony. It is widely accepted that
theories should be simple and economical. But what 'simple' and
'economical' mean depends very much on the particular context in
question. For a theory must do justice to all the facts it tries to explain and thus cannot distort them for the sake of simplicity and
economy. This means that it is not always the case that the simpler
theory is the best theory.[21] The Principle of Parsimony does not function as an absolute and single rule of philosophical explanation; it
needs to be taken in context and used in conjunction with other principles. Whence the use of the term 'should' rather than 'must' in the
expression 'entities should not be multiplied beyond necessity.'

Something similar applies to the Principle of Acquaintance. It is
a desideratum of theoretical descriptions that they refer to entities
which are directly observable. But in some cases such desideratum
needs to be subordinated to more pressing needs or desiderata. Indeed, in some cases observation is prevented for various reasons and
that should not preclude theoretical speculation, conjecture, and
formulation.

In contrast with the Principle of Parsimony and the Principle of
Acquaintance, it would appear that the Principle of Non-Contradiction is to be regarded as absolute both in the sense of being non-
negotiable and in the sense of being non-contextual. A theory which
includes or implies a contradiction must be regarded as false; and
contradictions cannot be explained away in terms of context.[22] Yet,
even here matters are not so drastic. A theory which appears to contain or imply a contradiction may still be useful and even correct on
the whole because the apparent contradiction may be the result of a
lack of a proper distinction among certain terms, for example. It

---

21. Quine, "On What There Is," p. 17.
22. Alternatively, one could speak of consistency, or of having various levels
    of theory "hang together." Smith, "Modest Reductions and the Unity of
    Science," p. 37, n. 18.

would not do, then, simply to throw out every theory which appears to contain or imply a contradiction without further study and investigation. Ideally, of course, the finished product should have no contradiction, but no theory is ever a finished product. So, we must use the Principle of Non-Contradiction, like the other two principles we have examined, as a desideratum, a guiding rule which we aim to apply in context, but not as an inflexible criterion.

The last principle, the Principle of Analysis, is the most controversial of the four mentioned. Whereas few philosophers would question the ultimate validity of the Principle of Non-Contradiction and the Principle of Parsimony, there are many who question the validity of the Principle of Analysis. The reason for the skepticism surrounding this principle rests on the view that a whole is nothing more than its components—that is the reason why the knowledge of the components yields knowledge of the whole. But this view is widely disputed by those who hold that a whole is more than its parts and that, as such, has properties which the parts do not have and thus cannot be explained merely on the basis of the properties of the parts.[23]

In short, then, although all four principles are widely accepted and muster considerable rational support, they cannot be applied across the board. For this reason, even if the use of reduction is justified on the basis of these principles, one cannot be sure it is always warranted.

Reduction is used as a means to develop theories intended as solutions to problems which arise in particular disciplines. It occurs in both the social and the natural sciences and is particularly prevalent in philosophy. The reason that it is so in philosophy is that philosophers have a larger field to cover. Their field includes all human experience and, therefore, they are more likely to employ reduction to bring order and unity into it. In metaphysics, the use of reduction is especially commonplace for obvious reasons.

---

23. Frondizi, *The Nature of the Self*, pp. 148–73.

CHAPTER NINE

Realism, Conceptualism, Nominalism

I have argued metaphysics is the part of philosophy that studies categories, although its specific aim varies with respect to the most or the less general categories it studies. But, is this sufficient? Can I rest by saying this about metaphysics? The answer is negative, for so far I have left the key notion of category unexplained. In order to be able to speak about categories, I adopted a provisional understanding of them as whatever is expressed by terms or expressions, simple or complex, that can be predicated of other terms or expressions. This formula, however, does not appear to tell us all we need to know about categories. How, then, are we to understand categories?

This question is important not just because it makes clear that the understanding of metaphysics I have provided thus far may be inadequate. It is also important, in particular, because it ties the question concerned with the proper understanding of metaphysics to perhaps the most consistent issue associated with the discipline, the issue of whether metaphysics studies things, concepts, or words; that is to say, it raises the question of realism, conceptualism, and nominalism.

I should perhaps clarify the way I use 'realism,' 'conceptualism,' and 'nominalism' before I go any further, because these terms are much used and abused in the literature. In order to make my use clear in this context, let me distinguish four senses of the terms. The first sense occurs in the context of universals. In this context there are various ways in which the terms are used, but in all cases they refer to the degree of reality, that is, to the ontological status, attributed to universals.[1] Usually, realism is taken to be the view that universals are something outside the mind in addition to being something in the mind.[2] There is such a thing as cat outside the mind in addition to the individual cats, Chichi and Minina, and the concept cat through which I think about them. Conceptualism is the view which regards universals as having ontological status only in the mind. Cat is nothing but a concept or some such thing in the mind. In the world outside the mind, there are only individual cats, such as Chichi and Minina. And nominalism is the position which identifies universals with words and nothing but words. Cat is merely a word and not a concept or anything extramental.

The second sense of the terms occurs in an epistemological context. In this context, realism holds that we are able to know reality, that is, the ways things are outside the mind;[3] conceptualism or, as it is sometimes put, phenomenalism, holds that we have access only to our concepts or to phenomena, that is, the ways we think about things;[4] and nominalism holds that we are able to know only words, namely, the ways we speak about things.[5] These positions are concerned with knowledge, that is, with our epistemic relation to an object. According to realism, taken in this sense, I can know Chichi; according to conceptualism, I can only know my concept or mental representation of Chichi; and according to nominalism, I can only know the word, or my use of the word, 'Chichi.'

The third use of the terms takes place in reference to metaphysics. Independently of the ontological status of universals and the access we may have to the object of knowledge, this position holds a view concerning the proper object of metaphysics. Realism holds that it is reality, that is, the ways things are outside the mind, that metaphysics is intended to study;[6] conceptualism holds it is con-

---

1. See Gracia, *Individuality*, ch. 2.
2. I have defended a different use in ibid., p. 60, according to which realism is the view which holds that only universals exist.
3. Pols, *Radical Realism*, p. 1.
4. Hume, *A Treatise of Human Nature*, I, 1, 1, p. 1, and I, 3, 1, pp. 69–73.
5. Quine, *The Roots of Reference*, p. 35.
6. Aristotle, *Metaphysics* 1003a24, p. 731, and other texts to which reference was made in chapter 3.

cepts, that is, the ways we think;[7] and nominalism holds it is words, that is, the ways we speak or write.[8] Accordingly, the realist thinks metaphysics studies, for example, God; the conceptualist holds that metaphysics studies the concept we have of God; and the nominalist thinks metaphysics studies the word 'God' and how we use it.[9]

Of course, someone may want to object that the third alternative is not really different from the first or the second, because the ways we speak or write are either ways in which things outside the mind are or are ways in which we think; words are extramental or intramental. But I shall ignore this complication because those who adhere to the nominalist position usually want to contrast it with both realism and conceptualism as I have described them. In any case, this position would still be different from realism and conceptualism in general insofar as metaphysics would study a particular kind of extramental or intramental thing.

The fourth sense of the terms concerns the nature of what there is. Realism in this sense maintains that there is a world of things existing independently of the mind.[10] Conceptualism holds only mind-dependent entities, that is, concepts, exist. Because many of those who adhere to this position identify mind-dependent entities with ideas, this position is generally known as idealism.[11] Finally, there are those who appear to speak as if nothing but names (or language, or texts) exist.[12] These could be called "nominalists," but they have also been called "textualists."[13]

It should be obvious that these senses of the terms 'realism,' 'conceptualism,' and 'nominalism,' are closely connected. Indeed, if

---

7. Strawson, *Individuals*, p. xiii; Ockham, "On the Notion of Knowledge or Science" (*Expositio super viii libros Physicorum*, Prologus), p. 11, and "The Possibility of Natural Theology" (*Reportatio* 3, 8), pp. 112–113.

8. Quine, *The Roots of Reference*, p. 35.

9. For Tugendhat, these different ways of understanding give us three disciplines: ontology, philosophy of consciousness, and linguistic analysis. *Logisch-semantische Propädeutik*, pp. 7 ff.

10. Moore, "Proof of the External World," pp. 127 ff.

11. Berkeley, *Three Dialogues*, p. 58. The empirical variety is also known as phenomenalism. Dummett, *The Logical Basis of Metaphysics*, p. 4.

12. The recent origin of this view can be traced to statements by Heidegger. *An Introduction to Metaphysics*, p. 11.

13. Rorty, "Nineteenth-Century Idealism and Twentieth-Century Textualism," p. 139.

the proper object of study of metaphysics is the ways things are outside the mind, then it would be natural to expect that we are properly equipped to know them.[14] Not all philosophers, however, have agreed to this inference. Kant, for one, did not. According to him, pure reason is naturally intended to know something it is not equipped to know, namely, noumena or things-in-themselves.[15]

The connection between the first senses of the terms and the second is also easily drawn. For those who are realists concerning universals, for example, it is also natural to hold that we do know the ways things are outside the mind,[16] but not everyone who is not a realist concerning universals need reject that we know the ways things are outside the mind. Ockham, for example, was a conceptualist in the first sense, insofar as he rejected any ontological status for universals outside the mind, but he was a realist in the second sense insofar as he held that we have access to reality and that what we know are not merely the ways we think, speak, or write.[17]

On the other hand, for those who hold that we have no access to reality, it is natural to identify the object of metaphysics with concepts, phenomena, or words, and to deny any ontological status to universals outside the mind.[18] Other connections among these different uses of the terms could be indicated, but it should not be necessary.

For our present purposes, it is only the third set of senses mentioned that is pertinent, because our concern is with the object metaphysics studies, not with the status of universals, the knowledge we can have, or what there is. Moreover, it should be clear that what has been said thus far about metaphysics and its object does not commit us to a particular stand in this matter: it does not tell us whether many pre-Kantians were right in holding that the object of metaphysics consist of the ways things are outside the mind; whether Kant was right and the object of metaphysics consists in the

---

14. Aristotle and his followers, for example, maintain that powers and faculties are appropriate to their objects. Aristotle; *On the Soul* 418a3–7, 428b18 and 26, 429a15–25, 430a2–10 and 20, 431a1, and 431b25–30; pp. 566–567, 589–593, and 595. Aquinas, *In III Sententiarum* d. 24, q. 1, a. 1, p. 374b, and *Summa theologiae* 85, 1c.
15. Kant, *Critique of Pure Reason*, preface to first edition, p. 7.
16. Armstrong's whole project in *Universals and Scientific Realism* appears to be predicated on this view.
17. Ockham, "Five Questions on Universals" (*Ordinatio* 2, 4), pp. 128–29.
18. Quine, "On What There Is," pp. 9–17.

ways we think; or whether contemporary linguistic philosophers are right who identify the object of metaphysics with the ways we speak or write. The reason it does not is that this position does not specify the status of categories; it does not tell us whether categories are to be taken as ways in which things are outside the mind, as ways in which we think, or as ways in which we speak or write. If metaphysics studies categories and categories are ways in which things are outside the mind, then metaphysics is to be understood realistically; if metaphysics studies categories and categories are merely ways in which we think, then metaphysics is to be taken conceptualistically; and if metaphysics studies categories and categories are merely the ways we speak or write, then metaphysics is to be understood nominalistically.

The issue amounts, then, to the status of categories. Do categories have some status outside the mind, or are they merely ways of thinking or speaking and writing? The answer to the question concerning whether metaphysics is a discipline of the real, the conceptual, or the nominal, consequently, depends on the ontological status of categories.

A. Ontological Status of Categories

The positions one may adopt with respect to the ontological status of categories closely mirror the positions one may adopt with respect to the ontological status of universals. Moreover, their strengths and weaknesses also mirror many of those adopted with respect to universals. This should not be surprising, for I have understood categories here as whatever is expressed by a term or expression which is predicable of some other term or expression, and a universal is usually described as that which is predicable of many.[19] I have discussed the ontological status of universals to some extent elsewhere,[20] in the context of individuality, but there are certain peculiarities of the discussion as it applies to categories which preclude me from simply referring the reader to that discussion of universals. Besides, as we shall see later, categories are not exactly the same as universals. For these reasons, I must provide a somewhat detailed discussion of the ontological status of categories here. I should point

---

19. Aristotle, *On Interpretation* 17a38, p. 43.
20. Gracia, *Individuality*, ch. 2.

out, however, that many of the references found in footnotes to this section are to texts which speak of universals rather than categories. The points made therein, however, apply to categories as well.

Note that, although most categories can have members, some do not. The members of the category universal are cat and three, among others; of the category woman are Mary and Jane, again among others; of the category the last Dodo bird is the last Dodo bird; and so on. But the category nothing, for example, has no members, and the same holds true of the category square circle.

Moreover, categories can be members of categories. For example, the categories cat and dog are members of the category species. This raises the question of the category "category" being a member of itself, but I shall postpone the discussion of this issue until later in the chapter. For now, let us concentrate on the issue of the ontological status of categories.

Philosophers have proposed many positions with respect to the ontological status of categories, but there are at least seven that merit discussion here.[21] They identify categories with transcendental entities, immanent constituents of things, similarities, collections, concepts, types, and tokens. Let me discuss each of these separately.

1. Categories as Transcendental Entities

Categories are sometimes conceived as entities which have an ontological status other than that of the entities which are part of the world we encounter in our experience. Usually, those who subscribe to this view regard categories as more real, or at least superior in some sense, to the entities found in our experience. For some, these categories are self-sustaining, whereas others believe they are sustained by a superior mind. In either case, categories are conceived to be outside the world of human experience and do not depend on it in any way.

The first position is often attributed to Plato. According to it, categories are abstract, absolute, immutable, and necessary entities on which the world of human experience depends. Whether Plato held such a view is a matter of scholarly debate and immaterial for

---

21. There are others also. Grossmann, for example, conceives categories as entities of some *sui generis* kind. *The Categorial Structure of the World*, p. 5.

our present purposes.[22] For us, it is important only to understand that, according to this viewpoint, categories transcend the world of human experience in the sense that they are somehow outside it. This position divides the world into two: the real world, composed of categories, and the world of appearance, composed of the entities we encounter in experience. The persons and trees we encounter in our experience are only shadows of the truly real entities, personhood and treeness, which transcend experience.

The second version of this position was common among medieval authors; they placed Plato's "forms" in God's mind, turning categories into divine ideas.[23] Ultimately, categories are not self-sustaining, according to this position, for they require a supporting reality. Nonetheless, they are outside the world of human experience and, thus, transcend it.

The strength of both versions of the transcendental position lies in the support they lend to knowledge and morality. Knowledge finds a secure object, insulated from the casualties of experience and varying circumstances. The category triangle is what it is and does not undergo change. Whether there are any triangles in the world of human experience or not, or whether we think of triangles or not, does not affect the category. The requirements of triangularity are independent of the world of human experience and the minds that have access to it. True knowledge of triangularity is secure in the immutability of its object. Moreover, the same applies to the founding notions of morality. Justice is independent of the actions of human beings, what human beings may think, and the circumstances in which actions take place. Based on those notions, moral principles become transcendental realities immune from changing opinions.

The view that categories are transcendental entities encounters many difficulties. Most of these difficulties have to do with the relation that categories have to their members. For example, one may ask, how can one explain the relation between the category black

---

22. Plato did not use the Greek counterpart of the English term 'category' to refer to these entities, but I believe we are not far off by identifying the entities Plato had in mind with what I call "categories" here. See, for example, *Republic* 507 ff., pp. 742 ff. There are not many philosophers today who argue for a Platonic theory of categories in this sense, but there are nonetheless self-described Platonic or Platonistic theories. See, for example, Chisholm, *A Realistic Theory of Categories*.
23. Augustine, *Eighty-three Different Questions*, pp. 79–80.

and the black color of my cat's coat? If black is real and the black color of my cat's coat is unreal, then how can the black color of my cat's coat be a member of the category black? Indeed, the category, we are told, is immutable and necessary, but the black color of my cat's coat is both mutable and contingent, so how can the category apply to the color of my cat's coat? In short, how can a category categorize its members when it is so different from them?

Again, it does not make any sense to say that black is more real than the black color of my cat's coat, for I am directly acquainted with the black color of my cat's coat, but my relationship with black is mediated through the black color of my cat's coat I see. Black is rather distant, so how can it be said that black is more real than the black color of my cat's coat? From experience, it is the black color of my cat's coat that is more real to me.

Aristotle, and even Plato himself, raised many of these objections against this view in the context of what has come to be known as the problem of universals.[24] But there is one particular objection which is especially pertinent for us in the case of categories. Given the very general conception of category I have proposed, nothing and nonbeing are categories. But, if this is the case, and categories are transcendental realities more real than the world of experience, it follows that nothing and nonbeing are real, and this leads to the contradiction that nonbeing is being and nothing is something. It also leads to the conclusion that nothing and nonbeing are more real than the things and beings we experience, and this makes no sense whatever.

This objection is important, because it reveals the root problem of the view we have been discussing. That problem arises because the identification of categories with transcendental realities is too narrow. There are categories that are not and cannot be transcendental entities, even if one were to accept that there are some categories that are transcendental. Hence, it is inaccurate to regard all categories as transcendental entities.

2. *Categories as Immanent Constituents of Things*

A way to avoid some of the difficulties of the transcendental view of categories is to make categories immanent constituents of

---

24. Aristotle, *Metaphysics* 990b1 ff., pp. 706 ff.; Plato, *Parmenides* 129 ff., pp. 923 ff.

things.[25] Categories are no longer posited as entities outside the world of human experience, but rather as constituents of that world. In this way, one can argue that we are acquainted with them. Black is not something outside the black things I perceive, for example, but something in those things.

This position, however, does not take care of all the objections encountered by the transcendental view of categories. For example, like the transcendental view, it fails to accommodate the category nothing. If it turns out that categories are immanent constituents of things, then nothing must be an immanent constituent of things and, therefore, turns out to be something. But this is untenable.

There are other difficulties with this position which are unrelated to the ones encountered by the transcendental position. For example, this position does not explain why members of a category vary in the degree in which they are categorized by the category.[26] The transcendental position does not have this problem, because according to that view the possession of features is always mediated by the relation to the category and that relation presumably could be affected by other factors. Thus, a transcendental category may apply to two things differently owing to the circumstances in which each of the things in question finds itself. My neighbor's cat, Lucky, may not be as sharp as my cat, Chichi, because its participation in sharpness is affected by its situation; there is a logical or ontological distance, if we may be allowed the metaphor, between sharpness on the one hand and Lucky and Chichi on the other, and that distance explains the different degrees of sharpness which Lucky and Chichi have. However, if, as those who favor the immanentist position hold, there is no distance between a category and its members, because categories are immanent in their members, then how can we explain that in Chichi there is a greater degree of sharpness than in Lucky?

This argument is not conclusive, however, for immanentists can answer that categorial degrees are possible in things because categories are by nature subject to degrees. For example, one could say that certain metals can get hotter than other kinds of materials because of the very nature of the metals in question. Although iron and water can both get hot, iron can be hotter than water. Something

---

25. Aristotle seems to think of what I call "categories" here as immanent entities in *Metaphysics* 1017a23, p. 760.
26. Armstrong, *Universals and Scientific Realism* 1, p. 76.

similar could be said about degrees of heat in the same thing at various times.

Another way in which immanentists may answer is by saying that degrees in a category simply indicate subcategories of a more general category. Thirty degrees Celsius and twenty-five degrees Celsius are two subcategories of the more general category heat. It is misleading, then, to talk about degrees of the category of heat in metal and water; there are no categorial degrees, but rather different subcategories of heat in metal and water.

A different objection argues that, although members of categories change, neither the category itself nor all its members need be affected and thus the category cannot be in the things it categorizes. Consider, for example, the color of the paper on which I have printed these words. I can take the paper and put it in the fire, and with the burning of the paper its color will also be destroyed. Yet, neither the color of the paper I have not yet used, nor the category itself of the color, is affected. This leads to the conclusion that the category of the color of the paper is neither something in the paper nor the same thing in all the papers that have that color.

One way to answer this objection is by introducing a new notion of the unity of categories. According to this notion, to say that X and Y are one with respect to S does not imply that S is one in the same sense in which X is one or Y is one, so that the destruction of X or Y does not entail the destruction of S. That is to say, the identity of a category cannot be destroyed because this language does not apply to categories.[27] To claim that the color of a paper burns when the paper burns is to confuse the issue and beg the question. It is to confuse the issue because categories are neither like their members nor part of them; color is not like the color of this paper nor part of the color of this paper. It is to beg the question because it treats categories as members of categories and that claim is precisely what is at stake.

This may in fact be so, but in arguing in this way the immanent position of categories has compromised itself. It has done so, because it has accepted a distinction between categories and their members such that it becomes impossible to argue that the first are immanent in the second.

A third objection argues that the position taken by immanentists does not solve anything, for it does not identify what categories

---

27. Ibid., p. 112.

are in their members. This leads to the two objections raised before as well as to others. For the position to be effective, it must specify what sort of thing categories are and how categories are related to their members and to other categories.

According to a fourth objection, the immanent view cannot account for empty categories, for it holds that categories are constituents of their members and empty categories have no members of which they can be constituents. So, either categories are not constituents of their members or there are no empty categories. The first alternative contradicts the position and the second is unacceptable.[28]

Finally, perhaps the most significant objection that can be raised against the immanent position is that it is, like the transcendental position, too narrow; it leaves out some categories which it must include. Consider the case of the category transcendental entity. If all categories were immanent constituents of the things which make up the world of experience, then a transcendental entity, which by definition would be a thing outside the world of human experience, would be a constituent of that world because it is a member of a category and all categories are immanent. This contradiction arises because the understanding of categories as immanent constituents of things is too narrow and does not take into account the fact that there are categories which are not, and cannot be, constituents of the things which are part of our experience.

3. Categories as Similarities

A way to try to avoid the difficulties of both the transcendental and immanent positions is to argue that categories are similarities.[29] There are two versions of this view. The first maintains that the similarities in question are dependent on knowers and, therefore, are mental phenomena of some sort. Understood in this way, this position is not different from a position I discuss later, and so I leave its consideration for that time. The second position is close to the views so far discussed, because it regards categories as somehow independent of knowers. This position has an answer to the question raised in the third objection to the immanent position: categories are similarities among the members of the category. It explains how a and b

---

28. This objection was suggested to me by Micheal Gorman.
29. See Plato, *Parmenides*; Price, *Thinking and Experience*, ch. 1; Butchvarov, *Resemblance and Identity*; and Armstrong, *Universals and Scientific Realism* 1, ch. 5.

belong to the same category by noting that there is a similarity between a and b. Lucky and Chichi belong to the category cat because Lucky and Chichi are similar in catness. But does this help? In the final analysis, it does not.

Many of the difficulties encountered by this position stem from the interpretation of similarity as a relation. One of the well-known arguments against relations is that relations lead to an infinite regress.[30] Consider the relation R between a and b, which I shall express as aRb. If R were other than a and b, then R could itself be related to a and to b through two other relations, call them $aR'R$ and $bR'R$. But these relations also would be related to a, R, and b. The relation of R' to a would be $aR''R'$, the relation of R' to R would be $RR''R'$, and the relation of R' to b would be $bR''R'$. And the same would have to be said, *mutatis mutandis*, about the new relations and so this process could be repeated in infinitum, which precludes the achievement of the goal—an effective explanation. Now this can be applied to similarity. If the similarity S between a and b is other than a and b, then S can itself be considered similar, with a similarity S' to a, for example, so that $aS'S$. But this process can be repeated. Of course, one could argue that S cannot itself be similar to a, and therefore there is no S' and, consequently, no infinite regress. But this response is not generally accepted as an adequate answer to this difficulty.

Apart from the difficulties which arise from the side of relations, there are other difficulties as well encountered by the view of categories as similarities. One source of these difficulties has to do with the fact that, regardless of what similarity is, and whether it is a relation or not, if similarity is not a mental, knower-dependent phenomenon of some kind, it must be either something in the things that are similar or something outside the things that are similar. But to say that it is something in the things that are similar is to revert to a form of immanentism, and to say that it is something outside the things that are similar is to end up either in an infinite regress or in transcendentalism. And neither of these alternatives is acceptable, as we have already seen.

Moreover, like the previous positions discussed, this view has problems accounting for degrees. For one thing, it appears that the degrees of similarity among things are infinite, so does this mean that the number of categories is infinite? Perhaps this is not an in-

---

30. Plato uses it in *Parmenides* 132b, p. 926: see also Weinberg, "The Concept of Relation," p. 90.

surmountable objection, but it is certainly an irritant to a theory motivated in great part by parsimony.

A final objection I shall mention argues that the understanding of categories as similarities is too narrow, for there are categories which do not involve any similarity. Two examples should suffice to illustrate the point. Consider those categories which, like the last Dodo bird and divinity, have only one member or categories such as nothing which have no members. These categories do not posit any similarity because similarity requires at least two things.[31]

4. Categories as Collections

Another view holds that categories are collections. 'Collection' is a traditional term that goes back to the Middle Ages and may be taken as a synonym of 'aggregate.'[32] In contemporary jargon we could use the terms 'set' or 'class' to refer to it.[33] Another, now rare version of this position, goes back to Plato and identifies categories with wholes of which the members of the category are parts.[34] There are, therefore, three different versions of this position, depending on whether categories are understood as aggregates, classes (or sets), or wholes. The first of these views reduces a category to the group of members that belong to the category. Cat, for example, turns out to be the same as the group of cats. The modality of the members the group includes may vary. It may include past, present, and future cats, or it may include only past and present cats, or it may include all cats, whether real or possible, and so on. But these distinctions are immaterial for us. The relevant point is that, according to this view, a category is nothing but an aggregate.

For those who identify categories with classes or sets, however, the situation is different, insofar as they usually make a distinction

---

31. I assume that similarity is not the same as identity, although the term 'similar' is sometimes used in that sense. One way of distinguishing similarity from identity is to stipulate that similarity requires more than one thing, whereas identity applies only to one thing. I have discussed these notions in *Texts*, pp. 48–9.

32. John of Salisbury ascribes this position to Joscelin, in *Metalogicon* II, ch. 17, p. 115; Abelard argues against it in "Glosses on Porphyry," p. 35.

33. See Williams, "The Elements of Being"; Wolterstorff, "Qualities"; Sellars, *Science, Perception and Reality*, pp. 282 ff; Price, *Thinking and Experience*, ch. 1; and Stout, "The Nature of Universals and Propositions."

34. Plato, *Parmenides* 131, p. 925.

between a mere aggregate on the one hand and a class or set on the other. If the distinction is not made, then the position amounts to the aggregate position. If a distinction is made between aggregates and classes (or sets), then the position has a different turn as we shall see.

The version of the position which understands categories as wholes is similar to the view that holds they are aggregates, insofar as the category is the sum of its members and nothing more. But it differs from it in that the members differ with respect to the category.

One often noted advantage of the view of categories as collections is that it avoids positing categories as empirically inaccessible. By identifying a category with a collection of things in the world of human experience, it appears to avoid some of the problems faced by the positions discussed earlier. But this view faces difficulties of its own. Some of these have to do with particular formulations of the view.

The version of the view that identifies categories with wholes fails miserably. The difficulties arise because categories seem to apply fully to each member of the category. A cat is fully cat. But it is not clear that parts have or must have all the features of wholes. A piece of a pie, for example, does not have the same weight and size of the whole pie.

The version of this view that identifies categories with classes or sets, and then goes on to distinguish those from aggregates encounters difficulties related to the nature of sets and classes and to the proliferation of entities. If classes and sets are something other than their members, what has the proponent of this view gained over the views we have discussed before? She still has an entity that is other than the members of the class or set. And if classes and sets are nothing more than the members of which they are composed, then this position has to answer to the general difficulties to which I turn now.

Apart from the specific difficulties which apply to particular versions of the view, there are others of a more general nature that apply to all versions of it.[35] One of these is related to predication. If categories are predicable and, as this view maintains, they are collections, we may ask how a collection may be predicated of its members. If cat is equivalent to the collection of all cats, what sense can

---

35. Armstrong, *Universals and Scientific Realism* 1, pp. 29–34.

we make of the sentence, 'Chichi is a cat'? For, according to this view, understood strictly, this sentence would be equivalent to the sentence, 'Chichi is a collection of all cats.' Collections do not seem to be predicable of their members and, thus, it makes no sense to say that categories are collections.[36]

The proponents of this view might wish to answer to this that 'Chichi is a cat' is not properly translated by 'Chichi is the collection of all cats,' but by 'Chichi is a member of the collection of all cats.' In this way the difficulty seems to be avoided.[37] In fact, however, it is not avoided, for it is one thing to say that something is a member of a collection and another to say that something is of one sort or another. The sentences, 'Chichi is a cat' and 'Chichi is a member of the collection of all cats' are not equivalent in meaning. The first one tells us something about what Chichi is; that is, it appears to specify some property or feature of Chichi, whereas the second only identifies Chichi as a member of a group. If the defenders of this position were to rejoin at this point by saying that it is not just any group that is in question, and therefore that belonging to the group of all cats implies having some feature or property, then, of course, the original point of the objection is granted, namely, that what is important and determining is not that Chichi belongs to a group but that, after all, she is a cat. Accordingly, we cannot claim that 'Chichi is a cat' is analyzable into 'Chichi belongs to the group of all cats,' but rather vice versa.

One way to dispute this entire line of reasoning is to argue that it is based on a mistake concerning predication. Predication affects only words, but the objection presented assumes more than words are at stake, because it speaks of the predication of a collection. In reality, what is predicated is a word such as 'cat,' which means or refers to the collection of cats.

I do not believe this is a serious retort, because in fact the same point can be put in a different way, without referring to predication. This position would have to hold that the features of things which constitute the bases of their belonging to a certain category are the result of grouping. But this seems contrary to experience. Things are grouped into collections because they have certain features which are similar to or, depending on one's interpretation, are the same as the features of other things in the collection, not vice versa. A thing is part of the collection of all cats because the thing in question is a

36. Abelard, "Glosses on Porphyry," p. 35.
37. Lejewski, "On Lesniewski's Ontology."

cat. To say that an animal is a cat because the animal belongs to the collection of cats provides no satisfactory explanation; it is like putting the cart before the horse.

Another general objection that might be raised against the position that cats are collections is related to the one just mentioned. It indicates that if this position were correct, then one would have to expect categorial changes with changes in membership.[38] Any time the population of cats changed owing to births or deaths, for example, the category cat would have to change. This is so because a category is nothing but its membership.

One way of answering this objection is to identify collections only with groups of possible members, understanding 'possible' as we did earlier in this book, that is, as including the actual and the nonactual which is not contradictory.[39] This solves the problem of changes in membership, but it does not solve other problems, for how can possible members be distinguished as members of the collection except by reference to some feature or other?

In short, the explanatory power of this position is inadequate. If collections are arbitrary, then the view does not explain how the nonarbitrary character of categories can be derived from them. But if collections are not arbitrary, then their nonarbitrary character must be due to a condition that the members of the collection meet, and it is the latter that should be regarded as the foundation of the category, not the collection.[40]

One may want to say, of course, that there are categories which are collections. The categories aggregate, set, and class, one might want to argue, are good examples. But, even if one were to grant this, not all categories can be understood as collections. The problem with the view that regards them as such is that it has a too narrow conception of what a category is. In this, it commits the same error as the other views we have been discussing.

5. Categories as Concepts

A popular view among philosophers is to regard categories as concepts which are in turn expressed by linguistic signs.[41] By con-

---

38. Wolterstorff, *On Universals*, ch. 8.
39. Armstrong, *Universals and Scientific Realism* 1, p. 37.
40. For a different line of defense, see Wolterstorff, "Qualities," pp. 206–08.
41. For Arnauld, who had Aristotle in mind, categories are confused, arbitrary ideas. *The Art of Thinking*, pp. 42–45.

cept is meant something present in someone's mind. Thus, cat is regarded as a concept in someone's mind.[42] When we speak of it, we use the term 'cat,' or any other conventional (e.g., spoken, written, or even mental) sign, to refer to it. The concept is something individual in an individual mind, although it is used to denote many things. By denotation is meant that the term or expression used to express this concept can be predicated of various subjects in true sentences. For example, 'Minina is a cat,' 'Misifus is a cat,' 'Chichi is a cat,' and so on, where 'cat' is predicated of 'Minina,' 'Misifus,' 'Chichi,' and so on. What the mental reality is (i.e., the ontological status of the concept and its nature), is a matter of debate.[43] Apart from Behaviorists, who reject their existence altogether, some philosophers identify concepts with images, whereas others identify them with qualities, and still others conceive them as acts.[44]

Empiricists, like Hume, tend to think of a concept as an impression that has lost some of its distinguishing features and has thus become a somewhat vague image.[45] It is the vagueness or indistinctness that makes possible its application to many things. When I first perceive a cat, for example, I have a very strong and particularized impression of it, because all its peculiarities, or at least most of them, are present in my perception. But with time I forget some of these, making possible the association of this vague image, sometimes called "idea," with other similarly vague ideas of other cats. For empiricists, categories amount to these vague ideas.

Those who understand concepts as qualities of the mind argue that a concept is like a qualifying feature.[46] Just as red qualifies a

---

42. A concept in this sense is a mental event or phenomenon of some kind and not an intension. The notion of concept we are discussing here is narrower than the one discussed in chapter 2 of this book. Kant conceived categories, such as substance, as "pure concepts of the understanding." *Prolegomena*, § 39, p. 7. Locke conceived them as ideas; see *An Essay Concerning Human Understanding*, III, ch. 6, s. 13, vol. 2, p. 56. And Husserl spoke of them as "objective forms." *Logical Investigations* 6, § 58, p. 815.

43. Cf. Armstrong, *Universals and Scientific Realism* 1, p. 25.

44. Ockham, "Five Questions on Universals" (*Ordinatio* 2, 8), § 91, p. 230. Among those who reject them is Quine, *The Roots of Reference*, p. 35, and "On What There Is," pp. 2 ff. Concepts have also been conceived as dispositions, relations, states, and so on.

45. Hume, *A Treatise of Human Nature* I, 1, pp. 1 ff.

46. Ockham, "Five Questions on Universals" (*Ordinatio* 2, 8), § 92, p. 230.

red flag, so they say, the concept cat qualifies the mind which enter-
tains it. Using the metaphor of the wax and the seal, they explain
that the concept cat is like the shape imprinted by a seal on the
mind; the mind is likened to the wax. For those who hold this view,
and also identify categories with concepts, categories turn out to be
mental qualities.

Finally, there are some who understand concepts as mental
acts.[47] The concept cat is nothing more than the mental act whereby
one understands what it is to be a cat. There is no quality involved,
but only the act of understanding. Just as running is nothing but an
act of a runner, the concept cat is nothing other than the act of a
mind when it understands what a cat is. Consequently, for those who
understand concepts as mental acts, and categories as concepts, a
category must also be conceived as a mental act.

All these views about concepts have problems which also undermine the view that categories are concepts. The image view of concepts explains how we come to have vague ideas, but does not
explain the similarity among the ideas of various things and not of
others. That some ideas, and not others, can be associated together
seems to imply that those ideas, and the things for which they stand,
have some similarities that other things and ideas do not have. For,
not even contiguity—something which does not always operate
insofar as, for example, our perceptions of cats are not always spa-
tiotemporally contiguous—could explain this association and ultimate assimilation.

The view that holds concepts to be qualities must likewise account for their origin as well as for their generality. But the fact that
they must arise, according to this view, from the perception of particular things creates difficulties. How can cat be a quality informing
the mind and denote, as it does, any cat, when it is a quality of this
mind and it arose from the consideration of an individual cat? This
is not a question to which a satisfactory answer has been found.

Finally, the consideration of concepts as acts must explain how
concepts are stored and memorized, for it is not clear that acts can
be stored and memorized after they have ceased to be in operation.
Just as my act of writing these words stops, so the corresponding
mental act ceases. One could, of course, argue that concepts are not
acts in just this way, but rather dispositions to act in a certain way
or dispositions toward certain acts. But then the position amounts to

---

47. Ibid., § 86, p. 229.

the quality view, for in that case acts become more like features of the mind that predispose the mind to act in certain ways.

These are serious difficulties that must be resolved, if the stated views of concepts are to be maintained. There are too, however, difficulties that arise not in connection with the understanding of concepts as images, qualities, and acts, but with the understanding of categories as concepts. First, this view seems to fall into a serious confusion. It holds that categories are concepts and, therefore, that things like cat need to be understood as the concept cat. But this creates a problem, for the members of the category cat are cats, whereas the members of the category, concept of cat, are concepts of cat.[48] Categories cannot be identified with concepts, because concept itself is but one particular category. In short, the understanding of categories as concepts is too narrow, leaving out all sorts of things which are categories and are not concepts.

Another difficulty arises when one considers a universe with no knowers. In such a case, the universe could not contain concepts because there would be no knowers to have them, and thus, presumably, the universe would also lack categories. But it makes no sense to say that the universe would lack categories, insofar as the individuals in the universe would certainly have some features and as such would be members of the categories of entities with those features, even if there were only one entity with the features in question. Indeed, we need not go so far as to stipulate a case like the one mentioned. In our own natural world, it is generally acknowledged there was a time when no thinking beings existed (the existence of a supernatural being would not make a difference in this case), and yet the world was full of things belonging to categories—there were plenty of sticks and stones. Moreover, even now, we lack many concepts of things and their features and relations that exist. The part of the universe known to us is infinitesimal, and yet it would be completely absurd to say that only what we know exists. The concept view of categories, then, makes no sense unless the notion of concept is reinterpreted to mean something other than what is usually meant by it, and made completely independent of knowers.

These are not the only difficulties with the view of categories as concepts, however. Indeed, we may ask, if categories are concepts, and there are no categories which are not concepts, then where do our concepts come from? A realist conception of categories does not

---

48. Quine puts this point in terms of ideas, in "On What There Is," p. 2.

encounter this problem, because it also accepts the extramental reality of categories. But the present view must look for another answer, and yet none suggests itself easily. One way out is to try to explain how we form our concepts/categories in terms of some epistemic process whereby individual perceptions are transformed into categorial concepts. Hume followed this path, but earlier conceptualists, like Ockham, although puzzled by this problem, did not give any clear, let alone satisfactory, answer to it.[49] It is only with modern philosophy and particularly the British empiricists that this issue is explored to any depth.

Apart from the ways of understanding categories as concepts we have discussed, one could also interpret this view in a Kantian fashion. According to this line of interpretation, categories are rather like mental structures which are the preconditions of the concepts we form within experience.[50] Apart from making categories prerequisites of experience, this position restricts the number of categories. Cat and mother are no longer to be considered categories because they are given, as it were, in experience. But substance and relation are, because it is through them that we understand concepts like cat and mother given in experience.

This change, however, does not significantly improve the position, for categories continue to reside in the mind, even if they are not presented as phenomena and their number is small. Because of this, similar objections to the ones proposed can be used to undermine this view.

6. Categories as Types

The linguistic turn in philosophy has provided us with a still another alternative to the understanding of categories. They are taken to be types.[51] A type is to be contrasted with a token. Terms and expressions function as *types* if they can be placed both before and after the copula in a true identity sentence which says something about those terms and expressions, such as 'A is A.' In this case 'A' would stand for the type, and the sentence would mean that the universal A is the same as itself. Terms and expressions function as *to-*

---

49. Ockham, "Five Questions on Universals" (*Ordinatio.* 2, 6), § 112, p. 172.
50. Kant, *Prolegomena*, § 39, p. 71.
51. For the classical distinction between type and token, see Peirce, *Collected Papers*, vol. 4, par. 537. The discussion of types and tokens that follows is taken from Gracia, *Texts*, p. 11.

kens when they fail to meet the condition for types and, thus, cannot be placed both before and after the copula in a true identity sentence. In the example provided, it would be false that *A* is the same as *A* because the individual *A* at the beginning of the sentence is not the same individual *A* at the end.

The notions of token and type are subsumed under the notions of individual and universal. A token is an individual sign or text; a type is a universal sign or text. A text or a sign is a type because it is the sort of text or sign of which token texts or signs are instances, and a text or a sign is a token because it is a noninstantiable instance of a type of text or sign.[52] Tokens occur only once, but several tokens may belong to the same type. The notions of token and type, then, should not be used to apply to objects except in cases where those objects are semantically significant. By contrast, the notions of individual and universal may be used in connection with all sorts of objects. To speak of tokens, or individual texts or signs, and of types or universal texts or signs, is in effect to speak of the same things.

Today many philosophers make no distinction between universal and type, speaking of things, as well as signs or texts, as types. If one accepts this way of speaking, then the position concerning categories we are discussing must be understood to mean that categories are universals, but not necessarily that they are linguistic in any sense. The category color, for example, amounts to the universal color. But if types are understood in a more restricted sense, to refer to signs or texts, then the position must be understood as holding that categories are universal signs or texts. For example, the category color, then, would amount to the universal term 'color.'

Another way in which this position has been expressed is by saying that categories are predicates, when predicates are understood to be no more than type terms with meaning.[53] This is primarily a logical theory of categories that depends on the understanding of categoricity as predicability. Its roots go back to Aristotle. It has definite advantages over all the other views that have been discussed. For example,

---

52. I am using the notions of universal and individual defended in Gracia, *Individuality*, ch. 1, according to which an individual is a noninstantiable instance whereas universals are instantiable.

53. Abelard, *Dialectica*, pp. 69 and 112; Searle, *Speech Acts*, pp. 105 and 120. A more sophisticated version of this view argues that a category is a certain position in a non-absurd sentence. Ryle, "Categories," pp. 174, 180. See also Carnap, "The Elimination of Metaphysics," p. 68.

it avoids the difficulties that the understanding of categories as transcendental or immanent entities have. And it also avoids the psychologization involved in the concept view of categories.

Still, this position encounters serious difficulties. Perhaps the most disturbing is that it cannot explain the nonarbitrary character of predication. That predication is generally nonarbitrary is clear from the fact that we do judge certain predications to be true and others to be false. If I say that cats are barking animals, I am quickly corrected and told they are not; rather it is dogs that bark. But, if it is the case that predicates cannot be arbitrarily applied, then there must be bases for their nonarbitrary application. Consider the following example: If 'black' is predicated of 'X' nonarbitrarily, then either 'X is black' is true or it is false, and that entails that either X is black or it is not. But if categories are mere words and nothing else, then to say that X is black would not be saying anything about Xs color, but rather it would be saying something about words. On what basis, then, could the truth of the claim be established? The problem with the position that categories are types is that it can point to no basis of nonarbitrary predication if it wishes to maintain the purity of the position.

Of course, there are categories that are types. The word 'cat' is a type. But not all categories are types. The position that understands categories as types makes the same mistake that the other views we have discussed make: it identifies all categories with only one kind of category, and in doing so it becomes too narrow.

7. Categories as Tokens

This view understands categories as mere tokens.[54] If one makes no distinction between individual and token, then this position holds that categories are individuals, but not necessarily that they are linguistic in any sense. The category cat, for example, amounts to an individual, presumably this cat. But if tokens are taken in a more restricted sense, to refer to signs or texts, then the position holds that categories are individual signs or texts. For example, the category cat, amounts to the individual term 'cat' just printed on this page.

Both versions of this view are highly inadequate, for in both the distinction between a category and the member of a category col-

---

54. Roscelin is reported by Anselm to have held a position like this. Anselm, *The Incarnation of the Word* 1, p. 13.

lapses completely. Therefore, we cannot be given any sort of explanation why anything is such and such or belongs to such and such category. In fact, if categories are tokens, then it is not clear at all what things are. Consider, for example, the same type sentence written twice on a piece of paper: 'X is black' and 'X is black.' According to this view, the first instance of the sentence does not assert the same thing as the second instance, for the token predicate of the first is not the same as the token predicate of the second. Indeed, even the subjects are different because they are different tokens. But where do we go from here? Of course, token itself can be a category, but no member of this category can be a category.

8. Another Look at Categories

The positions that have been discussed fall roughly into three classes. Some are realist positions insofar as they identify categories with extramental entities. This is clearly the case with the first three views and one version of the fourth view discussed. Transcendental entities, immanent entities, collections, and similarities (when understood as nonmental) have an ontological status outside the mind. The fifth position discussed, by contrast, understands categories exclusively as mental entities of one sort or another. As such, this position may be characterized as a form of conceptualism, for categories, according to it, are found only in the mind. Finally, the last two positions discussed, which posit categories as types or tokens, may be characterized as nominalistic insofar as categories have only a linguistic status.

Each of these three kinds of view concerning categories yields a different conception of metaphysics. For realists, metaphysics studies extramental entities; for conceptualists, metaphysics studies mental entities; and for nominalists, metaphysics studies linguistic entities. Yet, we found that none of the positions discussed is satisfactory. Although they encounter various difficulties which arise from their particular idiosyncracies, they all have also one common problem, namely, all of them are too narrow; every one of them excludes from study some categories which have been regularly studied by metaphysicians. This gives us the key, both to the proper understanding of categories and the proper understanding of metaphysics. The source of the trouble has always been the attempt at unwarranted reduction. If we are going to find a satisfactory conception of metaphysics, we must avoid any illegitimate attempt to reduce categories to what they are not. My proposal is to do just that by conceiving categories in such a way that we are not forced to commit ourselves to realism, conceptualism, or nominalism. Before I explain how this is to be accomplished, however, let me briefly illustrate the difficulties involved in the reduction implied by realism, conceptualism, and nominalism.

A category is whatever is expressed by a simple or complex term or expression which is predicable of some other term or expression. Bachelor is a category because it is what the predicable term 'bachelor' expresses. Socrates, in contrast, is not a category because Socrates is what the proper name 'Socrates' expresses and the proper name 'Socrates' is not a predicable term. 'Socrates' can only function as subject in sentences, and when it occupies the third position in a sentence of the form 'X is Y,' the sentence in question is an identity sentence rather than a predicative one.

True predication requires that the conditions specified by the predicate be satisfied by what is expressed by the subject. Thus, 'mammal' is truly predicated of 'bachelor' only if bachelors are mammals. This means that the conditions specified by a term that expresses a particular category must be satisfied by the members of that category. In the pertinent cases for us, that is, cases of necessary or essential predication, the conditions are given by the category's definition. If the category bachelor is analyzable into unmarried and man taken together because these are the conditions specified by the predicate bachelor (bachelor is defined as unmarried man), then 'unmarried' and 'man' taken together must be truly predicable of the name of every bachelor. Likewise, if the category human is analyzable into rational and animal taken together, then 'rational' and 'animal' must be truly predicable of the name of every member of the category human. Of course, in cases of nonnecessary or nonessential predication this is not so. In 'The paper is white,' the conditions specified by the predicate are not given by the definition of 'white' and therefore the *definiens* cannot take the place of 'white' in the sentence. But this is not the kind of predication that is pertinent for us here.

All this means that if such categories as human or bachelor, for example, were concepts (i.e., if 'concept' were included in their definitions), then 'concept' would be truly predicable of the names of the members of those categories, say, of 'Socrates,' with the unwelcome result that Socrates would turn out to be a concept. Likewise if, the categories human and bachelor were words (i.e., if 'word' were included in their definitions), then 'word' would be truly predicable of the names of the members of those categories, say, of 'Socrates,' with the unwelcome result that Socrates would turn out to be a word.

In a similar way, if the categories hallucination and afterimage, for example, were extramental entities (i.e., if 'extramental entity' were included in their definitions), then 'extramental' would be truly predicated of the names of the members of those categories, say, 'Jorge's hallucination' and to be extramental would apply to Jorge's hallucination. But, of course, Jorge's hallucination is nothing outside his mind.

These examples illustrate that the exclusive understanding of all categories as words, concepts, or extra-mental entities is too narrow, for it involves an unwarranted reduction. It is a reduction because extramental entity, concept, and word are themselves categories, and thus the reduction of all categories to one of them is precisely the reduction of a broader category to a narrower one. This situation is comparable to one in which, all of a sudden, we would decide to narrow down the category animal to the category human, making all animals human. Extra-mental entity, concept, and word are all categories, and it will not do to say that all categories have to be one of these to the exclusion of others.

To this one could reply that my argument is fallacious because it fails to distinguish between categories and the set of conditions that apply to the members of categories. To say that categories are extramental entities, concepts, or words does not imply that the members of the categories are such. The category bachelor can be an extramental entity, a concept, or a word without its members necessarily being so, because the conditions that apply to the category do not apply to the members of the category. In short, bachelorhood is not a bachelor; it is only this or that man that is a bachelor.

This objection sounds quite formidable at first, but upon analysis it loses its force. Consider the example: Bachelorhood is not a bachelor. The use of the abstract noun to refer to the category already tips the scales in favor of the position on which the objection is based. For, although strictly speaking, the definition of bachelorhood should be no more than unmarried manness, one is tempted to define bachelorhood instead as, for example, the property of being an unmarried man, the concept of being an unmarried man, or a word denoting unmarried men. But, if rather than speaking about bachelorhood, we speak simply about bachelor, or about being a bachelor, then matters are quite different. For it becomes clear that the definition of bachelor is unmarried man, so that to be a bachelor is nothing more or less than to be an unmarried man. Indeed, 'bachelor' is predicable of 'Peter' because Peter is an unmarried man.

The definition of a category, then, is an identity sentence in which the predicate is interchangeable with the subject, and this predicate specifies the conditions that are satisfied by the members of the category. This is why both the subject and predicate in the definition of a category are predicable of the names of the members of the category. The definition of a category is not a predicative sentence. 'A bachelor is an unmarried man' is not like 'John is a bachelor.' The first says that to be a bachelor is the same thing as to be an unmarried man; the second, that John is the kind of thing bachelors are, namely, what is expressed by the predicate of the first sentence.

One source of the view that categories are exclusively words, or concepts, or extra-mental entities, and yet the members of categories need not be so, is a confusion between the two sorts of predication mentioned earlier: necessary or essential and nonnecessary or nonessential. Indeed, human can be a word or a concept, say, but this is not what being human is, and it is not what Socrates and other humans are said to be. Being human has nothing to do with being a word or a concept, that is, the category human has nothing *qua* the category it is, with these. This is why the members of the category are not words or concepts and also why word and concept tell us nothing about the category.

Now, the attempt to make categories something other than what is expressed by predicable terms and are used as conditions to be satisfied by the entities which the subjects of predicative sentences express, leads to problems. These, I hope, have been amply illustrated in the previous pages, when we discussed the difficulties involved in the conception of categories as transcendental or immanent entities, concepts, and so on.

But, then, how should categories be conceived and what kind of ontological status should we accord them? Before I answer this question it will be profitable to apply what was said in chapter 8 concerning reduction to the case of categories.

9. Reduction and Realism, Conceptualism, and Nominalism

I have claimed that the origin of the confusion and disagreement concerning whether metaphysics is about the ways things are, the ways we think about things, or the ways we speak and write about things is a too narrow understanding of the object of metaphysics. Because I have argued metaphysics studies categories, it is a narrow understanding of categories that is responsible for the problem. This narrow understanding is the result of the reduction of categories to certain subcategories. Category comes to be understood always to refer to the ways in which things are (as extra-mental entities), the ways in which we think about things (mental entities), or the ways in which we speak or write about things (linguistic entities). Realists adopt the first alternative and reject the others. And sometimes, indeed even often, adopt a much narrower view of the object of metaphysics, maintaining that it is only transcendental entities or immanent entities, for example, that metaphysics studies. Some go as far as to restrict the object of metaphysics to very narrow categories, such as the divine. Naturally, this approach, in its most extreme form, leaves out much that metaphysicians have studied in the past and excludes from the object of metaphysics the entire realm of thought and language. In less extreme forms, this approach does not forget about other categories such as thought and language, but when it deals with them it understands them as realities of the same sort as cats and dogs. The result is unfortunate.

Conceptualists do not do much better than realists. They choose for the object of metaphysics the category of the mental and sometimes even narrower categories within that, such as the category of phenomenon, for example. Again, this leaves out of the purview of metaphysics much that has been traditionally associated with it and makes conceptualism inadequate and easily vulnerable to various objections.

Finally, nominalists defend the third alternative: the object of metaphysics is language or even some subcategories of language, such as tokens or types. Again, this narrow understanding of the object of metaphysics, resulting from the reduction of its object to a subcategory or subcategories, does not do justice to the history of the discipline and has the weakness mentioned.

Realism reduces metaphysics to ontology, or a branch of ontology; conceptualism reduces it to logic, psychology, or the philosophy of mind; and nominalism reduces it to linguistics. But logic, psychology, the philosophy of mind, linguistics, and ontology and its branches are all disciplines concerned with specific categories and thus cannot provide us with the breadth of understanding metaphysics is supposed to provide. The relation of metaphysics to these disciplines is like that of metaphysics to other subdisciplines of philosophy. Metaphysics, by contrast to these specialized disciplines, studies the most general categories and the relation of less general categories to the most general ones.

The reduction of the object of metaphysics involves the replacement of one object by another. It also involves the rejection of the original object. Thus, like all reduction, the reduction of the object of metaphysics involves ontology and axiology—a change and a preference. The reduction, however, cannot be classified as ontological or axiological—or for that matter epistemological, linguistic, or logical. For the object that is rejected is, as we shall see, neutral with respect to these subcategories insofar as it can include categories of being, knowledge, concepts, language, and values.

As far as the aims that have moved those who engage in the reduction of the object of metaphysics, most of the ones discussed in chapter 8 seem to be at work in one way or another. The Principle of Parsimony is perhaps the one that, more than any other, motivates reduction. It is particularly evident in conceptualists and nominalists who often identify it explicitly as their goal: what can be explained with less should be explained with less. The emphasis on this principle is helped by the belief that reduction necessarily involves a decrease, although this is not necessarily the case. A reduction in the object of metaphysics is supposed to produce simpler and more economical theories.

The Principle of Acquaintance plays a major part in reduction for empiricists. Suspicious of any entities which are not observable, they often argue for realism, phenomenalism, or nominalism. In the first case, because they also believe they have access to objects outside the mind; in the second, because they believe we have access only to mental phenomena; and, in the third case, because they believe we are only acquainted with language.

The Principle of Non-contradiction appeals to most philosophers and, therefore, is widely used in metaphysics. The easiest way to deal with a contradiction is to give up one of its terms, and that can be done by reducing the term to something else. But this might not always be the wiser way out. Sometimes contradictions arise because of some deeper problems which require attention. In metaphysics, those who argue for realism, conceptualism, or nominalism, are often motivated by a desire to do away with contradictions generated by some of these positions. But they miss the fact that all three positions generate contradictions resulting from unsatisfactory analyses and unwarranted attempts at reduction.

Finally, the Principle of Analysis is used as a means to get at effective metaphysical explanations. Because the properties of wholes seem elusive, it is sought to reduce them to the properties of parts or, when that is not possible, to eliminate them altogether. But this is hardly a satisfactory solution. One should always be suspicious of any view which summarily dismisses what is given in experience in order to accommodate an abstract theory.

These are the reasons that motivate metaphysical reductions of the sort we have discussed. Now, let me turn to a proposal intended to avoid these unwarranted reductions.

10. Neutrality of Categories

If the problems we have indicated arise because of the misguided attempt at categorial reduction, the solution to the problem is to avoid categorial reduction. My proposal, then, is to respect the integrity of categories. *Each category, qua category, should be considered to be whatever it is, as determined by its proper definition, and nothing more,* for that is what the predicable term that names the category expresses. Accordingly, the category human is no more and no less than what is established by its definition, for the category human is nothing but what the predicable term 'human' expresses. Likewise, the category afterimage is nothing but what the definition of afterimage includes. And so on with other categories. We must not be deceived by the use of the expression 'category' placed in front of categories, or by the use of abstract nouns to speak about them.

This means that the very notion of category should be understood to be neutral with respect to whether categories are extramental kinds of entities, concepts, or words. Categories need not be understood exclusively as extramental, or conceptual, or linguistic, but neither are they to be considered not to be extramental, conceptual, or linguistic. If categories are conceived, as I have proposed, as what predicable terms express, then categories can be words, for some predicable terms express words, which is to say that the term 'word' is truthfully predicated of the terms that name them. The category, the English definite article, is a word for the sentences, 'The English definite article is a word,' and " 'The" is a word' are true. And there are categories that are concepts in the sense that they are mental entities, for there are some predicable terms that express concepts, which means that the term 'concept' is truthfully predicated of the terms that name them. The category afterimage is a concept in this sense, for it is true to say, 'An afterimage is a mental entity,' and 'What Mary saw when she closed her eyes after seeing a bright light is a mental entity.' And there are categories that are extramental, again because some predicable terms express something extramental, that is, the term 'extra mental' is truthfully predicated of the terms that name them. The category, Dodo bird, is extramental for I can truthfully say 'The Dodo bird is a bird that existed in the island of Mauritius many years ago.'

These particular categories are words, concepts, or extra-mental entities because the conditions specified by the terms 'word,' 'concept,' or 'extra-mental entity' are included in the set of conditions specified by their definitions. To be an English definite article is to be a word, to be an afterimage is to be a mental entity, and to be a Dodo bird is to be something outside the mind, even if no Dodo bird actually exists. Hence, whether a particular category is a linguistic, mental, or extramental kind of entity, should not be determined before an investigation of the category is carried out and we have arrived at a definition, or at least a description, of the category. And this is precisely the job of disciplinary studies.

To reduce all categories to words, concepts, or extra-mental entities is like trying to reduce all buildings to houses, all animals to cats, or all humans to human males. Indeed, to ask the question whether to be a category is to be a word, a concept, or an extra-mental entity is to ask an illegitimate question, for neither an affirmative nor a negative answer will do. The question has no answer because it is the kind of question that should apply to particular categories or members of categories rather than to category itself. One may ask whether Chichi is a word, or a concept, or an extra-mental entity, and one may ask the same of human, or the English definite article. But it makes no sense to ask whether all categories are words, concepts, or extra-mental entities. To do so would be like asking whether cats are black or not. Well, some are black and some are not, which means that being black or not being black are not part of the conditions of being a cat. Likewise, when asked whether categories are words, one could say some categories are words and some are not. The question, then, does not properly apply to category, but to this or that category, just as black or non-black do not apply to cat, but to this or that cat, for to be a cat does not prescribe a certain color. In this sense, to ask the question is to commit what Carnap called a "type mistake," that is, to presuppose that a type can apply to something to which it cannot apply.[55]

Categories considered *qua* categories, then, cannot, in virtue of being categories, be exclusively conceived as words, or concepts, or extra-mental entities. And the reason is that, as Ryle put it, there is

---

55. Carnap, "The Elimination of Metaphysics," p. 75.

not one kind of thing that all predicates signify.[56] Indeed, even the term 'object,' which I have used to refer to what metaphysics studies, is misleading when used to speak about categories. For object itself is a category and cannot be taken, prima facie, to encompass all other categories.[57]

In short, human is just human, and the category human is just human and nothing more or less. The addition of the term 'category' to 'human' in the expression 'category human' adds to human only the recognition that human is what is expressed by the predicable term 'human' and as such is different from Socrates, which is expressed by the non-predicable term 'Socrates.' Of course, in order to think and talk about human we use concepts and words. There is something in our minds when we think of human, be that an act, a quality, a state, or whatever, and this is the concept whereby we think of human. In addition there is the word 'human' (*humano* in Spanish, and so on) which we use to talk about human. But neither the concept nor the word are the same as what I think and talk about when I think and talk about human, namely, human.

Some philosophers, as we have seen, identify categories with concepts—human becomes the concept human. And some identify categories with words—human becomes the word 'human.' And they justify this identification by the use of the term 'category.' But this is not helpful, for even if we identify the category human with the word 'human,' or with the concept human, neither of these is the same as human, and it is things like human that are the concern of metaphysicians. My proposal, then, is to recognize that categories are whatever they are, as determined by their definitions, nothing more or less. But this does not preclude us from also considering the words and concepts we use to talk and think about them. The key to avoid confusion is to keep these separate. Of course, if one keeps these separate, it does not matter much what one calls them. I prefer to call concepts whatever is in the mind when we think about such things as human; words, whatever linguistic means we use to speak and write about such things as human; and categories, whatever we think and talk about when we think and talk about such things as

---

56. Ryle, "Categories," p. 180.
57. This was Meinong's mistake. He considered object to be the most general subject of study and, therefore, he must be understood to have taken it as the most general category. "The Theory of Objects."

human. Different terminological conventions make no difference as long as the distinction is preserved and we understand that the metaphysician's object is such things as human. Of course, in that object are included also concepts and words, and all sorts of other things, for those are also categories. The metaphysician is not interested in just the category human, but also the category concept of human and the category word 'human,' in addition to all other categories, in the way noted in chapter 7.

Metaphysical nominalists think that by identifying categories with words they have disposed with concepts and realities, but they have not. For not all terms they use in predication express words. They have succeeded rather in creating puzzles which they cannot solve. And the same applies, *mutatis mutandis*, to metaphysical conceptualists and realists. Only the neutralist with respect to categories avoids these puzzles by treating categories simply as what they are, nothing more or less.

What has been said about categories in relation to words, concepts, or extra-mental entities can also be said about categories versus all sorts of other categories. Category is not just neutral with respect to the categories word, concept, and extra-mental entity; it is neutral with respect to all other categories. We have discussed these three because it is these which have been used by philosophers to explain categories and most others are clearly unhelpful. For example, no one has yet argued that categories are cats or that categories are colors. But the move to reduce categories to words, concepts, or extra-mental entities, is analogous to the move to reduce categories to cats or to colors. These reductions have not been attempted because they are too obviously absurd. The absurdities involved in the reductions of categories to words, concepts, or extra-mental entities, however, are much less obvious, and therefore these reductions have had many proponents.

B. Categories and Universals

Now that we have discussed the nature of categories, it is imperative that we say something about their relationship to universals, for much that applies to universals also applies to categories and vice versa. Indeed, as I said at the beginning of this chapter, the discussion of the ontological status of categories I have provided here closely mirrors the discussion of the ontological status of universals I have given elsewhere. Ultimately, categories turn out to be very much like universals in that they are in some sense neutral, although their neutrality differs in some important ways from that of universals.

The similarity of categories and universals should not surprise us. Remember that universality is often conceived as predicability and here I have adopted an understanding of a category as what is expressed by a predicable term. What, then, is the distinction between categories and universals?

The first point of difference between them is that universals are instantiables whereas instantiability has nothing to do with categories. A necessary, and indeed a sufficient, condition of universality is the possibility of instantiation. Cat is a universal because it can be instantiated; indeed, it is instantiated in Chichi and Misifus. But so is unicorn. Unicorn is universal because it can be instantiated, even though it is not in fact instantiated. To be instantiable in principle, then is of the essence of universality. This is the reason that square circle and nothing are not universals. Square circle is not instantiable because it is contradictory, therefore precluding the existence of square circles. Nothing, likewise, is not instantiable, because there cannot be any instances of nothing. Instantiability is not a necessary condition of categoricity, although it is a sufficient condition of it. Category is broader than universal. Every universal is a category, but not every category is a universal.

That a category is what a predicable term expresses means that there are categories for every term that is actually predicated or can be predicated in nonidentity sentences. Therefore, insofar as 'nothing' and 'square circle' are predicable terms, nothing and square circle, which these terms express, are categories. But we saw that nothing and square circle are not instantiable. Only some categories are instantiable, namely, those that are also universal. Cat and red are instantiable categories, that is universals, but nothing and square circle are not.

This should also serve to distinguish categories from individuals. Individuals are noninstantiable instances. Chichi, the cat, is individual because there cannot be any instances of Chichi. Any instances that appear to be like Chichi are rather instances of cat, of which Chichi is also an instance. One way to confirm that something is an individual is to see if its name is not predicable of something else in a nonidentity sentence. Chichi is individual because 'Chichi' cannot be so predicated. In contrast, red is a universal because 'red' is predicable. Now, because categories are what is expressed by predicable terms, it is easy to see how they are not individual. Individuals are excluded from the extension of both 'universal' and 'category,' although individual itself is both a category and a universal. It is a universal because it is an instantiable whose instances are this and that individual; it is a category because the term which expresses it, namely, 'individual,' is predicable.

C. Unity of Metaphysics

One of the issues that has concerned metaphysicians throughout the history of the discipline has been the question of the unity of metaphysics.[58] Indeed, much of the discussion concerning the object, method, and aim of metaphysics, and of the kind of propositions of which it consists, has been generated by the desire to find some unity for metaphysics and, thus, justify its existence. The search for unity amounts to a search for what is both common to everything that is metaphysics, or metaphysical, and what is different between metaphysics, or what is metaphysical, and everything else. This controversy has plagued the discipline from its very beginnings because Aristotle himself gave different descriptions of the discipline, thus tacitly putting into question its unity.

Now, the definition of metaphysics I have provided I believe is sufficient to answer the question of unity, for here is a discipline that has a clearly delimited kind of object and a clearly established aim. Metaphysics is the part of philosophy concerned with the determination and study of the most general categories and with the determination of how less general categories are related to the most general ones. To this extent, metaphysics is one and also justified.

Of course, the object metaphysics studies is not numerically one in the way Chichi or the paper on which these words are written is numerically one.[59] The unity of metaphysics, like the unity of other disciplines of learning, is rather like the unity of a collection

---

58. Aristotle raised the question of the unity of science in *Posterior Analytics* 87a40, p. 153. The issue involved in the unity of metaphysics is not the same issue as the contemporary issue involved in the unity of science. The latter has to do with whether all sciences can be reduced to physics. See Fodor, "Special Sciences," p. 128.

59. Ockham, "The Notion of Knowledge or Science" (*Expositio super viii libros Physicorum*, Prologus), p. 7.

of things which are considered as related in certain ways,[60] as for example, the citizens of a state and the organs of an organism are related.

D. Some Objections and Clarifications

I would like to finish this chapter by raising and answering some objections to the conception of metaphysics I have presented. Apart from preempting some obvious attacks, the discussion of these objections will further clarify some aspects of my view which may still remain obscure.

The first objection may be put as follows: Am I not begging the question in arguing that metaphysics studies categories but should not reduce them? Isn't the purpose of the discipline precisely to study categories with a view to reducing them, that is, identifying the most general categories and explaining less general ones in terms of them?

The answer is that the aim of metaphysics is not to reduce categories willy nilly. Its aim is to determine which are the most general categories and to establish the relation of less general to the most general categories. This entails reduction in certain cases, where such reduction is warranted by the categories in question, but it does not entail that metaphysics must always engage in reduction, and particularly not that it must engage in unwarranted reductions. I claim, moreover, that the reduction of categories exclusively to words, concepts, or extra-mental entities is precisely a case of unwarranted reduction. The explanations that metaphysics offers, then, need not be reductive even if some of them are. And, indeed, I do not believe all explanations require reduction.

A second objection might run along similar lines: Have you not de facto engaged in reduction when you claim that metaphysics studies categories, for doesn't your position entail the replacement of other objects by categories?

Again, I can answer that not all reduction is pernicious. So I need not avoid this characterization of my position. My point is that the particular reductions in which realism, conceptualism, and nom-

---

60. Aquinas, *Summa theologiae* I, 1, 3, p. 8. See also Aristotle, *Posterior Analytics* 87a38–40, p. 153, and *Metaphysics* 1064a1–3, p. 860.

inalism engage are indeed pernicious. In contrast, my reduction, if it can be described in this way, is not so because of my pluralistic and open conception of categories. This conception respects the integrity of particular categories.

A third objection runs like this: I claim that my position is not a form of realism, conceptualism, or nominalism. But, in fact, it amounts to a form of realism, for it holds that at least some categories are more than words or concepts. And that is precisely the way many philosophers understand realism.

First of all, it is true that in saying that metaphysics studies categories and some categories are the sorts of things which are extramental I have defended a form of realism. But this is not the kind of realism that one finds most often defended by those who claim themselves to hold a realistic conception of metaphysics. The realism most often defended is of two sorts, both equally coarse in my view. The first holds all that metaphysics studies is extra-mental entities; the second holds all that metaphysics studies is actually existing extra-mental entities. Neither of these positions is tenable for reasons I have already explained. My position, on the other hand, holds only that there are some categories that are extramental in the sense that they can have members which exist outside the mind. I am not committed to the naive forms of realism popular throughout the history of philosophy. Metaphysics studies categories whose members exist outside the mind, categories whose members can exist but do not exist outside the mind, categories whose members exist only in the mind, categories whose members are linguistic entities, and categories which can have no members.

Second, my position leaves open the question of the status of the categories which can have extra-mental members in those members. This is another issue, as noted at the beginning of this chapter. My position applies only at the level of the definition or understanding of the nature of metaphysics, for it is often at this level that metaphysicians argue for a commitment to realism, conceptualism, or nominalism. By defining metaphysics in a certain way, they tip the scales one way or another, with the unfortunate consequences that they automatically exclude certain views and discussions from the discipline. For example, if metaphysics is understood realistically, then all forms of conceptualism and nominalism are ruled to be non-metaphysical, and vice versa. But this makes no sense. Aristotle, Hegel, and Quine have all made metaphysical claims and a proper understanding of metaphysics should make room for them. If my understanding of metaphysics is adopted, the decision as to the ultimate nature of reality will depend on the detailed analysis of particular categories, and especially those which are studied under ontology. Only then can we expect to come up with a respectable theory. It is not in the definition of metaphysics that this work is to be done, but in the discussion of particular categories.[61]

A fourth objection raises the question of the categoricity of category itself. Is category itself a category and if it is, then does not this mean that we cannot avoid an infinite regress?

I see at least three ways of answering this question. One is by adopting Russell's theory of types and arguing that category is not a category in the sense that its members are categories. Hence, the infinite regress that is generated by treating category in this way is not pernicious.

A second answer could point out that the term 'category' when it refers to itself is not a predicate, but a name, and thus it cannot be treated as referring to a category. This is the reason why, when the term is used in third position, it is always in identity sentences. 'Category is a category' is a sentence of the form 'A is A' and not a predicative sentence of the form 'A is of kind B.'

A third answer says that category is the most primitive notion we have.[62] There is no possible analysis which can be given of it without reference to itself. That is why there is no possible definition of category. All we can do to talk about category is to give some criteria of identification. And that is precisely what I have done when I said that a category is what is expressed by a predicative term or expression.

But does not this make categories predicates, after all? No. The predicate is the term or expression; the category is what the term or expression expresses. Still, one may retort: Does not this, then, make categories meanings, for meanings are supposed to be what terms or expressions express? Again, no. A meaning is what we understand when we understand a term, an expression, or a text. Meanings are what we understand considered in relation both to bits of language in use and to the mind that understands those

---

61. I have done it in the context of individuality. See, Gracia, *Individuality*, chap. 2.
62. This point is acknowledged by some who, contrary to what they expressly claim, go on to analyze categories in terms of entities of one sort or another. See, for example, Grossmann, *The Categorial Structure of the World*, p. 5, where he calls them entities, and p. 6, where he calls them properties.

meanings. The meaning of 'The cat is on the mat' is "The cat is on the mat" considered in relation to the bit of language in use 'The cat is on the mat' and the mind that understands it. A category is not that at all, because it is not defined in the same way as meaning. The category triangle, for example, is whatever a triangle *qua* triangle is, say a geometrical figure with three angles, whereas the meaning of 'triangle' is that, namely "geometrical figure with three angles," considered in relation both to the word 'triangle' and a mind that understands it.

A fifth objection might point out that, at the end of chapter 7, I made room for the study and use of ontological priority in metaphysics, the nonreductive approach to metaphysics for which I have argued in this chapter implies the rejection of the use of ontological priority in metaphysics. The reason is that such use would appear to entail precisely the kind of reduction I oppose.

The answer to this objection is that the notion of ontological priority does not necessarily entail reduction, but rather ordering. Of course, it all depends on what one means by 'ontologically prior.' But if one takes 'X is ontologically prior to Y' to mean either that X is first in being, X is independent of Y, or X is more eminent than Y, then to be ontologically prior does not entail any kind of reduction.[63] The use of the category merely makes explicit certain relations between X and Y.

A sixth objection argues that, if it is true that what applies to a category also applies to its members, then to be neutral with respect to words, concepts, and things must apply to all categories and their members. But, then, words, for example, must be neutral with respect to word, concept, and thing and this creates a contradiction.

As noted earlier, category is not a category in the way cat and word are categories for reasons already explained. Second, that the members of a category satisfy the conditions specified by the predicate which expresses the category does not mean that they have to have the category's neutrality with respect to certain features. To say that category is neutral with respect to word, concept, or thing is precisely to say that to be a category tells us nothing about whether categories are words, concepts, or things; it is not to say that particular categories have themselves to be neutral with respect to these subcategories. For the neutrality of category with respect to those is not a condition specified in the definition of category. Consider the

---

63. Cf. Gorman, *Ontological Priority*, pp. 76–77.

case of human being. That human being is neutral with respect to a particular color of skin does not mean that individual human beings must be neutral with respect to a particular color of skin; it means that being human says nothing about having a particular color and that is why humans can have all sorts of colors of skin and still fulfill the conditions of being human.

But, one might want to retort: What of universals? If to be a universal is to be instantiable, does not this require that the members of the category universal be instantiable? Certainly, instantiability is passed on to cat, for example, but how come it is not passed on to Chichi and Misifus?

To this one could answer that the conditions specified by the predicate which expresses a category are satisfied by the members of the category (the conditions specified by 'cat,' such as the capacity to meow, are satisfied by the members of the category cat, namely, Chichi and Misifus), but not by the members of categories which are themselves members of the original category. The conditions specified by the predicate which expresses the category universal are satisfied also by the members of categories such as cat, but not the members of the category cat (Chichi and Misifus).

Unfortunately, this answer does not work for two reasons. First, the characteristics specified by some predicates are satisfied by the members of subcategories of the category the predicate expresses. The conditions specified by 'animal' are satisfied by mammals and insects, which are members of the category the predicate 'animal' expresses, but also by the members of subcategories of mammal and insect, such as human and primate in the case of the first and cockroach and mosquito in the case of the second. Second, there are some categories in which some conditions clearly are not so satisfied. Individual, for example, is multiply instantiable, but Chichi and this piece of paper are not. Obviously, to say that the conditions specified by the predicates which express categories are satisfied by members of subcategories of the category does not work in every case.

Consider again the category which pointedly creates the difficulty, that is, the presumed counter example to my view: individual. The difficulty is that the members of this category do not satisfy the condition of instantiability which is specified by the universal predicate 'individual.' Individual is instantiable, but the members of the category, the individuals Chichi and Misifus, are not. Now, let us consider exactly what are the conditions specified by the predicate 'individual.' These might be stated as follows: The category individual is characterized by the fact that its members cannot themselves have members. This means that it is the very nature of this category that its members not have members. Or, to use the language of universals, it is in the nature of the universal, individual, that its members be noninstantiable. It is this that generates the contradiction, because it turns out that the category individual is universal, that is instantiable, but to be an individual is precisely to be noninstantiable.

One possible way out is to say that the contradiction arises only in the context of categories such as universal and individual. It does not arise in the context of categories such as cat and mammal. This suggests that there are fundamental differences between these two sorts of categories, and one might want to argue that we need to make a distinction between them to account for these differences. But this entails, of course, the kind of work metaphysics does and which is out of the boundaries of our meta-metaphysical inquiry in this book. Moreover, leaving this issue unresolved does not undermine the viewpoint I have defended for two reasons. First, my view concerns categories in general and not particular categories; I have left open the logic of particular categories. Second, it should be obvious that the categories which are pertinent for us, such as the category word, is more like the category cat than like the category universal.

Finally, someone might still insist that I have not answered the important question I set out to answer in this chapter. By arguing that categories are neutral I have left open the question of their being. What is the manner of their being?

This objection missed the main point of the preceding discussion. This point is that, just as there are illegitimate questions concerning cats and triangles, so there are illegitimate questions concerning categories in general. That the questions are illegitimate means that they make no sense either because they are based on a logical mistake or because they make an unwarranted assumption. Any answer to them, then, compounds the mistake and leads to further confusion. To ask whether cats are black, whether cats have angles, whether triangles are large, or whether triangles beg for food are all illegitimate questions. The first and third are illegitimate because some cats may be black and some may not be, and some triangles may be large and others may not be. The other two are illegitimate because having angles is not something that applies to cats at all, and begging for food is not something that applies to triangles at all. Likewise to ask about the reality, being, or manner of being of categories *qua* categories is nonsense. To answer such questions would entail reducing all categories to some categories.

The last two objections and their answers should further bring out the point I have been trying to emphasize in this chapter, namely, that it is only the attempt to reduce categories to what they are not, either by reifying, conceptualizing, or nominalizing them that creates problems. A particular category, say, cat, is just that, cat, namely, what is expressed by 'cat' when cat is predicated of 'Misifus' or 'Chichi.' There is nothing more, or less than that, and it is the attempt to find something more or less in it, that creates the contradictions and confusions associated with nominalism, conceptualism, and realism.

CHAPTER TEN

Conclusion

With the boundless arrogance of a man of the Enlightenment, Kant claimed in the introduction to *Prolegomena to Any Future Metaphysics* that "he who undertakes to judge or, still more, to construct a system of metaphysics must satisfy the demands here made, either by applying my solution or by thoroughly refuting it and substituting another. To evade it is impossible."[1] Moreover, he went on to claim that, for those unfortunate ones who, in spite of his efforts, still find the *Prolegomena* obscure, there is no recourse but to give up the investigation altogether, and apply themselves to other enterprises, for not every one has the talent to engage in the analysis of abstract concepts. Obviously, Kant was very sure of himself and what he had achieved.

I make no such extraordinary claims for this book, for I share, rather, Whitehead's healthy distrust of the capacity of human beings to establish any conceptual scheme for all times and places. As Whitehead points out, "Philosophers can never hope finally to formulate ... metaphysical first principles. ... [for] [m]etaphysical categories are not dogmatic statements of the obvious; they are tentative formulations of the ultimate generalities."[2] Indeed, pessimistically speaking, it could be said that one's intellectual history is the history of one's mistakes. Still, I do hope what I have said in

---

1. Kant, *Prolegomena*, p. 11.
2. Whitehead, *Process and Reality*, pp. 6, and 12.

this book, if nothing else, promotes the discussion of issues which, I believe, are at the core of not just metaphysics, but all philosophy. To paraphrase Whitehead: Metaphysics is an adventure in the clarification of thought, progressive and never final, but it is an adventure in which even partial success has importance.[3]

My view is quite simple. I claim that metaphysics is the part of philosophy that studies categories: It tries to determine and define (when possible) the most general categories, and to make explicit their interrelations and the relations of less general categories to the most general ones. Categories, moreover, are conceived neutrally with respect to the subcategories word, concept, or thing. Each category is what it is, as expressed by its definition, and therefore cannot be reduced to any other category unless the conditions that it satisfies make such reduction legitimate. Metaphysics, then, turns out to be the categorial foundation of knowledge. For in it we attempt to establish and understand the most general categories and the relation of all other categories to them.

I claim, moreover, that the study of categories in the way noted is in fact what most metaphysicians have done throughout the history of philosophy when they engaged in metaphysics, although most of them describe metaphysics in a very different way from the one I have proposed. This, however, should not surprise us, for it is a common place for humans to misdescribe what they do for the simple reason that their descriptions are frequently guided by prejudices rather than observation.

Although my claims have significant implications for other issues concerning metaphysics, they are in fact quite narrow. I have stayed away from many issues that merit careful scrutiny, but the discussion of which would have lengthened the book considerably. For example, I have omitted discussion of epistemic questions concerned with the possibility or impossibility of metaphysical knowledge and the way we have access to categories, semantic issues involved in the meaning and reference of metaphysical terms, and metaphysical questions concerning the status of metaphysics. The treatment of these and other pertinent matters will have to wait for another occasion.

I began this book by raising the question of why metaphysics survives all attacks against it and continues to flourish in one form or another. And I postponed answering it until we had a clearer no-

---

3. Ibid., p. 4.

tion of the discipline. Now we do and, therefore, it is possible to answer the question with some confidence. First we can reject some answers which have been given to it. The reason metaphysics survives is not that it is concerned with being, God, transcendental reality, ultimate causes, or any of the other objects we have rejected as proper objects of metaphysics. Nor is the reason that in it humans find meaning for their lives or that metaphysics is natural for them. No, the reason metaphysics will never perish is that it is concerned with the most general categories and the relation of less general ones to them. As the view of these categories and their relations, metaphysics is *logically presupposed* by every other view that one may have. Any account of what we know or think we know, then, is incomplete until we provide its metaphysical foundation. We can, of course, practice other disciplines and hold other views without consciously practicing metaphysics or holding metaphysical views, but in these cases we do in fact vicariously engage in metaphysics and hold metaphysical views, for the views we hold logically presuppose views about the most general categories, their interrelations, and the relation of the less general categories we use to the most general categories. All our knowledge depends on metaphysical views whether we are aware of it or not, and all our thinking involves metaphysical thinking. Those who delude themselves in believing that they do not engage in metaphysical thinking nonetheless do. The only difference between them and declared metaphysicians is that the former are unaware of what they do and, therefore, do it surreptitiously and unreflectively, whereas the latter are aware of it and do it openly and deliberately. Metaphysics is inescapable.

Bibliography

Abelard, Peter. *Dialectica*, ed. L. M. de Rijk. Assen: Van Gorcum, 1956.

Abelard, Peter. "Glosses on Porphyry." From *Logica ingredientibus*. In *Five Texts on the Mediaeval Problem of Universals*. Translated and edited by Paul V. Spade. 26–56. Indianapolis, IN: Hackett, 1994.

Adorno, Theodor. *Against Epistemology: A Metacritique*. Translated by Willis Domingo. Oxford: Blackwell, 1982.

Aertsen, Jan A. *Medieval Philosophy and the Transcendentals: The Case of Thomas Aquinas*. Leiden: E. J. Brill, 1996.

Albert the Great. *Metaphysica*. In *Opera omnia*. Edited by Bernhard Geyer. Vol. 16. Aschendorff: Monasterium Westfalorum, 1960.

Allaire, Edwin B. "Bare Particulars." In *Universals and Particulars: Readings in Ontology*. Edited by Michael Loux. 235–44. Garden City, NY: Doubleday, 1970.

Anselm. "The Incarnation of the Word." In *Anselm of Canterbury*. Edited and translated by Jasper Hopkins and Herbert Richardson. 9–37. Toronto: Edwin Mellen Press, 1976.

Anselm. *Proslogium*. In *Saint Anselm: Basic Writings*. Translated by S. N. Deane. 1–34. LaSalle, IL: Open Court, 1962.

Aquinas, Thomas. *On Being and Essence*. Translated by Armand Maurer. 2nd rev. ed. Toronto: Pontifical Institute of Mediaeval Studies, 1968.

———. *Commentary on the "De Trinitate" of Boethius*, qq. 5 and 6. In *The Division and Method of the Sciences*. Edited by Armand Maurer. 3rd rev. ed. Toronto: Pontifical Institute of Mediaeval Studies, 1963.

———. *Commentary on the "Metaphysics" of Aristotle.* Translated by J. P. Rowan. Chicago: H. Regnery, 1961.

———. *Scriptum super libros Sententiarum.* In *Opera omnia.* Edited by S. E. Fretté and Paul Maré Vivès. Vols. 7–11. Paris, 1871–80.

———. *Summa theologiae.* In *The Basic Writings of Saint Thomas Aquinas.* Edited by Anton C. Pegis. Vol. 1. New York: Random House, 1945.

Aristotle. *Categories.* In *The Basic Works of Aristotle.* Edited by R. McKeon. 7–37. New York: Random House, 1941.

———. *On Interpretation.* In *The Basic Works of Aristotle.* Edited by R. McKeon. 38–61. New York: Random House, 1941.

———. *Metaphysics.* In *The Basic Works of Aristotle.* Edited by R. McKeon. 689–926. New York: Random House, 1941.

———. *Nicomachean Ethics.* In *The Basic Works of Aristotle.* Edited by R. McKeon. 927–1112. New York: Random House, 1941.

———. *Poetics.* In *The Basic Works of Aristotle.* Edited by R. McKeon. 1453–87. New York: Random House, 1941.

———. *Posterior Analytics.* In *The Basic Works of Aristotle.* Edited by R. McKeon. 110–186. New York: Random House, 1941.

———. *Prior Analytics.* In *The Basic Works of Aristotle.* Edited by R. McKeon. 62–107. New York: Random House, 1941.

———. *On the Soul.* In *The Basic Works of Aristotle.* Edited by R. McKeon. 533–603. New York: Random House, 1941.

———. *Topics.* In *The Basic Works of Aristotle.* Edited by R. McKeon. 188–206. New York: Random House, 1941.

Armstrong, D. M. *Universals and Scientific Realism.* 2 Vols. Cambridge: Cambridge University Press, 1980.

Arnauld, Antoine. *The Art of Thinking (Port-Royal Logic).* Translated by James Dickoff and Patricia James. New York: Bobbs-Merrill, 1964.

Aubenque, P. *Le problème de l'être chez Aristote: Essai sur la problématique aristotélicienne.* Paris: Presses Universitaires de France, 1962.

Augustine. *Eighty-Three Different Questions.* Translated by David L. Mosher. Washington, DC: The Catholic University of America Press, 1977.

Augustine. *The Teacher.* Translated by John H. S. Burleigh. In *Augustine: Earlier Writings.* Edited by John H. S. Burleigh. Vol. 6 of Library of Christian Classics, 69–101. Philadelphia: Westminster Press, 1953.

————. *Against the Academics*. Translated by John J. O'Meara. New York: Newman Press, 1951.

Austin, J. L. *How To Do Things with Words*. Edited by J. O. Urmson. Cambridge, MA: Harvard University Press, 1962.

Averroes. *Aristotelis Metaphysicorum libri xiii cum Averrois cordubensis in eosdem commentariis*. In *Aristotelis opera cum Averrois commentariis*. Vol. 8. Venice: Junctas, 1562–74; Reprint Frankfurt am Main: Minerva, 1962.

————. *Aristotelis de Physico audito libri octo, cum Averrois cordubensis variis in eosdem commentariis*. In *Aristotelis opera cum Averrois commentariis*. Vol. 4. Venice: Junctas, 1562–74; Reprint Frankfurt am Main: Minerva, 1962.

————. *On the Harmony of Religion and Philosophy*. Translated by G. F. Hourani. London: Luzac, 1961. This work is frequently known as *The Decisive Treatise*.

Avicenna. *Metaphysica*. Translated from Persian by P. Morewedge. New York: Columbia University Press, 1973.

Avicenna Latinus. *Liber de philosophia prima sive scientia divina*, I–IV. Edited by S. Van Riet. Leiden: Brill, 1977.

Avicenna. *La métaphysique du Shifâ'*. Translated by Georges C. Anawati. Paris: J. Vrin, 1978.

Ayer, A. J. *Language, Truth and Logic*. New York: Dover, 1936.

Ayer, A. J., ed. *Logical Positivism*. Glencoe, IL: Free Press, 1959.

Bambrough, Renford. "Universals and Family Resemblances." *Proceedings of the Aristotelian Society* 61 (1960–61): 207–22.

Barnes, Jonathan. "Metaphysics." In *The Cambridge Companion to Aristotle*. 66–108. Cambridge: Cambridge University Press, 19.

Baronius, Robert. *Metaphysica generalis*. Leiden, 1654.

Baumgarten, Alexander Gottlieb. *Metaphysica*. Marburg: Hemmerde, 1779 (first published in 1748); Reprint, Hildesheim: Georg Olms, 1963.

Beck, Lewis White. *Early German Philosophy: Kant and Its Predecessors*. Cambridge, MA: Harvard University Press, 1969.

Berkeley, George. *Three Dialogues Between Hylas and Philonous*. Edited by Colin Turbayne. Indianapolis, IN: Bobbs-Merril, 1954.

Blackburn, S. "Moral Realism." In *Morality and Moral Reasoning: Five Essays in Ethics*. Edited by John Casey. 101–124. London: Methuen, 1971.

Boethius, M. S. *In "Isagogen" Porphyrii commenta.* Edited by Samuel Brandt. 2nd ed. In *Corpus scriptorum ecclesiasticorum latinorum.* Vol. 48:133–348. Vienna: Tempsky, 1906; Reprint, New York: Johnson, 1966.

———. *On the Trinity.* In *Boethius: The Theological Tractates.* Translated by H. F. Stuart and E. K. Rand. 2–31. Cambridge, MA: Harvard University Press, 1968.

Bonaventure. *Collationes in Hexaëmeron et Bonaventuriana quaedam selecta.* Edited by F. Delorme. Florence, Ad Claras Aquas (Quaracchi): Collegium S. Bonaventurae, 1934.

Bradley, F. H. *Appearence and Reality: A Metaphysical Essay.* Oxford: Clarendon Press, 1930.

Brentano, Franz. "Genuine and Fictitious Objects." In *Realism and the Background of Phenomenology.* Edited by Roderick M. Chisholm. 71–5. Glencoe, IL: The Free Press, 1960.

———. *The Theory of Categories.* Translated by Roderick M. Chisholm and Norbert Guterman. The Hague: Nijhoff, 1981.

Broad, C. D. "Critical and Speculative Philosophy." In *Contemporary British Philosophy.* Edited by J. H. Muirhead. 75–100. London: Allen and Unwin, 1953.

Butchvarov, P. K. *Resemblance and Identity.* Bloomington, IN: Indiana University Press, 1966.

Butler, R. J., ed. *Analytical Philosophy.* New York: Barnes and Noble, 1962.

Calov, Abraham. *Metaphysica divina, pars generalis.* Rostock, 1636.

Calov, Abraham. *Metaphysica divina, pars specialis.* In *Scripta philosophica.* Rostock, 1650.

Carnap, Rudolph. "The Elimination of Metaphysics Through Logical Analysis of Language." Translated by Arthur Pap. In *Logical Positivism.* Edited by A. J. Ayer. 60–81. Glencoe, IL: Free Press, 1959.

Cartwright, K. "Propositions." In *Analytical Philosophy.* Edited by R. J. Butler. 81–103. New York: Barnes and Noble, 1962.

Charles, David and Kathleen Lennon, eds. *Reduction, Explanation and Realism.* 1–18. Oxford: Clarendon Press, 1992.

Chisholm, Roderick M. *A Realistic Theory of Categories: An Essay on Ontology.* Cambridge: Cambridge University Press, 1996.

Clauberg, Johann. *Metaphysica de ente, quae rectius Ontosophia.* In *Opera omnia philosophica.* Vol. 1:277–340. Hildesheim: Georg Olms, 1968; Reprint of 1691 edition.

Collingwood, R. G. *An Essay on Metaphysics*. Oxford: Clarendon Press, 1940.

Copi, Irving M. *Introduction to Logic*. 6th ed. New York: Macmillan Co., 1982.

Copleston, Frederick. *A History of Philosophy: Vol. I: Greece and Rome*. New York: Doubleday, 1993.

Dascal, Marcelo. "Philosophy, Common Sense, and Science." In *Philosophical Analysis in Latin America*. Edited by Jorge J. E. Gracia, et al. 285–312. Dordrecht: Reidel, 1984.

Davidson, Donald. "Mental Events." In *Essays on Actions and Events*. 207–227. Oxford: Clarendon Press, 1980.

Derrida, Jacques. "Signature Event Context." *Glyph* 1 (1977): 172–97.

Descartes, René. *The Philosophical Works of Descartes*. Translated by E. S. Haldane and G. R. T. Ross. 2 vols. Cambridge: Cambridge University Press, 1967.

———. *Principles of Philosophy*. Translated by John Veitch. In *The Meditations and Selections from the Principles*. 130–213. La Salle, IL: Open Court, 1988.

Desmond, William. *Being and the Between*. Albany, NY: State University of New York Press, 1995.

———. "Being, Determination, and Dialectic: On the Sources of Metaphysical Thinking," *Review of Metaphysics* 48 (1995): 731–69.

De Ulloa, Juan. *Logica menor*. Rome, 1711.

Dummett, Michael. *The Logical Basis of Metaphysics*. Cambridge, MA: Harvard University Press, 1991.

Dupré, John. *The Disorder of Things: Metaphysical Foundations of the Disunity of Science*. Cambridge, MA: Harvard University Press, 1993.

Fabro, Cornelio. "The Transcendentality of *Ens-Esse* and the Ground of Metaphysicvs." Translated by C. McKay, *International Philosophical Quarterly* 6, No. 3 (1966): 389–427.

Ferrater Mora, José. "On the Early History of 'Ontology.' " *Philosophy and Phenomenological Research* 24, No. 1 (1963): 36–47.

Feyerabend, P. K. *Realism, Rationalism and Scientific Method: Philosophical Principles, Vol. I*. Cambridge: Cambridge University Press, 1981.

Fish, Stanley. *Is There a Text in This Class? The Authority of Interpretive Communities*. Cambridge, MA: Harvard University Press, 1980.

Fodor, Jerry A. "Special Sciences (or: The Disunity of Science as a Working Hypothesis)." *Synthese* 28 (1974): 97–115.

Foucault, Michel. "Nietzsche, Freud, Marx." In *Transforming the Hermeneutic Context: From Nietzsche to Nancy*. Edited by G. L. Orminston and A. D. Schrift. 59–68. Albany, NY: State University of New York Press, 1990.

———. "Prison Talk." In *Power/Knowledge*. Edited by Colin Gordon. 37–54. New York: Pantheon Books, 1980.

Frede, Michael. "Categories in Aristotle." In *Essays in Ancient Philosophy*. 29–48. Minneapolis, MN: University of Minnesota Press, 1987.

Fredugis. "Letter on Nothing and Darkness." Translated by Allan B. Wolter. In *Medieval Philosophy: From St. Augustine to Nicholas of Cusa*. Edited by John F. Wippel and Allan B. Wolter. 104–108. New York: Free Press, 1969.

Frondizi, Risieri. *The Nature of the Self: A Functionalist Interpretation*. London: Southern Illinois University Press, 1971.

Gilson, Etienne. *Being and Some Philosophers*. 2nd ed. Toronto: Pontifical Institute of Mediaeval Studies, 1952.

Goclenius, R. E. *Lexicon philosophicum graecum*. Frankfurt: Becker, 1613; Reprint Hildesheim: Olms, 1964.

Gorman, Michael Jr. *Ontological Priority*. Ph.D. Diss. Buffalo, NY: State University of New York at Buffalo, 1993.

Gracia, Jorge J. E. "The Ontological Status of the Transcendental Attributes of Being in Scholasticism and Modernity: Suárez and Kant." In *Proceedings of the International Congress of Medieval Philosophy*. Edited by J. Aertsen. Forthcoming.

———. "The Language of Categories: From Aristotle to Ryle, via Suárez and Kant." In *Proceedings of the XXth Congress of the SIPEM*. Leuven: Leuven University Press, forthcoming.

———. "Scotus's Conception of Metaphysics: The Study of the Transcendentals." In *Essays in Honor of Girard Etzkorn*. Edited by Gordon A. Wilson and Timothy B. Noone. *Franciscan Studies*. 56 (1998): 153–168.

——— *Texts: Ontological Status, Identity, Author, Audience*. Albany, NY: State University of New York Press, 1996.

———. *Individuality: An Essay on the Foundations of Metaphysics*. Albany, NY: State University of New York Press, 1988.

———. *Philosophy and Its History; Issues in Philosophical Historiography*. Albany, NY: State University of New York Press, 1992.

———. *A Theory of Textuality: The Logic and Epistemology*. Albany, NY: State University of New York Press, 1995.

———. "The Transcendentals in the Middles Ages." *Topoi* 11, No. 2 (1992): 3–11.

———. "Suárez and the Doctrine of the Trascendentals." *Topoi* 11, No. 2 (1992): 121–133.

Gracia, Jorge J. E., ed. *The Transcendentals in the Middle Ages*. *Topoi*, 11, No. 2 (1992).

———. *Concepciones de la metafísica*. Madrid: Consejo Superior de Investigaciones Científicas, 1998.

Grice, H. P., Pears, D. F., and Strawson, P. F. "Metaphysics." In *The Nature of Metaphysics*. Edited by H. P. Pears. 1–22. London: Macmillan, 1957.

Grigely, Joseph. "The Textual Event." In *Devils and Angels: Textual Editing and Literary Criticism*. Edited by Philip Cohen. 167–94. Charlottesville: University Press of Virginia, 1991.

Grossmann, Reinhardt. *The Categorial Structure of the World*. Bloomington, IN: Indiana University Press, 1983.

———. *Ontological Reduction*. Bloomington, IN: Indiana University Press, 1973.

Gutke, Georg. *Primae philosophiae*. Wittenberg, 1618.

Habermas, Jürgen. *Postmetaphysical Thinking: Philosophical Essays*. Translated by W. M. Hohengarten. Cambridge, MA: MIT Press, 1992.

Hamlyn, D. W. *Metaphysics*. Cambridge; Cambridge University Press, 1989.

Hampshire, S. N. "Metaphysical Systems." In *The Nature of Metaphysics*. Edited by D. F. Pears. 23–38. London: Macmillan, 1957.

Hare, Peter H. "Religion and Analytic Naturalism." *Pacific Philosophy Forum* 5 (1967): 52–61.

Heidegger, Martin. *An Introduction to Metaphysics*. Translated by Ralph Manheim. Garden City, NY: Doubleday, 1961.

———. *Kategorien- un Bedeutungs-lehre des Duns Scotus*. Tübingen: J. C. B. Mohr, 1916.

Hegel, G. W. F. *The Science of Logic*. In *The Logic of Hegel*. Translated by William Wallace. 1–379. Oxford: University of Oxford Press, 1904.

Henrich, Dieter. *Konzepte: Essays zur Philosophie inder Zeit*. Frankfurt am Main: Suhrkamp, 1987.

Hochberg, H. "Ontology and Acquaintance." *Philosophical Studies* 17 (1966): 41–55.

Hooker, C. "Towards a General Theory of Reduction." *Dialogue* 20 (1981): 38–60, 201–35, 496–529.

Howard, Leon. *"The Mind" of Jonathan Edwards: A Reconstructed Text.* Berkeley and Los Angeles: University of California Press, 1963.

Hume, David. *A Treatise of Human Nature.* Edited by L. A. Selby-Bigge. Oxford: Clarendon Press, 1975.

Husserl, Edmund. "Phenomenology." In *Realism and the Background of Phenomenology.* Edited by Roderick M. Chisholm. 118–28. Glencoe, IL: The Free Press, 1960.

———. *Logical Investigations.* Translated by J. N. Findlay. 2nd ed. 2 Vols. London: Routledge and Kegan Paul, 1970.

Ingenieros, José. *Principios de psicología.* 6th ed. Buenos Aires: L. J. Rosso, 1919.

Izquierdo, Sebastián. *Pharus scientiarum.* Lugduni, 1659.

John of Salisbury. *The Metalogicon.* Translated by Daniel D. McGarry. Berkeley, CA: University of California Press, 1955.

Kant, Immanuel. *Critique of Pure Reason.* Translated by Norman Kemp Smith. London: Macmillan, 1963.

———. *Dreams of a Spirit Seer, Illustrated by Dreams of Metaphysics.* Translated by E. F. Goerwitz. London: Sonnenschein, 1900.

———. *Prolegomena to Any Future Metaphysics.* Edited by L. W. Beck. New York: Bobbs-Merrill Co., 1950.

Kripke, Saul A. *Naming and Necessity.* Cambridge, MA: Harvard University Press, 1981.

Küng, Guido. *Ontology and the Logistic Analysis of Language: An Inquiry into the Contemporary Views on Universals.* Revised edition. Dordrecht: D. Reidel, 1967.

Leibniz, Gottfried Wilhelm. *Philosophical Papers and Letters.* Translated and edited by L. E. Loemker. 2nd ed. Dordrecht: Reidel, 1969.

Lejewski, C. "On Lesniewski's Ontology." *Ratio* 1, No. 2 (1958):150–76.

Loar, B. *Mind and Meaning.* Cambridge: Cambridge University Press, 1981.

Locke, John. *An Essay Concerning Human Understanding.* 2 Vols. New York: Dover Pubs., 1959.

Long, Douglas C. "Particulars and Their Qualities." *Philosophical Quarterly* 18 (1968): 193–206. Reprinted in *Universals and Particulars*. Edited by M. J. Loux. 264–84. New York: Anchor Books, 1970.

Loux, Michael J., ed. *Universals and Particulars: Readings in Ontology*. New York: Anchor Books, 1970.

Lowe, E. J. *Kinds of Being: A Study of Individuation, Identity and the Logic of Sortal Terms*. Oxford: Blackwell, 1989.

———. *Subjects of Experience*. Cambridge: Cambridge University Press, 1996.

———. "Ontological Categories and Natural Kinds." Forthcoming.

Mandelbaum, Maurice H. "The History of Ideas, Intellectual History, and the History of Philosophy." *History and Theory*. Beiheft 5 (1965): 33–66.

Maritain, Jacques. *A Preface to Metaphysics*. New York: New American Library, 1962.

McGann, Jerome J. *The Textual Condition*. Princeton, NJ: Princeton University Press, 1991.

McGinn, C. *The Subjective View: Secondary Qualities and Indexical Thoughts*. Oxford: Oxford University Press, 1983.

McInerny, Ralph. "The Science We Are Seeking." *Review of Metaphysics* 47 (1993): 3–18.

McKeon, Richard. *Introduction to Artistotle*. New York: Modern Library, 1947.

McTaggart, John. *The Nature of Existence*. Cambridge: Cambridge University Press, 1921.

Meinong, Alexius. "The Theory of Objects." Translated by Isaac Levi, D. B. Terrell, and Roderick M. Chisholm. In *Realism and the Background of Phenomenology*. Edited by Roderick M. Chisholm. 76–117. New York: Free Press, 1960.

Mercier, Cardinal. *A Manual of Scholastic Philosophy*. Translated by T. L. Parker and S. A. Parker. 2 Vols. London: Routledge and Kegan Paul, 1960.

Miller, J. Hillis. "The Critic as Host." In *Deconstruction and Criticism*. Edited by Harold Bloom, et al. 217–253. New York: The Seabury Press, 1979.

Moore, G. E. "A Defense of Common Sense." In *Philosophical Papers*. 32–59. London: Allan and Unwin, 1959.

———. *Principia ethica.* Buffalo, NY: Prometheus, 1988.

———. "Proof of the External World." In *Philosophical Papers.* 127–50. London: Allen and Unwin, 1959.

———. "A Reply to My Critics." In *The Philosophy of G. E. Moore.* Edited by Paul Arthur Schilpp. 3rd ed. 533–677. La Salle, IL: Open Court, 1968.

———. "What Is Philosophy?" In *Some Main Problems of Philosophy.* 1–27. London: Allan and Unwin, 1953.

Nagel, Ernest. *The Structure of Science: Problems in the Logic of Scientific Explanation.* Indianapolis, IN: Hackett, 1979.

Ockham, William of. "Five Questions on Universals" (*Ordinatio,* d. 2, qq. 4–8). In *Five Texts on the Mediaeval Problem of Universals.* Translated and edited by Paul Vincent Spade. 114–231. Indianapolis, IN: Hackett, 1994.

———. "On the Notion of Knowledge or Science" (*Expositio super viii libros Physicorum,* Prologus). In *Willliam of Ockham: Philosophical Writings.* Edited and translated by, Philotheus Boehner. 1–16. London: Nelson, 1967.

———. "The Possibility of a Natural Theology" (*Reportatio* 3, 8). In *William of Ockham: Philosophical Writings.* Edited and translated by Philotheus Boehner. 97–113.

Oppenheim, P. and H. Putnam. "The Unity of Science as a Working Hypothesis." In *Minnesota Studes in the Philosophy of Science.* Edited by H. Feigl, et al. Vol. 2:3–36. Minneapolis, MN: University of Minnesota Press, 1958.

Ortega y Gasset, José. *Obras completas.* Madrid: Revista de Occidente, 1966.

Parfit, D. *Reasons and Persons.* Oxford: Oxford University Press, 1984.

Pears, D. F., ed. *The Nature of Metaphysics.* London: Macmillan, 1957.

Peirce, Charles Sanders. *Collected Papers.* Edited by Charles Hartshorne, et al. Cambridge, MA: Harvard University Press, 1931–58.

Plato. *Apology.* In *The Collected Dialogues of Plato, Including the Letters.* Edited by Edith Hamilton and Huntington Cairns. 3–26. New York: Pantheon Books, 1961.

———. *Cratylus.* In *The Collected Dialogues of Plato, Including the Letters.* Edited by Edith Hamilton and Huntington Cairns. 421–74. New York: Pantheon Books, 1961.

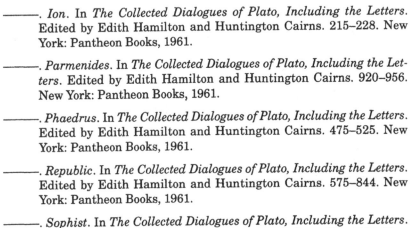

———. *Ion*. In *The Collected Dialogues of Plato, Including the Letters*. Edited by Edith Hamilton and Huntington Cairns. 215–228. New York: Pantheon Books, 1961.

———. *Parmenides*. In *The Collected Dialogues of Plato, Including the Letters*. Edited by Edith Hamilton and Huntington Cairns. 920–956. New York: Pantheon Books, 1961.

———. *Phaedrus*. In *The Collected Dialogues of Plato, Including the Letters*. Edited by Edith Hamilton and Huntington Cairns. 475–525. New York: Pantheon Books, 1961.

———. *Republic*. In *The Collected Dialogues of Plato, Including the Letters*. Edited by Edith Hamilton and Huntington Cairns. 575–844. New York: Pantheon Books, 1961.

———. *Sophist*. In *The Collected Dialogues of Plato, Including the Letters*. Edited by Edith Hamilton and Huntington Cairns. 957–1017. New York: Pantheon Books, 1961.

———. *Theaetetus*. In *The Collected Dialogues of Plato, Including the Letters*. Edited by Edith Hamilton and Huntington Cairns. 845–919. New York: Pantheon Books, 1961.

Plotinus. *The Enneads*. Translated by Stephen MacKenna. New York: Pantheon Books, 1957.

Pols, Edward. *Radical Realism: Direct Knowing in Science and Philosophy*. Ithaca, NY: Cornell University Press, 1992.

Popper, Karl R. "On the Status of Science and of Metaphysics." *Ratio* 1, No. 2 (1958): 97–115.

Popper, Karl R. "Metaphysics and Criticizability." In *Popper Selections*. Edited by David Miller. 209–219. Princeton, NJ: Princeton University Press, 1985.

Porphyry. *Isagoge*. Translated by Edward W. Warren. Toronto: Pontifical Institute of Mediaeval Studies, 1975.

———. *In Aristotelis Categorias*. In *Commentaria in Aristotelem Graeca*. Edited by A. Busse. Vol. 4, part 1. Berlin, 1887.

Price, H. H. *Thinking and Experience*. Cambridge, MA: Harvard University Press, 1962.

Putnam, H. "The Analytic and the Synthetic." *Minnesota Studies in the Philosophy of Science* 3 (1962): 358–97.

Quine, W. V. O. "Ontological Relativity." In *Ontological Relativity and Other Essays*. 69–90. New York: Columbia University Press, 1969.

———. *The Roots of Reference*. LaSalle, IL: Open Court, 1973.

———. "On What There Is." In *From a Logical Point of View*. 1–19. Cambridge, MA; Harvard University Press, 1953.

———. *Word and Object*. New York: MIT Press, 1965.

Quinton, A. M. "Final Discussion." See Ryle, Gilbert, et al., "Final Discussion." In *The Nature of Metaphysics*. Edited by D. F. Pears. 142–64. London: Macmillan, 1957.

———. "The *A Priori* and the Analytic," *Proceedings of the Aristotelian Society*. New Series 64 (1964): 31–54.

Randall, J. H. *Nature and Historical Experience: Essays in Naturalism and in the Theory of History*. New York: Columbia University Press, 1958.

Reale, Giovanni. *The Concept of First Philosophy and the Unity of the "Metaphysics" of Aristotle*. Translated by John R. Catan. Albany, NY: State University of New York Press, 1980.

Rescher, Nicholas. *Process Metaphysics: An Introduction to Process Philosophy*. Albany, NY: State University of New York Press, 1996.

Roberts, Mark. "The Bearer of Truth and Falsity." *Southwest Philosophy Review* 10, No. 2 (1994): 59–67.

Robinson, Richard. *Definition*. Oxford: Clarendon Press, 1954.

Rorty, Richard. "Nineteenth-Century Idealism and Twentieth-Century Textualism." In *Consequences of Pragmatism (Essays, 1972–1980)*. 139–59. Minneapolis, MN: University of Minnesota Press, 1982.

———. *Philosophy and the Mirror of Nature*. Princeton, NJ: Princeton University Press, 1979.

Rosen, Stanley. "The Limits of Interpretation." In *Literature and the Question of Philosophy*. Edited by Anthony J. Cascardi. 213–41. Baltimore, MD: Johns Hopkins University Press, 1987.

Royce, Josiah. *Metaphysics*. Edited by W. E. Hocking, R. Hocking, and F. Oppenheim. Albany, NY: State University of New York Press, 1998.

Russell, Bertrand. *Logic and Knowledge, Essays 1905–1950*. Edited by R. C. Marsh. London: Allen and Unwin, 1956.

———. "Vagueness." *Australasian Journal of Philosophy and Psychology* 1 (1923): 84–92.

Rutgers, Winand. *Universalis metaphysica*. Leiden, 1619.

Ryle, Gilbert. "Categories." In *Collected Papers*. Vol. 2:170–84. New York: Barnes and Noble, 1971.

———. "Are There Any Propositions?" In *Collected Papers*. Vol. 2:12–38. New York: Barnes and Noble, 1971.

———. "Systematically Misleading Expressions." In *Logic and Language*. Edited by Antony Flew. 11–36. Oxford: Blackwell, 1968.

Ryle, Gilbert, Mary Warnock, and A. M. Quinton. "Final Discussion." In *The Nature of Metaphysics*. Edited by D. F. Pears. 142–64. London: Macmillan, 1957.

Scharf, Johannes. *Theoria transcendentalis primae philosophiae*. Wittenberg, 1624.

Scharlemann, Robert P. *Thomas Aquinas and John Gerhard*. New Haven: Yale University Press, 1964.

Schiebler, Christopher. *Epitome metaphysicae specialis*. Giessen: Hampellius, 1617.

———. *Opus metaphysicum*. Giessen: Hampelius, 1617.

Schilpp, Paul Arthur, ed. *The Philosophy of G. E. Moore*. 3rd ed. La Salle, IL: Open Court, 1968.

Schleiermacher, Friedrich. *Brief Outline on the Study of Theology*, T. N. Tice. Atlanta, GA, 1966.

Scot, John the. *Periphyseon: On the Division of Nature*. Translated by Myra L. Uhlfelder. Indianapolis: Bobbs-Merrill, 1976.

Scotus, John Duns. "Concerning Metaphysics" (*Quaestiones subtilissimae super libros Metaphysicorum Aristotelis*, Prologus, and *Opus oxoniense* 1, 3, 4, and 1, 8, 3). Edited and translated by Allan B. Wolter. In *Duns Scotus: Philosophical Writings*. 1–12. London: Nelson, 1963.

———. *Ordinatio*. In *Opera omnia*. Edited by Carolo Balić. Vol. 3. Vatican City: Typis Polyglottis Vaticanis, 1950–82.

Searle, John R. *Speech Acts: An Essay in the Philosophy of Language*. Cambridge: Cambridge University Press, 1969.

Seifert, Josef. *Essere e Persona: Verso una fondazione fenomenologica di una metafisica classica e personalistica*. Translated by Rocco Buttiglione. Milan: Vita e Pensiero, 1989.

Sellars, Wilfrid. *Science and Metaphysics*. London: Routledge and Kegan Paul, 1967.

———. *Science, Perception and Reality*. London: Routledge and Kegan Paul, 1963.

Shillingsburgh, Peter L. *Scholarly Editing in the Computer Age: Theory and Practice*. Athens, GA: University of Georgia Press, 1986.

Simmons, Peter. "Categories and Ways of Being." In *Philosophy and Logic in Central Europe from Bolzano to Tarski*. 377–94. Dordrecht: Kluwer, 1992.

Smith, Barry. "Logic and Formal Ontology." In *Husserl's Phenomenology: A Textbook*. Edited by J. N. Mohante and William R. McKenna. 29–67. Washington, DC: University Press of America, 1989.

Smith, Peter. "Modest Reductions and the Unity of Science." In *Reduction, Explanation, and Realism*. Edited by David Charles and Kathleen Lemon. 19–45. Oxford: Clarendon Press, 1992.

Spinoza, Baruch. *Ethics*. Translated by Andrew Boyle. London: Dent, 1963.

Stout, G. F. "The Nature of Universals and Propositions." In *Studies in Philosophy and Psychology*. 384–403. London: Macmillan, 1930.

Strawson, P. F. *Analysis and Metaphysics: An Introduction to Philosophy*. Oxford: Oxford University Press, 1992.

———. "Analysis, Science, and Metaphysics." In *The Linguistic Turn: Essays in Philosophical Method*. Edited by Richard M. Rorty. 312–20. Chicago: University of Chicago Press, 1992.

———. *Individuals: An Essay in Descriptive Metaphysics*. London: Methuen and Co., 1959.

———. "Reply to Jorge J. E. Gracia." In *Ensayos sobre Strawson*. Edited by Carlos E. Caorsi. 112–17. Montevideo: Universidad de la República, 1992.

Strawson, P. F., et al. "Discussion of Strawson's 'Analysis, Science, and Metaphysics.'" In *The Linguistic Turn: Essays in Philosophical Method*. Edited by Richard M. Rorty. 321–30. Chicago: Chicago University Press, 1992.

Suárez, Francisco. *Disputationes metaphysicae*. In *Opera ommia*. Edited by Carolo Berton. Vols. 25 and 26. Paris: Vivès, 1861.

Suppes, Patrick. *Introduction to Logic*. Princeton, NJ: D. Van Nostrand Co., 1957.

Sweeney, Leo. *A Metaphysics of Authentic Existentialism*. Englewood Cliffs, NJ: Prentice-Hall, 1965.

Taylor, A. E. *Aristotle*. New York: Dover Publications, 1955.

Taylor, Charles. "Philosophy and Its History." In *Philosophy in History: Essays on the Historiography of Philosophy*. Edited by Richard M. Rorty et al. 17–30. Cambridge: Cambridge University Press, 1985.

Taylor, Richard. *Metaphysics.* 4th ed. Englewood Cliffs, NJ: Prentice Hall, 1992.

Timpler, Clemens. *Metaphysicae systema methodicum.* Hannover, 1616.

Tugendhat, Ernst and Wolf, Ursala. *Logisch-semantische Propädeutik.* Stuttgart: Philip Reclam, 1983.

Ulloa, Juan de. *Logica major.* Rome, 1712.

Vasconcelos, José. *Tratado de metafísica.* In *Obras completas.* Vol. 3:391–664. Mexico: Libreros Mexicanos Unidos, 1959.

Veatch, Henry B. *Aristotle: A Contemporary Appreciation.* Bloomington, IN: Indiana University Press, 1974.

————. *Swimming Against the Current in Contemporary Philosophy: Occasional Essays and Papers.* Washington, DC: The Catholic University of America Press, 1990.

Von Arnim, H. F. A. *Stoicorum Veterum Fragmenta.* 4 Vols. Stuttgart: B. G. Teubner Verlagsgesellschaft mbH, 1964.

Wachterhauser, Brice. "Interpreting Texts: Objectivity or Participation?" *Man and World* 19 (1986): 439–57.

Warnock, Mary. "Final Discussion." See Ryle, Gilbert, et al. "Final Discussion."

Weinberg, Julius R. "The Concept of Relation: Some Observations on Its History." In *Abstraction, Relation and Induction.* 61–119. Madison and Milwaukee, WI: University of Wisconsin Press, 1965.

Whitehead, Alfred North. *Process and Reality: An Essay in Cosmology.* New York: Harper Brothers, 1957.

Williams, B. A. O. "Metaphysical Arguments." In *The Nature of Metaphysics.* Edited by D. F. Pears, et al. 39–60. London: Macmillan, 1957.

Williams, D. C. "The Elements of Being." *Review of Metaphysics* 7 (1953): 3–18, and 171–92.

Wisdom, John. "Philosophical Perplexity." In *The Linguistic Turn: Essays in Philosophical Methodology.* Edited by Richard M. Rorty. 101–10. Chicago: University of Chicago Press, 1992.

————. "Philosophy, Metaphysics and Psycho-Analysis." In *Philosophy and Psycho-Analysis.* 248–282. Oxford: Blackwell, 1957.

————. "Philosophy and Psycho-Analysis." In *Philosophy and Psycho-Analysis.* 169–181. Oxford: Blackwell, 1957.

Wittgenstein, Ludwig. *Philosophical Investigations.* Translated by G. E. M. Anscombe. New York: Macmillan, 1965.

————. *Tractatus Logico-Philosophicus*. Translated by C. K. Ogden. London: Routledge and Kegan Paul, 1981.

Wolff, Christian. *Philosophia prima, sive ontologia, methodo scientifica pertractata, qua omnis cognitionis humanae principia contineatur*. Edited by Jean Ecole. Frankfurt: Libraria Regenriana, 1736; Reprint Hildesheim: Georg Ohms, 1962.

Wolff, Christian. *Preliminary Discourse*. Translated by R. J. Blackwell. Indianapolis, IN: Bobbs-Merrill, 1963.

Wolterstorff, Nicholas. "Qualities." In *Universals and Particulars: Readings in Ontology*. Edited by Michael J. Loux. 90–108. Garden City, NY: Doubleday, 1970.

————. *On Universals*. Chicago: Chicago University Press, 1970.

Wood, Robert, ed. *The Future of Metaphysics*. Chicago: Quadrangle Books, 1970.

Wundt, Max. *Die Deutsche Schulmetaphysik des 17. Jahrhunderts*. Tübingen: Mohr, 1939.

Zea, Leopoldo. *Positivism in Mexico*. Translated by Josephine H. Schulte. Austin, TX: University of Texas Press, 1974.

Zimmermann, A. *Ontologie oder Metaphysik? Die Diskussion über den Gegenstand der Metaphysik im 13. Und 14. Jahrhundert*. Leiden: Brill, 1965.

Zubiri, Xavier. *Cinco lecciones de filosofía*. Madrid: Alianza Editorial, 1982.

————. *Teoría fenomenológica del juicio*. Madrid: Revista de Archivos, Bibliotecas y Museos, 1923.

————. *Sobre la esencia*. Madrid: Sociedad de Estudios y Publicaciones, 1963.

————. "Filosofía y metafísica." *Cruz y Raya* 30 (1935): 7–60.

Author Index

239

Subject Index

Made in the USA
Monee, IL
27 August 2022

12686117R00149